ATC Tales

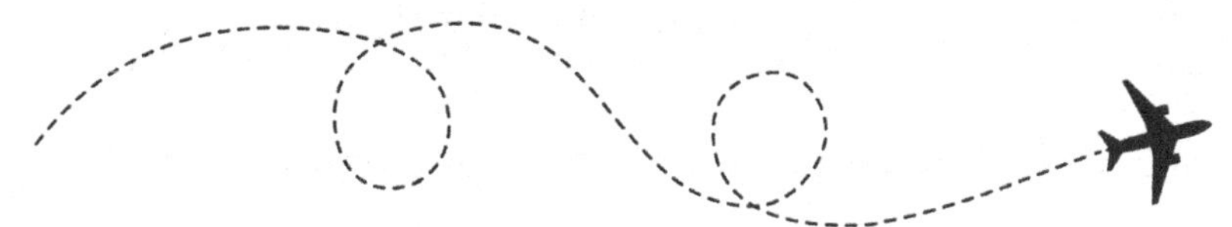

By Mac MacKechnie

ATC Tales

Editing and book design by Jansina of Rivershore Books

ISBN: 978-1-63522-155-8

Printed in the United States of America
10 9 8 7 6 5 4 3 2 1

Rivershore Books
8982 Van Buren St. NE • Minneapolis, MN 55434
612-208-3434 • info@rivershorebooks.com

A word about "ATC Tales." These are a collection of stories about people and airplanes, and people who worked those airplanes, mostly from Fort Worth Center but a few from other places. Most are stories I either worked or was familiar with. Sometimes you might recognize a name, maybe your name, maybe somebody else's name. This material is all copyrighted or is going to be. It's for your edification and enjoyment.

Sometimes the stories talk about what it's like to be an air traffic controller, sometimes how controllers perceive pilots, sometimes about people. I hope you enjoy them. To paraphrase Broderick Crawford and his 1950s TV Series, "These are the true stories of air traffic control."

One of the good things about writing these stories is that I can write all the cute little tales I want. You are, after all, a captive audience. These particular stories cater to the aviation sort and since you're of that sort. . .

Strange things happen in the nether world of ATC. I used to think that this world, the world of ATC, was normal, but after a while I realized, it ain't normal. A lot of abnormal things happen out there . . . and if you know some controllers, you know what I mean.

Dedication

This book is dedicated to Dwain Lankford. Dwain was a controller (and later a supervisor) for many years, serving at various facilities until he came to Fort Worth Center in, I believe, 1962. I met him through his son, Rick, with whom I worked at Harris Hospital. Rick invited me to supper one night at his parents' house and, over the course of the meal, Dwain talked me into applying for the ATC test. It was a life-altering moment.

Dwain was an interesting fellow. At age 18 he was a B-24 command pilot in World War II, flying 50 combat missions with the 460th Bomb Group in Italy. After the war, at 20 years of age, he applied to several airlines for a pilot position, but was turned down because he too young.

Thank you, Dwain.

Acknowledgments

I have many people to thank for all this, too numerous to mention them all, for fear of omission, but I do have to mention several. First, Laurie, my lovely wife, for her encouragement in getting this done. Next, to Beth Ball, with whom I carpooled and worked with, for many years. Even after she left, we stayed friends and she has, over the years, been very encouraging, telling me again and again, "You should write a book!"

A special word of thanks to my daughter, Sian Brannon, who took many typewritten pages, scanned them, formatted them, and arranged them to make it possible for this book to actually happen. Without her, this little creation would have remained a dream.

Thanks to Michaela Chorn who designed the cover, and to Jansina of Rivershore Books, who did all the final editing and actually got it into print.

ATC Tales I

Something strange happened to me out there yesterday, something I've not seen in the 23 years I've been there. I've heard of a lot of funny things, squirrelly things, nutty, off-the-wall, bizarre and oddball things, but until yesterday, never in my life did I think I'd see an American dash 80 overtake an F-16.

ZOOM02, what a callsign, just right for an F-16, at FL350, was on a cross-country from SSC (Shaw AFB, Sumter, SC) to Tinker, coming west to DFW and turning north toward Tinker AFB in Oklahoma City. This guy wasn't a ball of fire but hey! He was an F-16. American 1961 was off DFW northbound, coming up under the ZOOM. I'd already dumped the ZOOM to get under a JetLink southbound and then a northbound G4. No step for a stepper, I thought, but the boy was dogging it. Still, he got down to FL270 and everything was fine.

Just goes to show you how complacency can zap you. AAL1961 had launched into the blue and was rocketing northward as fast as the first officer's legs could pedal. This guy was a dash 80 and since I know a dash 80 captain, I know that the first officer has to do all the pedaling on departure ("Cause it's uphill," my friend told me.)

Six miles in trail of ZOOM, the American was doing a zoom job himself as he climbed to FL290. Of all a sudden I was realized things were not looking good in Mudville (soon to be Muckville if I didn't do something quick). "ZOOM02, a dash 80's overtaking you, turn 30 right for traffic and 'say airspeed.'" "2-3-0 knots," came his soulful reply.

"20 left for traffic" to the American. "20 left and where's the traffic?" came his reply.

"You're overtaking an F-16," I said, a note of urgency added to the usual cool, calm, and collected dulcet tones of the wise sage.

"You gotta be kidding!" he exclaimed.

It started working and now, feeling embarrassed for the F-16 pilot (think about it, a dash 80 running up your six o'clock) I said to the American, "I think the F-16's a maintenance flight." It didn't matter though 'cause the American knew that for once, just once, he'd bested an F-16.

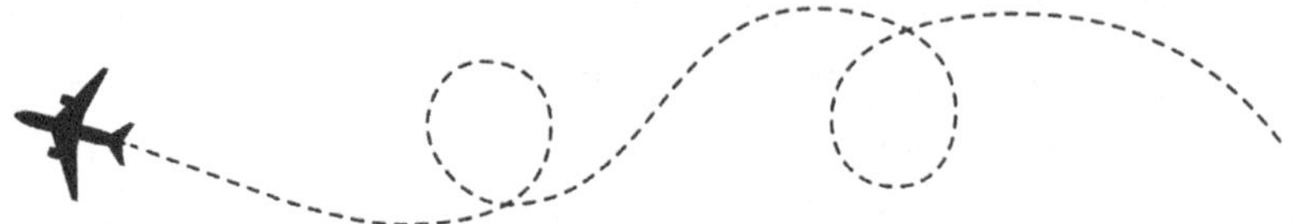

One night about eight o'clock on McAlester-high, eight or ten air carriers on frequency, I asked a slant alpha, a Delta, "Is your aircraft radar-vector equipped," thinking I'd give him a vector out west toward his destination. A pause, then a "Negative." From out of the aforementioned netherworld came another voice, "He means 'can you fly a heading?' Dummy!"

At DFW Tower a controller was tired of playing word games with a Cohlmia pilot, so he said, "CHL1240, let me talk to Beavis. I'm tired of talking to you."

ATC Tales 2

In Albuquerque Center a controller was being plagued by a pesky pilot who kept asking questions about hiring and benefits. The pilot then asked, "How do you like working as a controller?" The fellow replied, "I've been working here three days and I like it just fine." Not another word except "Roger."

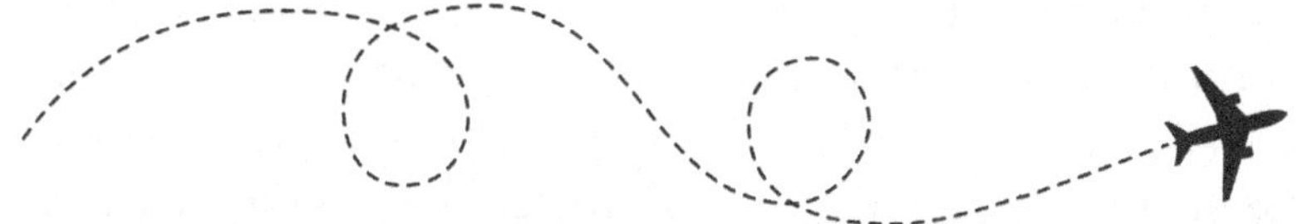

At Fort Worth Center a controller on the TXK specialty was plaguing a pilot at FL 210 with questions. The irritated pilot asked the controller, "What altitude does your airspace go up to?" The perplexed controller responded, "flight level 2-3-0." The pilot replied, "Roger. Requesting flight level 2-5-0."

An Idaho Air National Guard flight of four, callsign SPUD01, checked on my frequency saying, "Spud check, One potato." Then came, Two potato, Three potato, Four!" Then, "Fort Worth Center, Spud01, flight level 3-5-0."

One fine day I was sitting on Frisco-lo when John Tittle, a controller on my specialty, checked on frequency, wanting VFR flight following. John is a greeat guy with a heart of gold. Aiming to have a little fun with him, I replied: "November 4-2-4-4 Alpha, roger. For radar identification, throw yourself out of the aircraft." John told me much later that my reply got responses from several other aircraft on frequency.

ATC Tales 3

A friend who's in the Air Force, Paul Erbacher, was an Electronic Warfare Officer in the 4018th CCTS, flying B-52s out of Carswell AFB, with a pilot named Kominski, a captain in his squadron. This captain was recently divorced and had picked up a girlfriend (Marie) who called him everywhere on base, tracking him down at the most obscure and/or remote locations. (She even tracked him down at a Macy's store in Dallas.) Erbacher and I worked out something where I would pass a message along to his aircraft sometime when they came flying through my sector, a message to the effect that he (Kominski) should call Marie as soon as he landed. I finally got the chance.

He came through on FILTH14, refueling on AR313, down in MLC-lo where I was working. I called them up and asked if they had a CPT Kominski on board. At first, they said they weren't allowed to release that information, but I went ahead, saying "If he's on board, have a message from Albuquerque Center for CPT Kominski. He's to call Marie as soon as he can after he lands." They didn't acknowledge for the message, so I asked them, twice, if they copied and they finally said, "We copy." I bet they did.

What makes it all the sweeter is that the squadron commander was on board in the right seat and it was he who took the message. When Erbacher called me at home later he said there were nine guys on board and all of them, including Kominski and the CO, heard the message. It went over great and Kominski has heard a lot of ragging since this afternoon. He's trying to keep everyone quiet about it but there's no chance of that, you can bet on it.

A couple of others onboard knew about it before it happened and the rest found out after, except Kominski. When they landed at Carswell AFB, the CO got off first to ride back in a staff car. Erbacher got off with him and explained the situation, not wanting Kominski to take a fall for something he wasn't responsible for. The CO thought it was a good laugh. So did everybody at work, especially when I got to the part about the Squadron CO being on board and taking the message. Who says you can't have fun and work for the government at the same time?

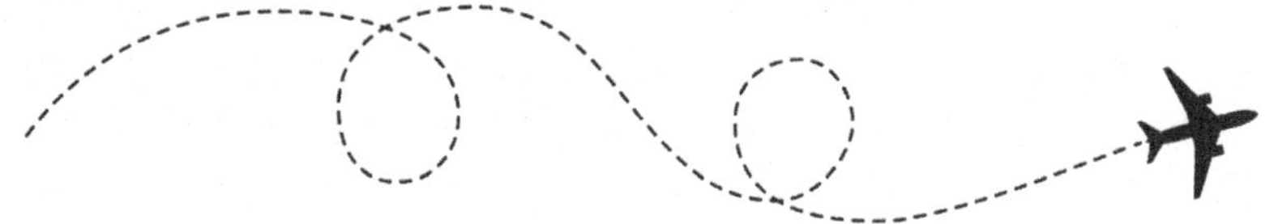

On MLC-lo N71CR was flashed to low by high. N71CR had been at FL260 and requested lower, so high-altitude put FL220 in the computer and handed him off. 71CR came over saying, "Fort Worth, 71CR, out of FL260 for 240, looking for lower." Not knowing the Gulfstream wanted a descent all the way into Addison, I said, "descend and maintain FL220, is that low enough for you?" The Gulfstream came right back with, "Not if we're going to land on the first pass."

ATC Tales 4

John Mock, called "Chopper" because when he was an evaluator he used to "chop" a lot of careers off in the bud, has a very loose style of controlling airplanes. He gave an aircraft a 30 degree turn for traffic, but the pilot argued, "We'd rather go direct, where's our traffic?" John's reply? "If you don't turn now, he's going to be in your cockpit!" I suppose he made his point.

John's brother-in-law, the recipient of a Ph.D., visited John at work once and John showed him around. At the end of their short tour John's brother-in-law told him, "For a man with no college degree, you're pretty smart." John, who had been a Navy P-3 pilot for four years and is a whiz at anything dealing with electronics, said, "For a man with a college degree you couldn't pour piss out of a boot unless the directions were written on the heel; and then the piss would come out only because you turned the boot upside down to read them."

ATC Tales 5

Tom Deppmeyer didn't take many fam trips but those he took have been eventful. Before he went on first trip his supervisor took in the office, sat him down and gave him the do's and don'ts of fam tripping. "Keep your mouth shut; speak only when spoken to; and don't do anything to embarrass the agency!" It's a DC-9 trip, Tom's sitting there minding his own business, being ignored by the crew when he smells smoke, a faint whiff but a whiff nevertheless.

"Should I say something about it?" The lecture came flooding back to him and besides, "these guys know what they're doing." The crew doesn't notice anything. Now it's much stronger and looking around he sees a puff of the white stuff coming out of a panel. "Surely these guys will notice it in a minute." In the meantime, he locates his own oxygen mask and makes sure it's working. By now the smoke is, while not billowing out, is coming out at what Tom feels is an alarming rate. He can wait no longer. Casting all inhibitions aside, and with his own mask firmly in hand, he taps the captain on the arm.

"Excuse me," he says, his voice ever so polite, and when the captain cocks his head around toward him, "but is that," he now points up to the smoke above and behind the co-pilot, "supposed to be like that?"

The captain was out of his seat in one motion, trying to scramble up, over and around Tom all at the same time, a mean feat in itself, as Tom is a big boy and the small DC-9 jumpseat was still down and Tom still in it. A stewardess had left something in the microwave which had self-destructed, with the resulting smoke coming forward through a panel into the cockpit. The problem was taken care of in short order and for the remainder of the flight Tom wondered if his bugging the captain to point out the problem could be construed as embarrassing the agency.

Tom wasn't much of one to take static off anybody. He was at a stoplight in Hurst one time when the fellow in the pickup next to him chucked a soft drink can on the ground. Tom told him he ought to pick it up and the fellow told Tom what he could do with himself. Tom got out of his truck, picked up the can and threw it in the back of the man's pickup, then leaned over in the fellow's window and started discussing the man's shortcomings with him. Needless to say, the man was a bit disconcerted and took off as soon as the light turned green. Tom's hand had been wrapped around the rearview mirror and it, the mirror, stayed with Tom as the car sped away, its driver hurling epithets back at Tom. Tom, not to be denied a parting shot, and not wanting the man to leave the mirror behind, took his best shot, throwing the mirror in a perfect arc, with it landing in the pickup's bed on the far side of the intersection.

ATC Tales 6

I got a note from a friend who flies for American Airlines. He's a big bad captain on Boeing 757s and 767s. He flew F-4s as a Navy pilot and while he doesn't walk on water, he sometimes thinks he does. Those Navy pilots . . .

He's been flying to England, slinking out of this hot weather we've been having, sliding over there for a few days every week, all the while telling his daughter and me and everybody else how he really wants to be here, suffering with all the rest of us. Yeah, right.

I worked some Navy pilots at work today. A fleet of P-3s came through on their way west from Hurricane Floyd, this half-dozen or so going to Dyess AFB in Abilene as the Navy seeks to protect their aviation assets from the ravages Floyd is sure to bring. You see this every time a hurricane comes through. All the military airplanes flee to the west until the hurricane's gone and then they gather up like a flock of mosquitoes and head back east.

I worked a 737 today, a fat little airplane that Southwest Airlines has hundreds of. This thing was a 200 series, and they aren't the world's best climbers. Needing the fellow out of 24,000 in a hurry, I asked him if his airplane was a 7-3 that climbed like a fast mover or one that climbed a rock. "We're a rock today," said the pilot, and so I stopped 'em at 22,000. He was never going to jump that Kingair. Some 7-3s, the 700 series, 800 series, climb like jet fighters. They rocket straight up and keep going until you tell 'em to stop. The 200 series stops its climb whenever the word "maintain" is issued in a clearance.

There are some Kingairs that climb pretty good, too. I was on Frisco one evening and was stepping up N65CR, a Kingair to Des Moines, under AAL50, a heavy DC-10 out of DFW to

London. The -10 was lumbering up slow but steady with me climbing N65CR a thousand feet at a time under him. I was ready for supper so Chuck Andrews was letting me go. In the briefing I told Chuck my plan, but I could tell he was eager to get in there and climb the Kingair, which he did as soon as I unplugged.

When I came back from chow a while later, Chuck stopped me to say that maybe he should have gone with plan A. He climbed the Kingair with the DC-10 steaming up behind him and the Kingair almost climbed right into him. Chuck had to tell the Kingair, "Maintain your present altitude," not descending him so the Kingair wouldn't arc over the top before starting back down. As it was, he had the separation, a thousand feet at five miles, but barely. Chuck's a little bit older now and a much more seasoned controller . . . and he doesn't climb Beech Rockets up in front of DC-10s.

ATC Tales 7

When the Training Department was taken over by a civilian contractor it conducted an "F.I.T." (Facility Instructor Training) course, a week-long course which trains instructors. One of the students was a fellow named Dave Davison from Albuquerque, a former supervisor there who had the infamous William B (WB) on his crew at Albuquerque Center.

William, it turns out, still owed him thirty-eight dollars and had done so for eight years, until one day when Davison caught WB on the control room floor and asked for his money back. WB, working a 0600-1400 shift, getting off at 1330, told Davison, "OK, come back at 1405 and I'll give it to you." Of course, WB would've left 35 minutes before. Davison, suspecting something's wrong, strolls down on the floor at 1315, when WB is writing up a trainee's grade sheet, and hangs around, waiting to talk to WB. WB stalled as long as he could but couldn't any longer so he got in an argument with Davison and finally gave him twenty dollars, now owing him only eighteen and telling him to "Come back tomorrow and I'll pay the rest." That placated Davison, who started talking to Don McKinney, telling him what was going on. McKinney started laughing, saying that he'd be lucky to catch WB tomorrow because he (WB) was leaving for a week's vacation in Chicago as soon as he got off work that afternoon. Davison started running after William, but I don't think he caught him.

ATC Tales 8

The Army used to teach Iranian students to fly helicopters at the Army's primary flight instruction facility at Fort Wolters, Texas. Once the students got checked out on solo flight, they were given the opportunity to do a low-level tactical navigation sortie. Normally, the students (10 or so, US and foreign trainees) would all get the same low-level routing and would be dispatched at approximately 5–10-minute intervals. They would all be in a string, so to speak, with a pathfinder (read instructor pilot) in the front and another at the rear of the string.

One of the intrepid Iranian students took off and was flying the route just fine when Mother Nature called, advising the student that Number Two was about to come calling. The student looked for a place to land in order to take care of business. The landing site came into view (a small open area right next to a brushy ravine). The Iranian student left the helicopter running while he went down into the ravine. As he was doing his business, the helicopter vibrated itself to the edge of the precipice and tumbled into the ravine. Big fireball, smoke, etc. . . .

Just about that time, the next student pilot, another Iranian, arrived on scene and spotted the wreckage. He landed on the freshly vacated site and ran down to see if there was a survivor. The sharp-witted (first) Iranian student quickly scrambled out of the ravine and jumped in the waiting helicopter and took off, leaving the Good Samaritan standing by the smoking hole. Try explaining that one to your instructor.

There was once a Turkish student undergoing T-38 training at Sheppard AFB. He was doing solo touch-and-goes and had to abort his takeoff, running the jet off the end of the runway. He shut down the engines and egressed the aircraft. When the crash truck got there, there was no pilot in sight. There was a big search for the student, but no one could find him. Then someone spotted the guy in the Officers' Club. When asked why he left the scene, he calmly claimed "I was not flying today; it must be someone else." That's one way to handle an aircraft accident.

ATC Tales 9

On the mid a while back we, Merv, George, and I, got to talking about off-the-wall situations of airplanes and people that we've worked over the years. You don't really think about all the stuff you've seen until you start telling "there I was" stories. I've written a few of them down just for the heck of it. Some are pretty good, and some aren't but they're almost all interesting—to me—which is why I write them down.

One of the best "good job" feelings I've ever had out there was one night on Mcalester-low when I was working a Beech Baron off Tulsa going to Dallas Love. He departed VFR and then, at 6,500 feet, got stuck on top of a layer. No problem, he figured, because Love Field was VFR and he'd have no problem at destination. Just after coming on frequency, however, he lost "everything but the alternator and the radio." He wasn't feeling very good about this and wanted to get it on the ground immediately if not sooner. Problem was that Tulsa was now socked in; so he headed south.

Near Henrietta, Oklahoma, still at 6,500 feet, I told the pilot he was near the airport and asked him if he wanted to go over it to see if he could see the ground. He replied in the affirmative and so I vectored him a bit to the southwest, got him over the airport where, lo-and-behold, there was a hole. He spiraled down below the clouds and then I vectored him to the field. It must have been a decent vector because he all but shouted, "We've got the runway! It's a beautiful sight. We're coming in to land!"

It was like watching the end of a dramatic movie, the plane on the verge of something potentially dangerous for cast and crew, and then the great finish.

I cleared him to advisory frequency, and he said, thanks, then left. There I sat, the feelings of a job well done ebbing and flowing through me, wanting to tell someone, but how do you tell someone stuff like this without seeming to want a pat on the back? Can't be done—at least not until well after it's over. [If I had to choose the best incident of my entire career, this would be it.]

BJS211 checked on frequency. Not knowing what BJS was, Pete Moss asked the pilot.

FW: "What's your callsign?"

BJS: "It's 'Solution,' like if you've got a problem, we've got a solution."

FW: "Do you have a teenager department?"

BJS: "No, we don't handle those problems. We barely have an adult department."

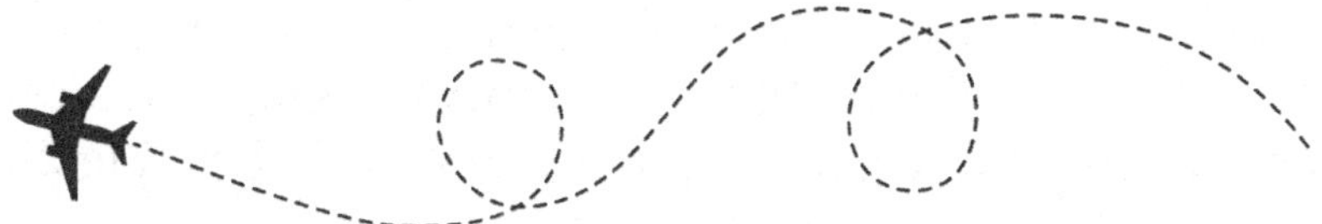

Pete Moss and a couple other fellows recently attended a hockey game. Spotting a couple of young lovelies, Pete said, "It isn't that I couldn't handle it. I'm so old I wouldn't know what to do anymore." Greg said, "I would; I remember."

ATC Tales 10

I worked an emergency on the mid once. Well, more than once but this one stands out. I had low altitude and was working a tanker and a C-141 receiver in AR-313 up by Tulsa. I'd pointed out the C-141 to Stillwater-low and they said, "keep him." They would watch him, and I would work him up to and down from the IP, keeping him in the block of 200B220.

George had high altitude. He was working an American Airlines Dash 80 out of Kansas City to DFW that was over Tulsa headed for Ardmore enroute to DFW when the aircraft had a sudden decompression and started down. George gave me a shouted warning across the aisle, and I assigned the C-141 flight level 2-0-0, then turned a heading of 0-9-0. I told him, "Make it a combat turn!" and he wrung it around like a fighter.

When the Dash 80 checked on frequency I assigned him flight level 2-1-0 to keep it legal. He said, "Yeah, right," but added, "but we can take vectors!" I turned him out to heading 2-6-0 and he kept it coming down to ten thousand.

I coordinated as best I could with Stillwater-low, then Tulsa Approach. The American went on down to 10,000 and on to DFW. He never did declare an emergency. The C-141 turned back to the AR track and life went on.

On jury duty one day, I found another fellow from work there, a fellow from Automation. Don S. Don's an interesting fellow; used to be a mortician before going into the Air Force as a controller. We saw each other late in the afternoon and visited until he got selected for a panel.

Mostly we talked about different people at work but started swapping airplane stories. Callsigns are a good starting point and I related the tale of FAGOT69, a B-52 I worked. Considering all its implications, it's a very strange callsign. When he checked on, I called him "Faggot six-niner" to which he replied, "Negative! Negative! It's Fajoe! Fajoe!"

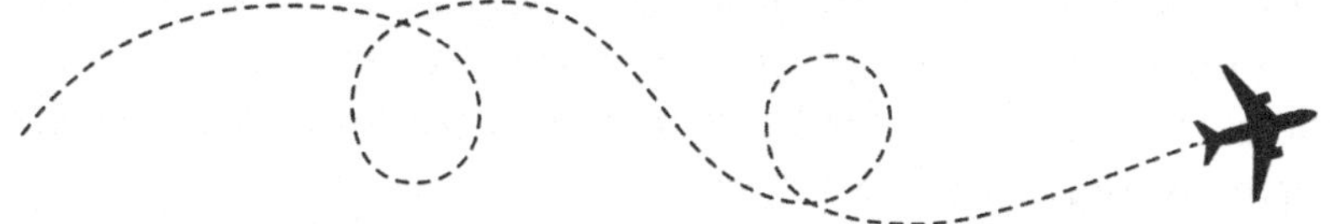

Don was inbound to San Diego on an American 727 being followed by a Delta 727. Needing some more space, the controller, obviously a trainee, told the Delta, "Slow to one-two-zero knots."

The Delta pilot couldn't and said, "If we slow to 120, we'll fall out of the sky," to which the American first officer on Don's flight quickly keyed his mike and said, "Report leaving even altitudes." Tower started saying, "I didn't say that; I didn't say that!"

Don has been collecting off the wall weather sequences for years and several stand out. A Lubbock sequence showed snow, rain and blowing dust, all in the same sequence. A Wink, Texas, sequence showed nothing except the time and "SOSNO," which nobody could figure out. Later, when the sequences returned to normal, an inquiry was made of the weather observer as to what it stood for. "Snakes on stairs; no observation," he said. Understandably so.

ATC Tales II

Years ago, I came back from a break to find Bob Hoover working a SLOP71, a KC-135 tanker out of Carswell AFB. Bob said he had asked the pilot if he had ever refueled the fighter group at Fort Smith. "Why?" inquired the pilot. Bob replied, "Because their callsign's 'HAWGs.'"

"That's not funny," came the reply.

I took the sector and Bob, with some glee, related the above. Never one to pass up a chance to have a go at a pilot, I called the pilot saying, "SLOP71, got time for a question?" answered by a laconic "Go ahead."

"I'm just back from break and I wondered if y'all ever refueled the fighters out of Fort Smith?"

"We didn't think it was funny when your friend asked it either," said he.

One day I worked a C-130, SCUM71, asking the usual question, "Where did you get the callsign?"

He was quick to say, "I wish I could get my hands on that guy because yesterday we were SCOW71."

Joe Purcell had been an Air Force controller in the early 50s and then came to work for the FAA. He had a penchant for Snickers bars but that didn't explain his nickname, "Joe Peaches."

One day Joe was working a Georgia ANG F-100, PEACH91. The radios weren't at their best and Joe couldn't understand the pilot's callsign. The strips hadn't been delivered to the sector yet, so Joe was going on what the pilot said. He asked the pilot to repeat the callsign several times and now the exasperated pilot said, "It's soft and fuzzy and sweet to eat." Joe said, "PUSSY91, Fort Worth Center, roger!" and the pilot shouted, "Negative! PEACHES, PEACHES, PEACHES!" He was Joe Peaches from then on.

A young lady was working an arrival push on HICOE-high. Kim Welte was in the jumpseat on an American inbound and actually heard her tell an arrival:

FW: "American 820, descend and maintain FL240."

AA: "Is that at our discretion?"

FW: "If I'd wanted to give you discretion, I'd have said 'pilot's discretion.' Start down now!"

A moment later a voice said, "Wasn't I married to you once?"

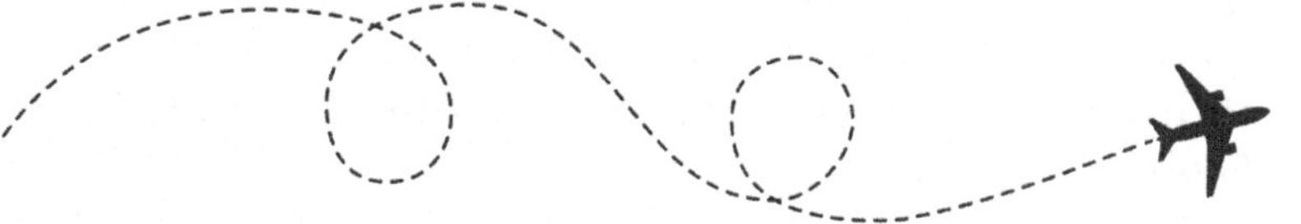

Coming from the south to land south at Tulsa there was a restriction to cross 30 miles south at or below 15,000, descend to ten thousand. Larry Foreman was training Kim Welte one day when they got a business jet 40 south, still at 41,000 feet. Kim, a brand-new trainee, gave the standard restriction, 30 out at or below fifteen, down to ten. The pilot, still at forty-one and having to lose over 25,000 feet in ten miles said, "Center, I couldn't make that restriction if I was a manhole cover."

ATC Tales 12

Ham Moses was getting a little busy on ADM-hi when he climbed an American off DFW. As he got to the altitude assignment part of the clearance his eye caught something it should have caught some time before: "AAL-348, climb and maintain . . . WHAHHH!"

Working OKC-lo D one day, I found myself sitting there with Randy Jordan on the R-side. Randy was fairly new with just four sectors under his belt—and brand new certified on OKC-lo. There were only two strips on as many aircraft, a C-141 out of high altitude inbound to Tinker AFB down J20 and an outbound BE90 off OKC to Dodge City, requesting FL220. Vance MOAs were hot and that sweetened the pot a little bit.

We obviously weren't busy so, in order to give Randy something to think over, I said to him, "I'll give you five bucks if, when that KingAir comes over, you ask him, 'Feel lucky today?' If he says yes, you have to give him direct Dodge City and climb him to FL220."

I knew that would cut him right across the C-141 descending and it would be tight. To be honest, I didn't expect him to do it (I wouldn't have) but when the KingAir came over Randy climbed him to twenty-two and then said, "N90DC, feel lucky today?"

When the pilot answered "Affirmative," Randy got a big old smile on that little bitty face and cleared the boy direct Dodge City with the C-141 screaming at him out of the northwest. He sure got my attention, and I came to the ready position immediately. The C-141 bobbed and weaved, dancing around western Oklahoma but Randy never turned the KingAir. The C-141 eventually got down and I stopped hyperventilating. That's when Jordan turned to me and said, "Where's my five bucks?"

I owed him five bucks, no mistake about that, but I wanted this to be a lesson to us both, so I gave him five Susan B. Anthony dollar coins. It taught me not to be so casual with my money, especially with Jordan, and it taught him never to bet with me if I'm carrying a lot of change.

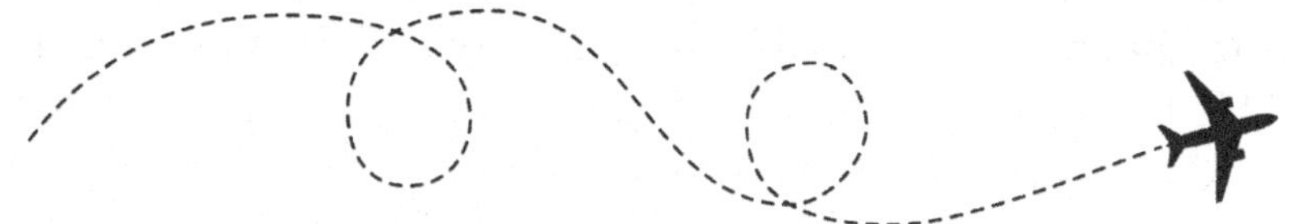

One day on Ardmore-hi I had five air carriers with their callsigns ending in "69," three Americans. 169, 369, and 569, and a Delta and a Continental each with a "369." After cautioning each and every one of the five of the similar-sounding callsigns, an interested voice said, "Wow! 69 must be a popular number!"

ATC Tales 13

A couple of nights ago a Twin Beech (BE-18) landed with its gear up at DFW, sometime in the late evening. Last night on the mid-shift I asked a Springair BE-18 if he knew "what company owned the Twin Beech that augured in to DFW, or should I say, landed with its gear up last night?" He said, "Curious choice of words 'cause I'm the pilot that 'augured in.' He had gear problems, so he decided to land gear up (as if he had a choice). Then he developed engine problems though of what nature he didn't specify. I asked him about damage to the aircraft and props. He said props on that plane were two-bladed so after he shut everything down, he kicked the starter a couple times to line the props up horizontal to the ground. Good thinking, I thought.

He was curious about the TV coverage. "What did they show? What did they say?" etc., etc. I asked him, tongue-in-cheek, if he was afraid the FAA would find out who he was and he just laughed. As I recall, the news report mentioned only the gear problem, nothing about the engines and I told him as much. I asked if he was in the plane in question and he chuckled on frequency. No, he said, "that plane has a lot of other problems than just gear and engines and it'll be in the shop for a while."

I asked him if they foamed the runway and he said that as a rule they don't do that anymore. He didn't explain why and I didn't ask. This particular plane's wheels don't entirely retract into the wells so although he bellied in, there wasn't too much damage.

Kind of interesting, this discussion. Rather like going straight to the horse's mouth for information. I told him I was glad he was OK and sent him off to Memphis Center. Another night by the boards.

ATC Tales 14

Brian Throop was working AQN-lo when a Delta started giving him a ration about the weather. Brian let it go until he could take it no more, telling the pilot, "DAL145, your disposition and attitude are incompatible with the flow of traffic. Turn right H180."

The pilot evidently couldn't believe his ears. "Say again?" came the query.

"DAL145, I say again, your position and altitude are incompatible with the flow of traffic. Turn right H180."

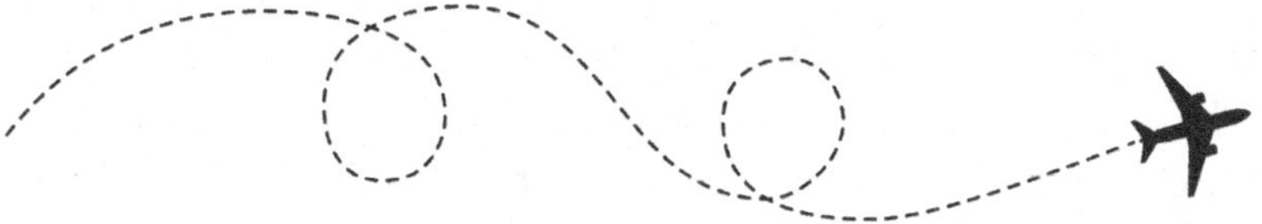

Brian was on HICOE-hi-R with Bob Pate on handoff when an American just west of Abilene in a chunk of weather wanted to know the best way to get to DFW. Just as Brian keyed his mike, Bob shouted, "Tell him to land at Abilene and take the f-----g bus!"

Mike McCully got into a conversation with a pilot one evening and asked, "What are y'all doing up there?"

The pilot replied, "Oh we're just eating cookies and milk."

And a female voice came out of the netherworld, "This is Cookie."

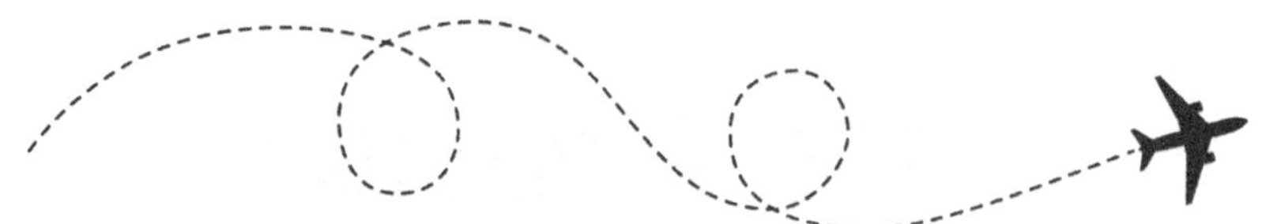

A friend of mine who flies for American came through one evening. We shot the breeze for a moment and then a soft female voice came on saying, "Center, it sure is fun flying with Dave."

"Dave," I said, "you'd better check that seatbelt 'cause I think it's cinched up a bit too tight."

Chad Etheridge was on OKC-hi D with Dudley Doright on the R-side. The sector was chock full of T-38s, all of them with callsigns of BILBO, BOBO, and DODO. Dudley was about to switch BILBO32 when Chad interrupted, saying "Don't you dare call him DILD032," admonishing DD several times.

Sure enough, "DILD032, contact . . ."

AFR086, Air France 86, came through, checking on, and ZFW replied: "Afro86, Fort Worth."

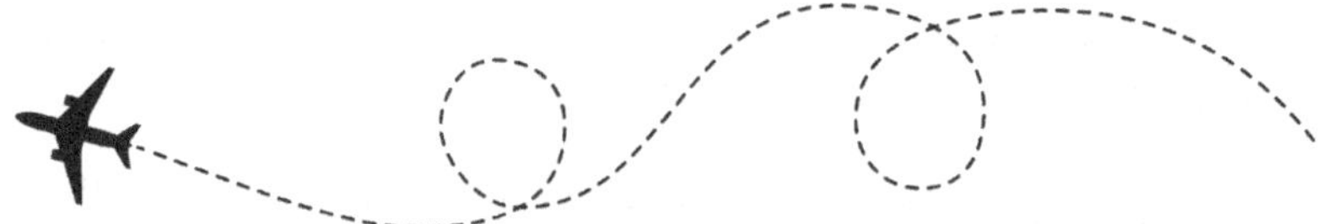

TAC01, Tac zero-one, the head of the USAF Tactical Air Command (TAC), came through. "Taco one, Fort Worth." When the pilot emphasized his callsign on this one, the controller was all the more adamant about calling him Taco.

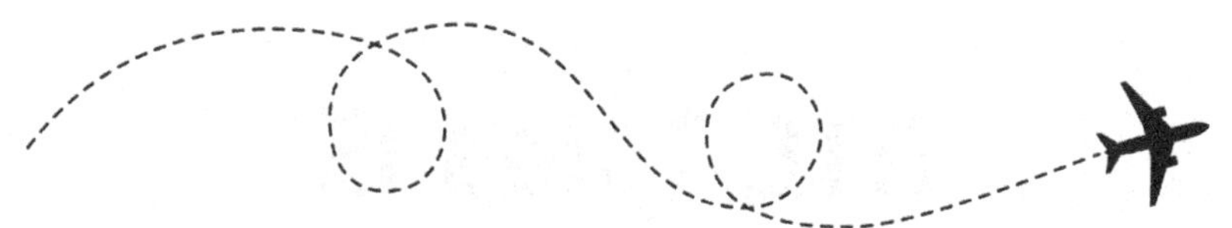

Britain's Royal Air Force uses the callsign "Ascot" in this country, the three-letter identifier being "RRR." A new controller seeing this for the first time called him, "Army Army Army." (Army's identifier is a single R.)

ATC Tales 15

Shorty Bush was working Mcalester high when a Kingair was drifting south off the airway. Shorty asked the pilot, "How's the visibility up there?"

"Oh, it's just fine," replied the pilot.

"Well," Shorty drawled, "look up north there about fifteen miles. That's J6. Go get on it."

Pete Moss asked an Eastern 727 over Oklahoma City heading east to Atlanta, "How's the visibility?"

"It's so clear I can see the tax increases in Washington," he said.

Chet May was on Oklahoma City-hi when he got a handoff from Liberal-high on a Delta 727, originally bound from San Francisco to Atlanta, who had declared a medical emergency and was diverting to Oklahoma City, requesting that the plane "be met by ambulance with a straight jacket."

Turned out a passenger had jumped out of his seat, ran to the aft galley, and started rummaging through the doors and drawers. He finally found the peanuts and started throwing the packages up into the cabin shouting, "There's microwaves in the peanuts and they're going to get you!" Then he started trying to open the aft door but was unable to do so.

At this point the crew was able to subdue him and made the early landing. They continued on to Atlanta in short order, without the passenger in question.

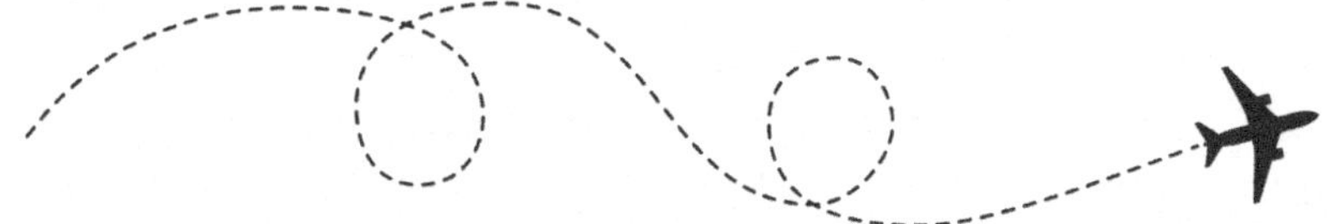

Pete Moss was on Oke City-high working two airplanes, an A-7 inbound to Tinker followed by a Mitsubishi MU-3 Diamond Jet inbound to Will Rogers. The MU-3 was about seven miles behind and 4,000 feet above the A-7 when he asked if there were any other airplanes in the vicinity. "We think we may have had a mid-air," the pilot said as he asked the question.

Pete told him there was an A-7 out there, four miles in front and 7,000 feet below him, but that was the only other airplane and was he ". . . declaring an emergency?"

No, he said, hut something had hit the front of the airplane and continued along the top to the back. There was no loss of control, but they were checking into it.

Pete switched him to low altitude, and he proceeded on to Will Rogers. Outbound Lisa Simonds worked him, and she asked him what had happened. The pilot said the windshield wiper motor had separated from the front of the airplane and evidently had traveled up over the top of the airplane, all the way down the top of it and then sailed off into space.

Too bad it wasn't raining. He'd have figured it out right away.

ATC Tales 16

Shorty Bush worked a Lear into Tulsa and the pilot, as Lear pilots are prone to be, a bit less than attentive. In fact, Shorty had nothing but problems with the boy, finally telling the lad he was incompetent and ought to pay more attention. The pilot, incensed at his treatment at the hands of ATC, said he was going to report Shorty to his chief pilot. Shorty told him that if the chief pilot hired him, then the chief pilot must be incompetent, too.

That didn't win Shorty any friends that day and the company sued for slander. An out-of-court settlement was agreed upon with Shorty having to apologize in writing. He apologized for calling the two pilots incompetent on the radio; not saying they weren't incompetent, just for calling them such on the air.

I occasionally ask controllers about the ATC experience that stands out most in their minds. Greg Peterson was a Navy controller for four years, serving in several places, including Midway and at an auxiliary training field in south Texas. He told me of one day when a brand-new Naval Aviator came into the tower asking if he could let his wife stay there and watch while he took an aircraft up to show off for her. He tried doing a roll right off the runway, flamed out and crashed, killing the pilot.

From Pete Costilow (PC) of OKC Approach: While flying out west somewhere, I heard a flight of F-16's call center for their clearance out of some bombing range and the call sign was FAGOT61. The center asked the pilot to repeat the call sign and the pilot said in a very effeminate voice, "Hey, we don't make 'em up, we just use 'em." As the controller keyed his mike to reply you could hear several people in the background laughing and the controller said, "Oh, we thought maybe you guys had your own air force."

Again PC: A friend of mine in the Army National Guard was flying a C310 one day when he lost both alternators. He was at 6,000', in the clouds, and asked the controller at Ft. Worth Center if he could have a lower altitude to get below the clouds as he had lost both generators and thought he might lose his radios. She said very excitedly, "Are you declaring an emergency?" He calmly replied, "No ma'am, I'm trying to prevent one."

While working a mid-shift one night, PC got an inbound to Tinker AFB on a C141, call sign, PUSAY69. When the aircraft called on frequency, PC asked him about his call sign and the pilot said, "The funny thing is, we're hauling a load of WAF's (Women's Air Force)."

Another inbound to TIK . . . a KC135, call sign DUMAS50. When PC asked the pilot how to pronounce the callsign he replied, "It depends which one of us you are talking to."

Pete told a VFR to squawk 0411 one time and after a long pause he said in a frustrated voice, "Approach, you better give another code, I can't get this last digit past seven."

Overheard in ABQ Center's airspace years ago on a mid, "TWA122, I've got to go to the bathroom, if anybody calls just tell them to ident."

A C130 reported in holding over the ABI VOR one night at 6,000′. This report was immediately followed by an excited voice that said, "Approach, approach, we're over the ABI VOR at 6,000′." This was followed by, "You oughta be, you dumbass, you're sitting right next to me."

Pete Costilow was working a flight of two Air Force Reserve F-4s, OKIE91, who said they wanted to split up into two single ships.

OKC: "Roger. What's your wingman's name?"

OKIE91: "Marvin B Case."

OKC: "OKIE91 roger. Tell Marvin to turn 40 degrees right, vector for spacing."

OKIE92 was "Marvin" all the way to Tinker.

ATC Tales 17

Walt Gilbertson was an army controller at Fort Rucker, Alabama. He enjoyed flying private planes as well so one day he and a friend were out tooling around in a small Cessna. They pulled up alongside a big helicopter, an army CH-47 Chinook, as it lumbered through the skies. Walt's friend looked over at the army pilot with a big "We're as fast as you" grin. The army pilot waved and then boom! They were in the chopper's dust. The helicopter took off. (Chinooks can do 170 mph; small Cessnas maybe 130.) Talk about being left at the altar.

Alan Neace was working a Braniff to DFW who requested "Direct to the dam," meaning the Lake Grapevine dam just north of DFW for a south landing. Alan queried, "Direct to the dam what?"

ATC Tales 18

Mugwump was working a Grumman American from TUL-MLC-BUJ-DAL at 8,000. These aircraft are generally pretty slow anyway, 100 knots with no wind but this guy had a 40-knot headwind and a groundspeed that averaged about 55 knots. Dismayed, the pilot said, "I might as well go back to Tulsa 'cause cars, buses, and even slow trucks are passing me."

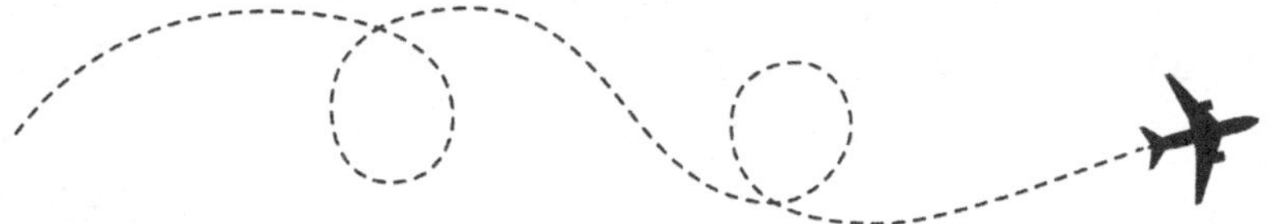

Helicopters are generally pretty slow and a pain for controllers to work. Sometimes they have their advantages though, as Merv Newman found out one night when Waco Approach closed up shop and went home, giving him the airspace. Waco Approach had a Jet Ranger helicopter doing an ILS approach to Waco Municipal and a DC-9 on a visual approach at TSTC Airport. There's enough separation for an approach control to do that but not Center. When the helicopter reported intercepting the ILS, Merv snapped, "Stay where you are!" Talk about being grateful the fellow was a Jet Ranger.

N680HH, a Convair 640, was given a pretty tight crossing restriction off BYP. Concerned about the aircraft making the restriction, Pete Moss asked the pilot if he could do it.

"We'll do it. We're coming down like a chicken-wire submarine."

ATC Tales 19

Overheard in the control room:

1. In a discussion about GPADs (performance evaluations), said by a fellow who is not the best controller in the world: I'm gonna be fully successful no matter what happens. If everybody else is going to do my work, I'm certainly not going to complain.

2. Someone asked an American, "How's your ride?" AAL: As smooth as the thighs of a high school cheerleader.

Every once in a while, you get a real groaner, a pilot who would probably complain about everything. Pete Moss had one a few days ago. On DAL-hi and needing to sequence a couple airplanes to Houston Hobby Airport, he turned and slowed N335H to follow a Southwest. N335H queried the turn and speed control and Pete told him why. The pilot shot back in a bitter tone, "Yeah, anything for Southwest," implying favoritism. Pete muttered something under his breath about having the pilot come sequence airplanes for a while but it ain't gonna happen.

I was working McAlester-low and cleared an American flight up to 22,000, telling him that would be his final altitude rather than the 28,000 he requested initially. I then re-cleared him on a shorter route and, as I'm supposed to do, restated the altitude, then waited for his readback. Instead of reading it back, he said, "Roger," meaning he understood. I could have let it go at that, but something told my little brain that I'd best get a full readback and pressed the issue with him. He then proceeded to read back the old clearance down the longer route. I re-cleared him, again, down the shorter route and asked for a full readback to which he got bent out of shape and said, "We read back what we had, Slick."

Another fellow happened to be plugged in with me and heard the "Slick," so for a few days the crew called me "Slick." I managed to restrain myself from chewing out the pilot. He wasn't paying as much attention as he should have been and, for once, I was.

ATC Tales 20

I worked a crash last night on the mid, a VFR Cherokee-six that probably ran out of gas about 10 miles west of Ardmore, Oklahoma. The guy said he had a rough engine, but I think that was the sputtering of the engine as the gas ran out. I figured the gas part out later, after realizing he had been in the air at least 800 miles. 800 miles at night! And then the guy runs out of gas 10 miles from his destination. It's a sick feeling sitting there knowing that somewhere up north there's a guy, in trouble, that he may be going down, that in all likelihood disaster has passed the impending stage, has passed the imminent stage, and has in fact occurred. You feel helpless knowing you can't help the guy.

I did what I could, called Radio and started a search and rescue effort, but that's always an after-the-fact item. The plane's out there somewhere, already down, passengers hurt—or worse. Last night we were lucky. Although he was VFR, he was talking to ATC so someone was watching him. I had some trouble talking to him for a while but when push came to shove, he was on frequency long enough to mention his rough engine and thus, albeit indirectly and unintentionally, get the search process started.

I called Radio to have them do the basics and called the front desk to see if the supervisor wanted the Ardmore Police to do a ramp check at Ardmore Downtown Airport. "We want," he said. Radio had that started before I got back to them. I had another airplane, CKE532, Checkmate 532, monitor the airport's unicom frequency, 122.7, to listen for calls from the aircraft. Nothing.

At a loss for a "good" way to phrase the next transmission, I said, "Checkmate 532, I don't know how to say this, but can you do a 360 to look for a fire?" I felt like I was writing the

Cherokee off. Nothing there either. "They don't always burn on impact," the supe said. The Checkmate did get a strong ELT signal at the spot where I lost the guy on radar. That's not a good sign, especially since the Checkmate said he didn't even have to break squelch to pick it up. That means it's close.

Eventually Radio called and said the Lone Grove Police Department had found the aircraft on the ground "near US70." Offhand I'd say the fellow was trying to land on the highway, but I have no way of knowing. There were two injured and they were "transported to the hospital." I don't know the extent of their injuries but at 0400 they were still alive.

After all the above, next comes the bad part—for any controller who happens to find themselves in a situation of this sort. Once the mill starts to grind, it starts spewing out paperwork. There are all sorts of procedures to follow, forms to fill out, people to be notified, a lot of stuff that needs doing. It's an inexorable process that takes its time to gear up but once started, seems to go on and on and on. Part of that process is to remove the controller from the position he's working until some sort of official determination is made as to whether or not he had any part toward the cause of the incident or accident, either directly or indirectly. Tapes are pulled and listened to by some fellow a lot higher up the food chain than I am. He then makes a determination as to whether or not the controller can go back to work.

Last night the man making that decision was the facility chief. He has to be called in an event like this, especially if there's a possibility of fatalities. The plane went down about 0135. The chief got out here about 0250 and the three of us, him, me, and the supervisor, went back in some room way back in the back somewhere, some room I can never find unless someone else shows me the way. Together we sat around listening to the tape. It was pretty much as I thought—they found nothing wrong and, after some consultation, I was told I could go back to work.

I'll still have to write a statement but that can wait until next week when I come back. Considering that he was VFR, not IFR, I might not even have to do that. I'd not mind skipping the statement; don't want the old John Henry on too many official documents. It's on enough already.

As a follow up to last night's crash, today the following appeared on an OKC TV station: It went down on a farm in Lone Grove, west of Ardmore. The plane barely missed a farm house occupied by a volunteer firefighter and his girlfriend who just happened to be paramedics. The pilot husband made it to the farmer's door, asked for help in extracting his wife and collapsed in the farmer's arms. The farmer and the paramedic got the woman out of the aircraft (no fire) and they are in serious condition in an Ardmore hospital. The story being told is that they lost all electrical power, everything just went black and he tried to make an emergency landing on the highway, landing in the farm instead. The accident is under investigation.

[A few days after the above was written, I spoke with Ardmore Tower about this incident. The tower controller said the pilot got out of the aircraft, crawled to the door, and began banging on it as best he could. When the farmer opened the door, he saw nobody standing there but, on looking down, he saw the pilot who explained the situation, saying he and his wife both needed serious help. The farmer said to the pilot, "Today's your lucky day! I'm an EMT with the volunteer fire department and my girlfriend is spending the night and she's an EMT too."]

I don't like working crashes, nobody does really, but they happen. Some people never work them and some work several in their career. In 1982, '83, somewhere back there, I was relieving Roy Newsom for a break on Mcalester-low. He wasn't too busy but there was some weather out there in southeastern Oklahoma. He'd finished the briefing part and was giving the traffic when I pointed to the track of a VFR Cherokee Six at 10,500 feet, the beacon of which had disappeared.

This guy was skirting a thunderstorm and to see a beacon disappear wasn't a good sign. Roy stopped the briefing and called the aircraft to say he'd lost the beacon and to recycle. The guy came back saying they were going down. They had lost the engine, lost the wing, and they were going to crash. I stayed on the D-side, moving Roy over to the R-side, and we got started on everything I mentioned above. There were three people on that one, the pilot along with the owner and his wife. The pilot talked but the woman was screaming in the background, all the way down.

Turned out Roy knew the male passenger, the aircraft owner. He had been a controller at Houston Center with Roy some years before. Fortunately, we didn't find this out until later. The last position Roy had them at was the MLC117023. Amazing how little details like that stick with you, even after all these years. Something else that still hits me on occasion is the chill I get when I see a beacon disappear. At least in last night's accident, there were survivors. That part makes you feel better.

ATC Tales Extra
(William Bester)

William Bester died last Friday after a long struggle with bad health, congestive heart failure, a heart attack or two and as many strokes. He was big and fat and you knew it was coming but it was still a shock when I walked in to work yesterday afternoon and heard the news.

He left here three or four years ago after getting his ticket pulled with no chance of getting it back. He didn't fit in upstairs and he didn't want to fit in anywhere else, so he retired.

Not many people were sorry to see him retire. He was obnoxious, always stirring up trouble, causing it, doing whatever he could to stir the pot. He was what you might call a true "character of ATC." He transferred here from Albuquerque Center in 1978. A big-boned Black man, he was as big around as he was tall. And he was as big a talker as he was around. He would spin a tale that went on forever. If it was so outlandish that you called him on it, he'd just spin it off in another direction. William was known to stretch the truth on occasion. I'd say he saw the truth as being elastic.

He had been here a year when he remembered he was divorced and that his ex-wife and kids were still in Albuquerque. He filed an amended travel voucher and got a suspension. The girl he'd been dating, the one who tipped him off he was being investigated for fraud, she got fired.

He led a charmed life. When he arrived here, he was the Executive Vice President of the National Coalition of Black Air Traffic Controllers. I don't think management really knew what to do with him so consequently they didn't do much. He came and went pretty much as he wanted. He had a whole flock of guardian angels up in the FAA somewhere because whenever he did something that mere mortals would have been fired for, he either got away with it or got a light punishment. And it wasn't, as some people said, just because he was "Black," but because he was William.

He was one of the three Blacks in the Southwest Region who didn't go on strike in August 1981. He caught a lot of flak for it, too. He caught a lot more flak one day shortly after the strike when he waved over Shorty Bush and Bob Hoover as they drove to work on SH183. He wanted to ride in with them, so he got in the back seat and hid while Shorty drove.

William hunkered down in the back seat as Shorty turned off American Boulevard onto FAA Road and proceeded through the picket line and all the strikers. Shorty kept pointing to the back seat as if to show the strikers there was somebody back there. Hoover, who had voted to go on strike, then came to work two hours later, was catching a lot of static from the picket line but matters soon changed when Shorty parked right by the fence.

Parking spaces were a dime a dozen after the strike. You could park pretty much anywhere you wanted, including right up front, which is where William thought Shorty was parking. Shorty parked as close to the gate as he could, and William caught beaucoup flak when he crawled out of the back. The crowd screamed at him all the way to the door.

William ran a LogAir off Tinker AFB up into Kansas City Center's airspace without a handoff one night on a mid. That was bad enough, but he compounded the matter by going to the Waffle House without telling anybody. He said he did but the other two fellows said he didn't, so he bought it. Initially he got 30 days off for that but later it was reduced to 15 days. Only William.

William turned up in the most unusual places. Mike Copp saw him at Chicago Midway one time when a Learjet taxied up and let him off, purple hat with a-big feather on his head and a good-looking woman on his arm. I saw him at DFW a week before he retired. I was in the back on an AmTran charter to Las Vegas. William's current girlfriend was in the back and he was doing a flash-and-dash. I was walking through the crowd at DFW and heard the familiar, "Cheeney Cheeney," his "nom de jour" for me. I introduced him to my wife, her saying later she now believed every story I'd ever told her about him.

He borrowed a lot of money from folks and always took his sweet time paying it back, if he ever did. He sold a lot of stuff out of his trunk. Some of it was good and some not so good. Sometimes you paid for something and never got it. You always got a line of BS though, and you got it with a smile.

Four guys showed up at the gate one day, there to collect money for a gambling debt from William. The guard called the specialty desk, telling the supe that the four wanted to see WB in the worst way. William, knowing why they were there and not wanting to confront them himself, enlisted John Frey to be the delivery boy. John, a fairly short young man, took the handful of money WB gave him and went out to the gate to speak with the assembled crowd, all of whom were a lot taller than him. The leader was not happy about the amount of money John presented to him but he told the fellow that William had said, "That's all I got." The leader took the money and started getting in John's face. John later said that he didn't know he could bend himself in half, backwards, until that day.

I guess I got along with William because I recertified him when he came back from Chicago Center in 1983 or '84, somewhere in there. Joe Woodard, my supervisor, was getting him on the crew and I was the only journeyman without a trainee, so I got him. He had his own unique way of working air traffic but while I trained him for recertification, he worked the sector the way I wanted him to. I didn't hassle him, and we always got along, sort of, after that. I think it helped that for many years we were on different crews. With William that always helped.

He was always getting onto pilots. He'd give a clearance and if a pilot didn't snap to, he didn't mind getting on their case. He cleared an F-16 to FL310 westbound off Tinker AFB, and the pilot read back 3-1-0 and went to 330, right in the face of a Southwest at 330 inbound to OKC. Instead of chasing the boy back down to 310 and chastising him later, he started in on the pilot's case, then got him back down. That was typical.

He was obstinate to the nth degree. On the mid he'd work high altitude all night. Memphis Center would call up saying all the FEDEXs would be direct destination. "Leaves 'em on da route!" he'd shout, and on the route they'd be. If a direct slipped into his sector, WB wouldn't change the fellow's heading, no matter how bad the heading might be.

On the other hand, the guys he flashed-and-dashed with, he'd give them direct all the time. Starcheck to Chicago would come off Love and check on climbing to 230. "Climb and maintain FL370 and out of 2-4-0 you knows what to do!" The Starcheck would read it back, "3-7-0 and out of 24 direct to the big house!" and away he'd go to Joliet out of 24,000.

The same to Denver. "Climb and maintain FL390 and out of 2-4-0 you knows what to do!" "3-9-0 and direct Centennial out of 24."

Even after William left, he still had an "in" at the Regional Office. Before personnel announcements were made for the facility he'd call out and say who was going to get what, days before it was announced officially. Where he got his information nobody knew, but it was generally accurate. That was William. Even after he was ATC history, he still knew what was what.

Was he all bad? No, he was one of those larger-than-life characters that used to permeate this place. They're fading away now, going into the netherworld of retirement, some never to be seen again. William was a rogue; to some a loveable rogue and to some, far from loveable. Still, he was a person you remembered. Almost anyone who knew him had a story about him, usually with some sort of twist that left you wondering how he either got away with it, or out of it. In his own inimitable way, he was quite a guy.

ATC Tales 21

One night on a mid-shift the controllers working east Texas were taking it easy, the last rush already having gone out and the next arrival push not due until well after they would leave in the morning. An American Airlines freighter off DFW to New York was climbing to FL 330. A series of voices came over the speaker:

AA818 requesting direct JFK

Roger, AA818 direct JFK

AA818 direct JFK.

The controller, realizing all was not right in this situation, asked AA818 how he got the clearance to JFK. After all, he, the controller, had never said a word. Turns out it was very dark in the cockpit and the two pilots were facing away from each other. One asked for direct JFK without telling the other he was doing so. The other pilot heard the request, thought it was a clearance direct and acknowledged for it. The first, thinking the other's acknowledgement was the clearance, answered for what he thought was the clearance direct JFK.

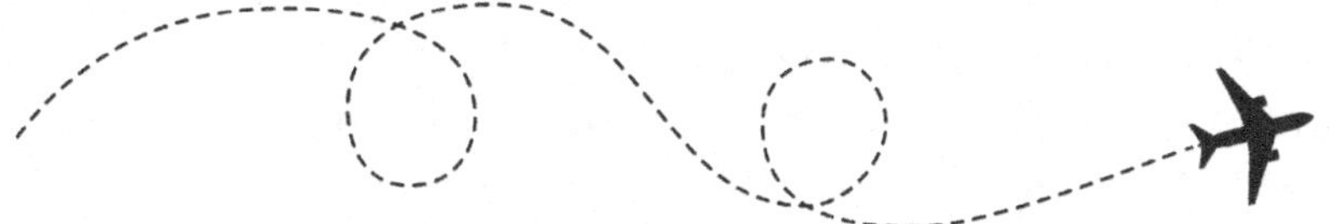

Don Frenya was working an inbound rush when he turned a Delta out for spacing. The Delta started giving Don a ration of static about why he had to turn, why not somebody else, why was he being picked on, so and so forth, you get the picture. Don let him run on and on and then just keyed his mike and uttered a short "waah, waah," just like a baby crying. I love it.

ATC Tales 22

Pete Moss got a "Letter of Superior Performance" for helping a VFR Cessna find his way to safety after blundering into bad weather while trying to traverse the mountains in southeastern Oklahoma. He told Pete, "We're near Wilburton, Oklahoma," which up east of Mcalester. Remember all this was in a non-radar environment and there's isn't that much radar anyway, out where he was. Pete had to use a VFR chart to help the pilot navigate his way through a valley in the mountains. After all was said and done and the pilot got out of the mountains to the plains, he told Pete he had been near Atoka, not Wilburton, earlier, which meant he was near 40–50 miles southeast of where he said he was earlier. When Pete started giving him suggested headings, and he started taking them, Pete was looking at one section of the map and the pilot was looking at another. No wonder he could never find the railroad tracks.

As it turned out, the headings Pete gave him also put him into a valley though that valley wouldn't have taken him to Fort Smith, Arkansas, as the valley Pete was looking at would have. Eventually, when he got to the end of the valley he was in and the cloud bases were coming down to the ground, thereby forcing him down into the same, he made a wise decision and reversed course. I'm sorry to say not all pilots are that smart.

Alan Neace's favorite Mexicana story:

Alan (AL) was working a day watch on Acton low (the DFW I s southwest cornerpost). Mexicana 855 came on the frequency descending to FL240. AL cleared him to cross Burleson at

7,000 and gave him the altimeter to which he said "Royer." Burleson was about 15 miles inside Acton, so when Alan recognized the pilot would not make the restriction, he coordinated the descent with Feeder West. It was approved.

Then, as the airplane sailed past AQN out of about FL 180, Alan asked the pilot if he was going to make Burleson at 7,000. He said, "Well, seenter, I tell you, yesterday we make it; today we don't." To which AL said, "Royer," cancelled his crossing restriction, and switched him to Feeder West.

(As most folks know, AAL flights showing four digits and beginning with a "9" are ferry flights.)

FW: "AAL-9191, are you a ferry flight?"

AAL: "The plane is, the crew isn't!"

FW: "AAL-9524, are you a ferry flight?"

AAL: "Center, you better watch how you say that!"

Pete Moss found himself on Frisco-lo when a strange three-letter identifier (CDL) came through, a Merlin at ten from the east coast to Abilene. He strained to hear the callsign but couldn't catch it.

CDL9163: "Fort Worth, umbly umbly 9163 with you at 1-0-thousand."

Repeating what he thought he heard, Pete charged on:

FW: "Tailhunter 9163, Fort Worth Center, roger."

CDL9163: "Negative! Negative! It's Carolina! Carolina! (then after a discreet pause . . .) but we like 'Tailhunter.'"

ATC Tales 23

Jim Elkins worked a Navy C-9 off Tinker AFB to Navy North Island in San Diego. Jim asked the pilot if he wanted direct and the pilot said he did. Jim got the coordinates from the pilot and gave them to Allen Arnett, who started putting it in the computer. The pilot said, "I've got 90 sailors off the Nimitz sitting in the back who thank you very much." Jimmy said, "I've got an ex-Marine typing it in right now."

There was a short pause and then, "Help him with the big words, will you?

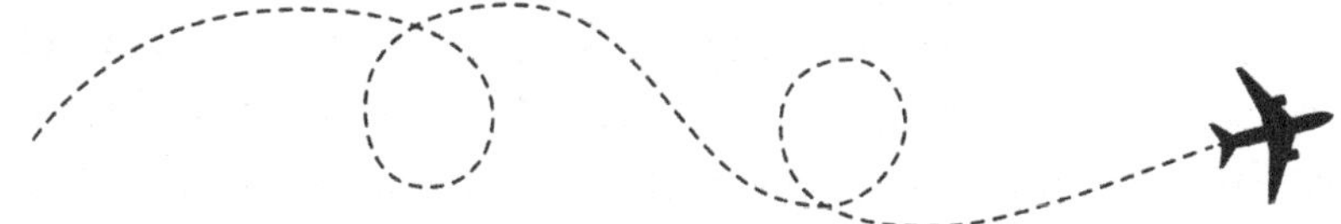

There used to be a guy at work whose nickname was "Black Cloud." This guy had incredibly bad luck, to the point where people hated to work with him because they knew bad things would happen.

To give you an idea of how bad his luck was, I'm told that he married his first wife on a Saturday afternoon at two o'clock. Three hours later while driving off on their honeymoon, they hit a bridge abutment and she was killed.

Years later he had remarried and had several kids. He was up on his roof one winter day when his wife came out to say that their son, who had been visiting down the street, had broken his leg and needed to go to the hospital. As he started down, he slipped and fell off the roof, nearly missing a stockade fence as he hurtled toward the ground. On his way down, he said later. "I wondered how much sick leave this is going to cost me." He wasn't seriously hurt in the fall, so he and his wife picked up their son and headed off to the hospital, having a wreck on the way.

He would sit down at a sector and the radios would fail. He would plug into a sector and an airplane might declare an emergency or even crash. He answered a ringing pay phone (in the old Center on Blue Mound Road in north Fort Worth) and heard a man say he wanted to declare a near miss. He worked the first C-5 aircraft as it crashed at Clinton, Oklahoma. The eight-man crew made it OK. The Clinton runway, the whole runway, was destroyed.

At Vance AFB for a T-38 ride, his pilot told him Vance hadn't had a flameout in several years. His aircraft lost an engine on takeoff, barely making it back to the runway. On a fam trip to Tulsa one day, his American Airlines 727 was cleared to land and descended out of a very low cloud deck, almost landing on a bulldozer sitting on the runway.

He was assigned to the training department for a while, working with a radar class that finished on a Thursday. He was asked if he would work in the control room the next day to help staffing. He was working Mcalester-low with a flight of four F-105s in the Rivers area. Near the end of his shift, a 7-3, one went back to Tinker as an emergency. The aircraft crashed on the runway though the pilot survived. Asked to stay an extra hour because staffing was short, he stayed on the same sector, and one other F-105 crashed in the Rivers area. The pilot was killed

With 18 months to go before retirement, Dick couldn't take it any longer. He quit and didn't come back. He was offered a job upstairs just to get him through to retirement. He didn't want it. He wanted out and nothing more to do with the FAA. After the PATCO strike the FAA called, asking him to come back as a GS-14 and work until retirement. He mentioned it to his supervisor where he now works and the fellow said, "I'll give you a six cent an hour raise." Dick said, "I'll take it!" He's a photographer now and is perfectly happy where he is.

ATC Tales 24

There was a crusty old fellow named Francis Frantz (FJ) out there when I first hired on. A bit of a grump, he didn't take much static from anybody, especially pilots. A B-17 co-pilot in the 95th Bomb Group during WWII, he was shot down on his second mission in January 1943 and spent the rest of the war in a POW camp. One day in the coffee shop some people were swapping war stories and he discovered that he and another controller had been in the same POW camp, nearly the same barracks, but alas, had not known each other.

Frantz didn't like airline pilots and generally refused to talk to them unless necessary. Used to be, all the DFW terminal arrivals over Tulsa went to Mcalester, then Blue Ridge, no exceptions, and daily we would get hundreds of requests for direct Blue Ridge to get out of that (itty-bitty) dogleg. Since the DFW departures came out over Mcalester it wasn't a good idea to approve direct Blue Ridge if you had any departures, but some people wouldn't approve it, period, especially Francis.

One day a Braniff over Tulsa came on:

BN: "Fort Worth, BN125 requesting direct Blue Ridge."

No answer from Fort Worth, 'cause like some radio stations, Francis didn't take requests.

BN: "Fort Worth, BN125 requesting direct Blue Ridge. "

Again, no answer. Now the pilot hasn't heard a word from Center and he's beginning to get a little antsy

BN: "Center, BN125."

FJ: "Go ahead, BN125."

BN: "This is the captain of BN125. Did you hear our request for direct Blue Ridge?"

FJ: "Affirmative."

BN: "Well, how about it?"

FJ: "Negative. "

BN: "I guess we definitely settled that, didn't we?"

FJ: "Affirmative."

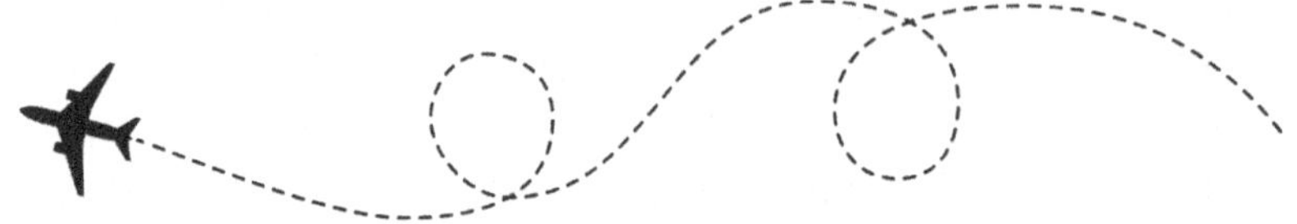

As a rule, Frantz didn't give VFR advisories. He didn't really like VFRs and would just as soon see every one of them grounded for life. He rarely even gave advisories on VFR aircraft to IFR aircraft but if he did, you knew the two would be close. One day a Continental inbound to Oklahoma City was, FJ thought, going to smack a VFR as he descended. Francis even went so far as to turn the Continental 20 right to go behind the VFR.

CO: "What's the reason for this turn?"

FJ: "There's a VFR aircraft at . . ." (and gave the position)

CO: "We're running late, and we don't have to turn for a VFR aircraft. We're going direct Oke City."

Francis never liked pilots anyway and by now he hated this one.

FJ: "Roger. It's your life."

The pilot called in on that one.

One day an Eastern at FL350 was out of Atlanta, over Will Rogers J6 Twenty-Nine Palms, LAX, and ran into a line of weather just west of Sayre, Oklahoma (SYO). FJ explained that the only way anybody was getting through by going down to FL310 and heading straight west out of SYO.

EA: "We don't want to go down to 3-1-0. We want to stay out at 3-5. Can we take a heading?"

Francis knew that wouldn't work but he had already explained the situation he said . . .

FJ: "What heading do you want to fly?"

EA: "Heading 1-8-5."

FJ: "Roger, fly heading 185, vectors around weather "

The plane headed south and there was no end to the weather in sight. FJ pointed him out to several sectors but kept him on frequency. Finally, with no end to the weather in sight, the pilot asked:

EA: "How long do we have to stay on this heading?"

FJ: "You picked the heading, you fly it!"

ATC Tales 25

Joe Purcell was an old sort who had been an Air Force controller in Japan and was now working for the FAA. He usually had one hand wrapped around a Snickers bar and the other free for everything else, mostly scratching.

One night a TWA off OKC westbound was running into weather and asked, "Which way are the deviates going tonight?"

Joe snapped back, "The ones in the airplanes are going south!"

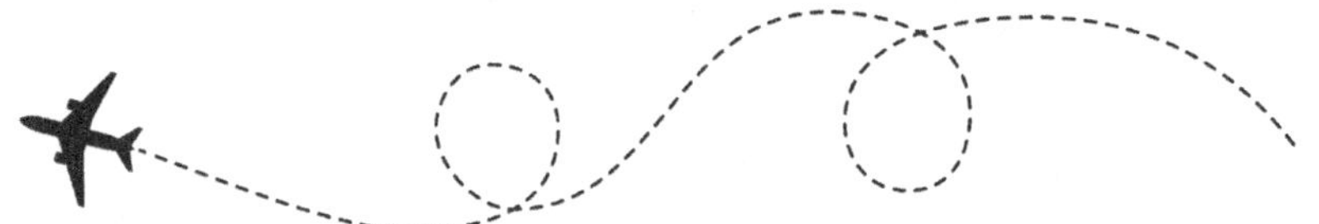

When he was on his way out, which in those days consisted of a couple months at the Schick Center having your head examined before getting your medical, Joe confronted one of the psychologists there with a perplexing situation. Asked if he drank, Joe said he had two beers a day.

"Why two," the psychologist wanted to know. "Why not one or three?"

Because he "wanted two, no more, no less," he countered.

The shrink went on, "What do you when you go to bed?"

Joe said he "read a while."

"You should use the bed only for sleep! If you're not tired when you go to bed," he insisted, "get out of bed and do pushups until you are tired, then go back to bed!"

Joe asked, "What should I do, f--- on the floor?" That was one of Joe's last sessions.

When Chuck Yeager's book, "Yeager," came out I read it as did any red-blooded American boy who loves aviation. There's a part in there about the true-blue fighter pilot who thinks only of the mission, never about anything else. If the engine quits you get out, Yeager said. You don't worry about what the airplane's going to hit, where it will wind up. You get out so you can fly another day.

A week or two after reading that I was sent to work Bill Barfield's D-side on OKC-low. A Navy A-7 at 29,000 feet, southwest of Gage inbound to Tinker lost its engine and was now a glider trying to make Clinton-Sherman (CSM) and its 10,000-foot runway. The pilot still had his radios and was riding the plane down as he tried to restart the engine. It wasn't working and Barfield wanted the pilot to get out. The pilot, very cool considering the situation, said he would leave at 13,000, if he couldn't make CSM

Barfield had his face pressed to the scope and was wrapped up in what was going on. There wasn't much other traffic, and he devoted all his attention to the A-7, now passing through thirteen, far enough from CSM to where it was obvious that he wouldn't make the runway. "Are you baling out?" Bill demanded, very agitated

"Negative," the pilot came back, "I'm gonna stay with it a while."

This didn't make Bill happy at all. He kept mumbling to himself and the scope, "get out; get out; get out!"

Now down through 8,000 Bill started shouting at the pilot, "Bale out! Bale out!" and the laconic reply, "Not yet."

The elevation out there is about 1600 feet above sea level, so at 6,000 MSL this guy was less a mile above the ground. As the plane left 5000, Bill, almost screaming now, said, "Get out! Get out!"

The pilot's next transmission caused Yeager's words to flash to mind as he, ever so calmly, said, "I'm just looking for a place to put it. I wouldn't want to hit a school."

The pilot, a Navy Lieutenant, aimed the A-7 at a field and then left the aircraft just below 4,000 feet some 7 miles north of CSM. Bill vectored a T-37 over the spot who saw the pilot land safely and start waving that he was OK. The tower had the Oklahoma Highway Patrol in the vicinity almost immediately. They found the pilot below the T-37 as he climbed over a fence going to the road. He was OK, though he spent a day in a Clinton, Oklahoma, hospital just to be sure.

Aside from the loss of an A-7 making a big hole in some farmer's field, the biggest problem of the day was getting Barfield to calm down.

(This story appeared in the Naval Aviation Museum Magazine, Foundation, under the title, "Navy Rock.")

ATC Tales 26

Skip Carlton was working a couple of United's at 310 that didn't look too good. He turned UAL485 20 right to go behind the westbound . . .

FW: "UAL485, turn right 20 degrees for traffic."

UAL: "5 left for traffic."

FW: "No, Skip said patiently. That'll make you hit the front of the airplane, not the back. 20 right."

When UAL485 was almost by the westbound, Skip started to wrap him around the traffic to get him back on course.

FW: "UAL485, turn 10 left."

The UAL turned left about 40 degrees and Skip's heart jumped.

FW: "UAL485, is that 10 left?"

UAL: "The lever stuck."

FW: "UAL485, you have traffic 10 o'clock six miles, turn right 30 degrees for traffic."

UAL: "We see him. We'll separate ourselves from him."

FW: "UAL485, I'll thank you for your help, but I'll separate you from him. Turn right 30 degrees."

Larry Stafford (LY) was facing a couple of weeks of bachelorhood as his wife went to Germany on the American flight from DFW to Frankfurt. Wanting to say hello and goodbye to her as he worked the American out on Frisco-low, he asked if the crew would say as much to her.

(At the same time, unbeknownst to Larry, his D-side gave DFW Apch a higher on a bizjet climbing right up under the American.)

LY: "My wife's on your flight. Will you say hello to her?"

AAL: "Sure. What's her name?"

LY: "S-T-A-F-F-O-R-D—AHHH! Turn 40 degrees right for traffic!"

No doubt whose deal that would have been. He even spelled his name for the Quality Assurance Office.

DECOD-hi sector has a reputation for being Restricted Area-42 and a lot of the sectors around it get fed up with it. John Bull on DAL-hi had enough one day when he pointed a bizjet at FL410, DFW direct SGF. Mike Olzewski (OJ) was the DECOD D-side who almost took the pointout. "Keep him out of our sector. We're too busy to watch him."

Bull wasn't happy with that, demanding, "Why don't you show me all your traffic at forty-one and I'll miss them."

Wrong thing to say to OJ. He's a supervisor who doesn't take stuff like that lightly. Bull found that out quick.

ATC Tales 27

Just a note about work. It was a very busy day today, one that I'd just as soon not see repeated anytime soon. I had MLC-low for a while and it went right to the top of the bays real quick. A few incidents stand out, including one involving FREBY81, a flight of three A-37s from the Michigan Air National Guard. They were out of SPS direct SGF to BLV, cruising along at FL210. They had no sooner crossed the ADM boundary when I saw they were descending so I asked the pilot, "FREBY81, say altitude; I show you at FL205." He said he needed lower, that one of his wingmen lost his oxygen they were starting down.

There was a Cheyenne out there at 140 westbound, twelve o'clock and 30 miles so I assigned him 150 and told him if he needed lower to turn right, H070 and descend to 110. "Turning right to 070, down to 110," and down he went. Right after I told him "Leaving 130 cleared direct SGF," he said, "Can you give my wingman a code? I've lost him. He's no longer with us."

Great, I thought, and started typing in a code request, at the same time asking what the aircraft's callsign was. FREBY82, he said, so I gave him a squawk, 2305, and told him to ident. He was north of SNL northbound, almost in Kansas City's airspace before I found him. As soon as I saw him I turned him right to 080, away from ZKC and back in the general direction of the rest of his flight. I asked FREBY81 if he wanted vectors to join up with 8-2 and when he replied, affirmative, I turned him H350 to join 8-2, descending 8-2 to 100 so I could maintain separation until they had each other sight and could climb safely. They soon had a visual, told me they were MARSA and I climbed 8-2 to 110 and the flight went on its way.

I thought it was great myself, a heck of a job, and my D-side seemed to think so. Joe Bumbles, my supervisor and the one who had the floor, thought it was OK, ho-hum, routine. I don't know what I expected, a big pat on the back maybe, a check (that'd be nice). I don't think the pilots will say anything to anybody because anything they say or do will show that they screwed up.

The whole time on MLC-lo was very busy. There was a lot of off-the-wall stuff that one rarely sees, a non-radar IFR departure cleared to 50 that climbed to 80 and then couldn't talk to me and we weren't sure he was cleared to 50, 80, or 100. A whole bunch of squirrelly stuff. The FREBY was the worst though, and the most interesting, that's for sure.

An astute reader [Mark Miller] had a comment about FREBY81:

I remember back in 1985 when I was still a fledgling, we had what was supposed to be a pair if B52's south of BNA 'til an Eastern DC9 got a very big eye full of another B52 at FL290 where there wasn't supposed to be one.

Seems the pair had tried to run IR174 west of BYH and had lost each other so the front one bugged out early and went on eastbound for his celestial navigation leg. Only problem was they didn't tell anyone they had split up until my R-side asked the one we had identified if he was a flight of one or two.

He said they were still a flight of two, but his wingman was about 50 nm in trail trying to catch up to him . . . no tag, no target, no talky. The R-man gave him one severe dressing down and made the lead ship do a 360 'til the other one caught up. The buff pilots didn't see the big problem but if they could've heard that DC9 driver on VHF they would've changed their minds!

ATC Tales 28

At Fort Worth's Meacham Airport there are a lot of foreign pilots, not all of whom speak good English, or understand it either. To one of these on short final for a touch and go, tower asked

FTW: "N62L, say your intentions. "

N62L: "I intend to become a private pilot!"

Also at Meacham there was a disabled aircraft on the runway. An inbound on short final for the same runway, piloted by another foreign student, was told several times to "go around" for the disabled aircraft, each time followed by a "Royer." The aircraft proceeded to land, roll a bit, and then take off into the blue. The tower asked, "Didn't you hear me tell you to 'go around?'"

" Affirmative," came the reply. "I land. I taxi around the airplane, and I take off. "

There are a lot of foreign military pilots at Sheppard AFB in Wichita Falls, Texas. It's a NATO training facility where the weather is good most of the year. Some of the pilots are a bit hard to understand, and not all of them speak good English . . . or understand it either (just like their Meacham counterparts).

A certain Falls specialty controller was working RAKE25 out in a training area. Thinking his transmission wasn't going out (it was), he said, "RAKE25, verify you're a raghead."

The pilot obviously didn't understand the intent of the question . . .

"Negative. We are a T-38 slant papa."

The controller is still called "Raghead."

ATC Tales 29

Early one morning Larry Foreman was working AAL1879 off Tulsa to DFW. He checked on, then almost immediately started the passenger PA, "Ladies and gentlemen, we apologize for the rough ride . . ." and then realizing he was on the ATC mike, stopped, then re-keyed and said, "And thanks for flying Continental."

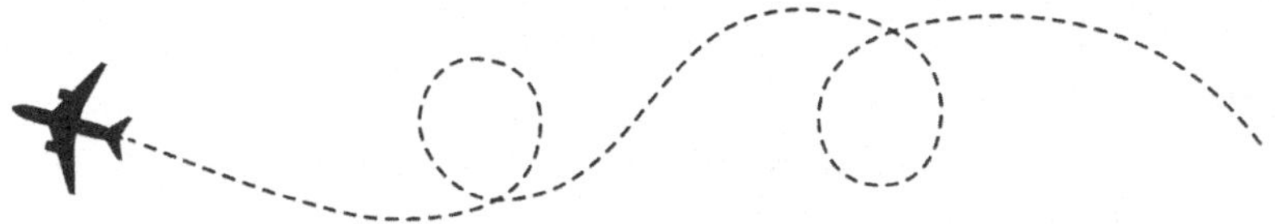

Early one afternoon during a big arrival push Seavr-low had all aircraft slowed to 250 knots. Out of the blue came . . . "Fort Worth, AAL1427. I've just found out my wife's gone into labor in Dallas right now with our first child How long are we going to have to be at 250 knots?"

He went straight to the airport, normal speed.

How many times have you had a NORDO airplane that hasn't heard a word you've said. Many, no doubt. But do you start a transmission to him with, "SNTRY36, you obviously can't hear my transmitter; standby." One OKC-hi controller did.

One night on a mid-shift with a lot of weather a FLIB came out of OKC climbing to 6,000 feet. Down around Lindsay the icing got really bad and the guy started falling out of the sky. His wife and kids were on board and they started screaming in the background every time he keyed his mike, and that was a lot.

He came out of the stuff about 4,200 and leveled off, got it under control and then tried climbing back to 6,000 (at his request). It all started again, the falling out of the sky, the screaming, the getting control of the aircraft and then, yes, once more a request to climb to 6,000. Figuring the fellow might be south of the weather the controller approved it and away he went back up.

The ritual began again, the falling, screaming, regaining control, and then the request. By this time at least the controller had learned his lesson.

FW: "Are you in the clear and safe at 4,000?"

FLIB: "Affirmative."

FW: "Roger. Maintain 4,000."

A note about ATC Tales. These are airplane stories, most of them mine, but several others have contributed. They all relate, in some fashion, to the world of ATC. One thing I've noticed about airplane stories is that the only thing that changes about them is the callsign(s). The stories I hear the young guys tell today are essentially the same stories I heard the old guys tell many years ago, when they spoke of their young days. Now I'm an old guy but the stories are still the same, timeless. Some of these happened years ago, some yesterday, some today, and the likes of them will be happening for years to come.

I have written these stories down over the years and kept them in a journal where everything about them remains. From time to time I haul one out, like this one, 'cause it fits the ATC Tales criteria.

ATC Tales 30

I was working OKC-high one morning and it was a busy little bear when I first sat down. Wes Wygle was going home—I'd probably be more accurate in saying he was going to play golf—and he wanted to get out of there so in I went. The briefing wasn't much, and it took me a few minutes to catch up. There was some weather out there and a little deviation though nothing spectacular that anybody had to go way out of their way for.

For a while in there I had a D-side, a young guy named Jimmy Elkins who will, in the long run, be a good controller. Right now, he needs to learn to talk to his R-side. We beat the sector down to a pulp and he went to chow.

Over the years various panels, study groups, and other bodies of interest to ATC have met to discuss and debate the system error situation. Their goal has been to determine just what might be done to avert and avoid system errors. One conclusion every such group has come up with is that most system errors happen not during, but after busy periods, during that "letdown" period when the controller thinks the situation is well in hand

Such was this noon when all but a handful of airplanes had disappeared and I had three (and soon four) airplanes on frequency.

One of the main players was AAL61, heading over ADM onto the great circle route going to Japan, level at FL310. Today's flight was an MD-11, one of those "stretch-10s" with a shrunken crew. (Actually, the overseas flights have several extra people on board to spell the primary crew.)

There were two other planes on frequency, neither of them a factor, and there was MANIAC1, an F-16 out of Tinker AFB, climbing to FL230 on a heading of 260. He was looking for direct Gage and FL 350, going to Hill AFB. Before MANIAC1 checked on I asked the American if he had TCAS and when he answered affirmative, I told him there was an F-16 ten o'clock, six miles, doing a rocket climb and he might get a TCAS alert, but the guy was only going to FL290.

When MANIAC1 checked on I climbed him to FL270 and he read it back, "2-7-0." He was going to clear the bizjet I'd stopped at 280 (thinking I'd be able to top him with the F-16) so I climbed MANIAC1 to FL290, stopping him for the American. The F-16' s heading would take him just behind the American and I'd be able to get him up that much quicker.

MANIAC1 didn't read back the first clearance to FL290 so I reissued the clearance and this time he read back "2-9-0." When I saw the F-16's Mode C show "2-8-7" I said, "MANIAC1, verify level FL 290." He replied, "I overshot." I saw his ModeC at FL 300 with the American off his right wing (3.907 miles and FL307, according to the sheet). I could hear the Area Manager's computer beeping up front as I turned to call for the supervisor and I knew the two had printed. Not a pretty picture.

The F-16 leveled at FL 290 as the American proceeded north. As the F-16 cleared the MD-11, I turned him northwest and climbed him to FL350, his requested altitude, I asked MANIAC1 how high he overshot and he said "300 feet." No way. I don't blame him for saying it and I suppose he'd best stick to it.

Before I shipped him to Kansas City Center, I read him his rights, "Mirandized" him, telling him there had been a possible pilot deviation and giving him the Center phone number and that he needed to call in. He went through the "what for" routine but said he would.

The supervisor, Joe Bumbles, and watch supervisor, Tom Thornbrough, were there over my shoulder asking what had happened. I told them, hoping they'd let it go without pulling the tapes but since the aircraft were so close, they decided they'd best be pulled.

Up to that point there was no doubt in my military mind what had happened. I gave the guy 2-9-0 and he read back 2-9-0. When I asked him to verify level 2-9-0, he said "I overshot." If I'd assigned him anything else, he'd have said, "You assigned me . . ." but he didn't; he said, "I overshot." I was relieved from the position shortly after it happened and was told to go to chow, that the tapes would be pulled in short order and we'd listen to them later.

Then the doubts set in. "Did I give him 2-9-0 and he read back 3-5-0?" Did I do something else or miss something altogether? All sorts of things go through your mind and they all went through mine. Bumbles asked if I wanted a NATCA representative present in the tape room. No, I said, if I screwed up, I screwed up. I must admit, when the tapes were set up and started to roll, I felt the butterflies start flying in my stomach.

There it was, clear as a bell, MANIAC1's readback of "2-9-0" and then, "I overshot." That cleared me, I thought, but the supe wanted to hear more. He ran the tape back to five minutes before MANIAC1 checked on and let it run for about as long after, looking, he said, for anything I might have said that could have mislead the MANIAC. This didn't endear this particular supervisor to me. When the supe heard the pilot acknowledge the clearance to 2-9-0 and then say he overshot, he should have quit there instead going on looking for something else.

Finally, he said he had had enough, something I felt like ten minutes before. I was "exonerated" and while I felt sorry for the pilot, I was relieved to know I was in the clear.

ATC Tales 31

On a light traffic day, one aircraft on freq, AAL77 called, "Fort Worth, are you there?"

"Yes, but I'm maintaining radio silence so as not to give away my position."

EJA297 was inbound to Tulsa, through FL260 for FL240, when RDP and FDP failed. MLC-lo could not accept a handoff on him so he was cleared to the OKM VOR to hold at FL240 and told that a lower altitude was being coordinated.

"What we need," said he, "is a little less coordination and a little more air traffic control!"

Lee Murrell was working a Braniff experiencing chop at FL 350 on TXK-hi and requesting FL310. Lee asked a Delta at 3-1-0 how his ride was.

ZFW: "DAL311, how's your ride?"

DAL: "Better than some, worse than most."

BNF: "Sounds like my wife."

DAL: "Maybe it was; what's her name?"

The Braniff stayed at 350.

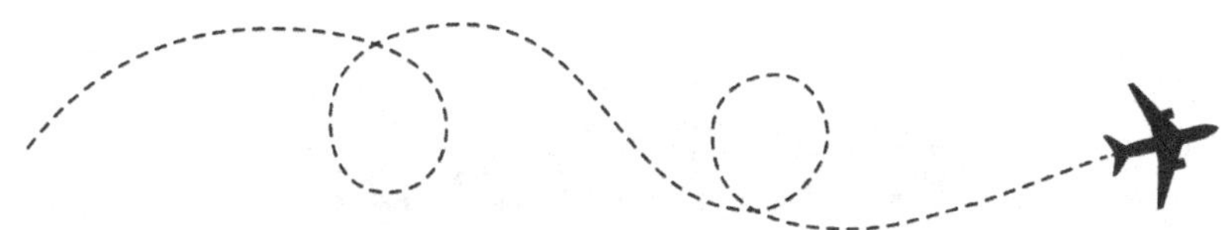

Greg Garcia was working DAL-hi R one day with Don Frenya on the D side. A Learjet was shooting up to FL410 southbound when he had a double flameout and ever so calmly keyed his mike saying, "Mayday. Mayday. Mayday."

Before Greg could respond, Don leaned over to say, "Did he say 'Mayday,' or 'Have a GOOD day?'"

Greg started laughing to the point where he couldn't even key his mike without laughing. The Lear did get one started though, and made a safe emergency landing at Carter Ranch.

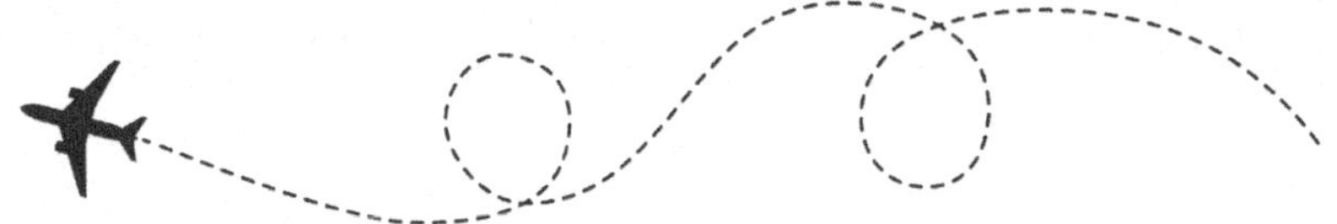

Speaking of Don Frenya . . . On Frankston one day he forced a Delta down to FL240 and the pilot wasn't happy about it, complaining all the way down. There was training in progress on FZT, so Don moved to DONIE where the same Delta was checking on, still complaining about being forced down early. Don asked the Delta,

Don: "DAL414, how do you hear Center?"

DAL: "Loud and clear."

Don keyed his mike and started, "Wah! Wah! Wah!"

ATC Tales 32

John Pearsall worked seven years as a controller at Seattle Center before going to work for flight inspection. One day there was lots of weather, lots of reroutes, and lots of frustration. He called a Kingair heading through SEATAC Approach with yet another reroute.

SEA: "4-2 alpha, I have a reroute for you when you're ready to copy."

42A: "Center, this will be the 15th reroute we've gotten since we took off. I've broken the lead in all my pencils; both pens are out of ink and I just can't remember any more. Cancel my IFR."

Pete Moss was working a BE76 Duchess, N6006D, piloted by a foreign student, out of Guthrie, Oklahoma to Dallas Redbird. Originally cleared over Ardmore, Pete gave him:

PM: "Cleared to the Redbird Airport via direct Bonham Finger one arrival."

06D: "Roger. We go direct Redbird direct Bonham Finger one arrival."

PM: "Negative. Cleared TO the Redbird Airport via direct Bonham Finger one arrival."

06D: "Roger. We go direct Redbird direct Bonham Finger one arrival. "

PM: "Negative. You're reading back 'direct' Redbird direct Bonham. I think you're getting what I'm trying to say but you need to read it back, 'Cleared TO Redbird via direct Bonham

Finger one arrival.'"

06D: "Roger. That's what I try to say. We go direct Redbird direct Bonham Finger one arrival."

Now Pete had wearied of the exchange and emitted a weary, "Roger." And an American voice floated out of the frequency netherworld: "Give it up."

N7287R departed Ardmore Municipal (ADM), cleared to Corpus Christi via direct to the ADM vortac V163 CRP, climbing to 100. Out of 4200 he was still heading southeast so I asked him if he was going to be turning toward the Ardmore vortac anytime soon.

"That's the plan," he snapped and trucked on off to the southeast.

If this segment had a title, it would be "The 10 Second Miracle."

Todd Lowy (LW) was on OKC-hi with a NORDO Kingair bound for Dallas at FL310 coming south that finally showed up on his frequency requesting a lower to land at OKC. LW coordinated with Kansas City Center's high and low sectors and descended the Kingair, not consulting with OKC-low which had a flight of T-37s blocking 160B170. The aircraft had long been switched to OKC Approach before Todd realized the two would be a factor for each other. The rub was, he had a bad "map" on his VSCS with no line to OKC Approach.

The Bonham supe started cycling maps through OKC-hi R but LW hardly had time to look up. He was shouting across the aisle to OKC-lo, finally taking a moment to glance at the VSCS map overhead, just as it changed for the umpteenth time. His eyes focused on one line, "OKC 25," the line he needed.

Jabbing his finger at the map, he seized the line and shouted, "Dump that Kingair now!"

"Wilco!" came the reply, and the map disappeared, the connection broken. It was enough though, as the Kingair began a rapid descent through 150 . . . and Todd could breathe again. Truly a 10 second miracle.

ATC Tales 33

The silkened-voice controller, so I was called, as perhaps hundreds of other controllers have been called over the years. Why that? I guess because we're down there on the other side of the microphone offering soothing words of comfort when a pilot is in distress, finds themselves in trouble or having a bad go of it.

What brought forth the comment was a reference to something that happened at work a few months ago. A student pilot, a young woman from Tulsa, was lost in central Oklahoma. At 4,500 feet and thought herself to be in desperate straits. The weather was good, and she had plenty of fuel but other than knowing she was above Oklahoma, she had no idea where she was.

Contacting Flight Service (she had the sense to do that, a lot of student pilots wouldn't) she got the Center frequency for where she thought she was, and gave me a call. I put her on a discrete beacon code and found her in short order, milling about near Ada. Then I suggested a heading for Ardmore Municipal, an old Air Force base that has great big runways and can be seen for miles and miles. Once there she decided she wanted to continue on to Dallas Addison, her original destination. I asked her if she was familiar with the interstate system down that way and she said she was, suggested she follow I-35 to Denton and then I-35E to Dallas. There she could contact DFW Approach for vectors to Addison.

It worked like a charm. She eventually got down safely but more than that, she is probably still flying today, the 90 minutes flying time between Ada and Addison were enough to let her confidence rebuild to the point where she will keep flying.

Once you're assigned to a specific specialty, you work the same airspace all the time. Some years ago, on Mcalester-low, I was working a Cessna 172 out of the DFW area to Fort Smith, Arkansas. 30 miles east of Mcalester the pilot said, "Center, we have an emergency. I have a passenger bleeding heavily through the rectum and we need to land and get him to a hospital."

The aircraft had already been handed off to Memphis Center. It would have been easy enough to ship him to Memphis and let them deal with it. Couldn't do it though and I don't think many would have. Instead, I suggested the airport at Mcalester, about 30 miles to the west. "This guy won't make it to Mcalester," the pilot said, "Is there anything closer?"

There was, Talahina and Wilburton, with Wilburton being the better of the two because the runway was a little longer and the airport would be easier to find. My D-side called Flight Service who in turn alerted the Highway Patrol and got an ambulance out there. That area is non-radar below 5,000 feet so while I still had the aircraft in radar, I set the pilot up for a north landing, a vector to the south end of the airport for a quick turn on final and a waiting ambulance and escort. The pilot later wrote saying that even as it happened, it was touch and go but fortunately the passenger made it.

(A month later I learned that the pilot had written a very nice "thank you" letter to the facility chief. He, in turn, recommended that my supervisor at the time, Frank Dixon, write up an award for me. The chief's letter was still sitting in Frank's mailbox six months later. In typical FAA fashion, no letter, no award, nothing.)

The life-and-death situations are few and far between, thank goodness. One night about midnight a pilot and his family took off of Fountainhead heading for Oklahoma City, a 265-degree heading at a distance of about 120 miles. Somehow, he wound up on a 230 heading and became lost. He called Flight Service and we went through the old routine, again with a safe and happy ending.

What got me about this last one was the pilot's casual attitude toward the whole thing. I'm sure he never realized that when Flight Service got his call for help, the whole federal government swung into action as we started looking for him. As I recall, this happened on a Saturday night, and I'll bet he woke up the next morning, read the paper, ate a few donuts, and never gave it another thought.

At work we go through various phases of training. In the radar phase we practice "no-gyro vectors," a series of "start turn; stop turn" instructions to pilots who have lost their navigation equipment and have to rely on the controller for turn assistance. Very few controllers ever give no-gyro vectors. I never had to give one until I had Chad Etheridge as a radar trainee.

One day right in the middle of one his busiest sessions an F-4 lost his nav equipment, requiring a no-gyro vector to Tinker AFB. That went very well as I let Chad work everything else and I worked the F-4 on a different frequency. Worked out great.

So the next time an aircraft lost his gyros I was ready. I was by myself and a little busy when a T-38 inbound to Tinker requested a no gyro vector because of malfunctioning equipment. He was 100 miles east of Tinker westbound at 22,000 feet. Any aircraft with a problem goes right to the head of the line for service but when you can do both, that's best.

I asked him if he was in visual contact with the ground. When he said he was, I asked if he saw Interstate 40 down there. Again, affirmative. "Stay north of the interstate," I told him, "and follow it into town. As soon as you start seeing Oklahoma City, Tinker will be just south of the highway; proceed direct Tinker when able." Away he went to the west, right to the airport. It worked, which was the important thing.

I guess this is enough ATC Tales for the night. One thing about stories like this: with exception of the call signs, these are essentially the same stories I heard old controllers tell when I first got there lo those many years ago. Now I hear the young guys tell the same stories, again with the only difference being the callsigns. I guess some things never change.

ATC Tales 34

At Salt Lake City a Delta 737 cleared for takeoff on the 12,000 feet runway advised the tower, "We're going to make a longer than normal takeoff roll."

"Don't make it longer than 12,000 feet," came the reply.

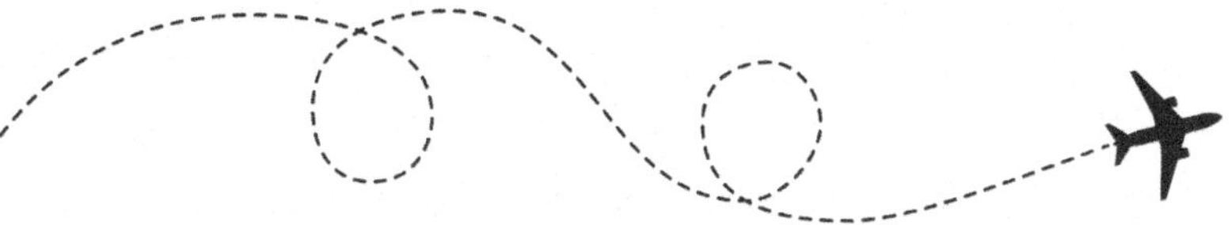

Occasionally callsigns don't make sense . . .

Wayne Coley on MLC-hi saw VVRAM21 (Navy RAM21) and until the aircraft left the sector it was "Vee Ram 21."

ABX191 was inbound to Waco's TSTC Airport (CNW) on a recent mid-shift . . .

ABX: "Fort Worth, ABX191, inbound TSTC. Landing 1-3. We have the weather."

FW: "ABX191, what is the weather at TSTC?"

ABX191: "We don't know yet."

FW: "I thought you just said you had the weather."

ABX191: "Oh yeah, I did say that. Let me find it."

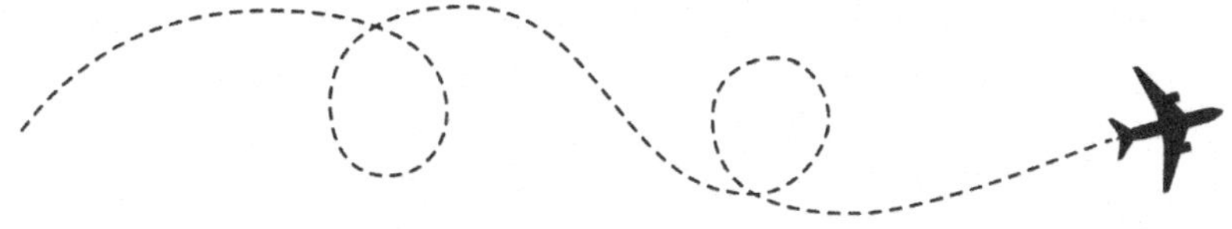

The occasional medical emergency is declared by an air carrier. AAL455 declared one a while back and was cleared direct DFW. His computer ID number? 9-1-1

Doug Plume was working TXK-hi when DAL421 checked on "climbing to FL230 with a request."

Doug: "DAL-423, I can't take you off your route. Climb and maintain FL330."

DAL423: "3-3-0. Does that mean you're omnipotent?"

Doug: "Yes, and there's a new drug out for it, too."

DAL423: "Does it start with a V?"

ATC Tales 35

It seems USA631 was a NORDO forever. Karen's plaintive plea came forth . . ."Earth to USA631; earth to USA631," but to no avail.

Shorty Bush was working the old MLC-hi one night, working a DFW departure requesting FL330 with a 3-1-0 overflight southwest bound in his face.

He told the 3-1-0, "Put on your landing lights." The pilot did so.

Shorty told the departure, "Your traffic's 12 o'clock, 60 miles, southwest bound at 3-1-0, with his landing lights on."

XXXXX said, "We see him."

XXXXX he's your traffic. Miss him; climb and maintain FL 330.

XXXXX no snitch patch back then.

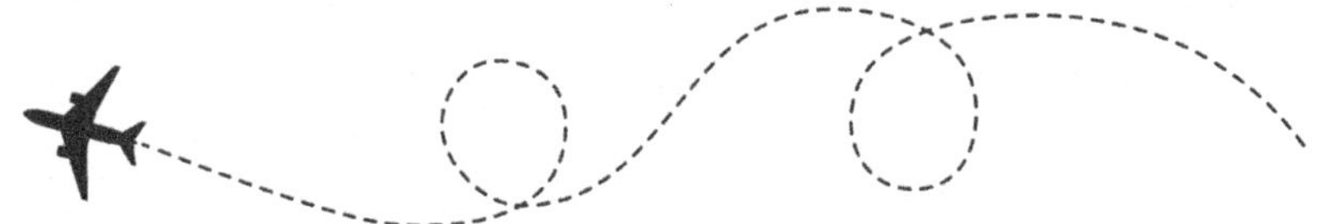

SAME40 at FL280 filed a flight plan that took him through the army's Fort Sill restricted area, hoot up to FL320. Pete Moss explained there was ". . . live artillery fire up to FL320 and you need to go around the area," and put the aircraft on a radar vector. The pilot, wanting to stay on his filed route, argued about it so Pete went through the "live artillery fire" litany again, to the same result, the pilot arguing about it.

Finally, another pilot on frequency shouted at the SAME: "No comprendez Swiss Cheese?"

FGT (Farmington, Minnesota) is a fix in Minnesota southeast of Minneapolis. Pete Moss didn't know what it was but wanted to clear some NWA direct there for the arrival into MSP. He shouted, "Does anyone know what F-G-T is? Corky Erickson shouted back, "Yeah, it's Fajoe up in Minnesota." So Pete called F-G-T "Fajoe" until someone finally asked, "Do you mean, Farmington?"

Ed Gleason was working a DC-9 westbound off Tinker AFB to the west coast, climbing him to FL230. The pilot read back, "FL3-3-0."

Ed said, "Negative. 2-3-0. You're a DC-9, not an F-18."

ATC Tales 36

Frank Dixon saw, finally, He had two coming together at FL310. His reaction? He (inadvertently) keyed his mike as "Oh shit," escaped his lips. Then came a ten degree right turn for one airplane followed by another "Shit" from the D-side who exclaimed ten degrees wouldn't work. 40 degrees more to the same plane and they barely scraped by.

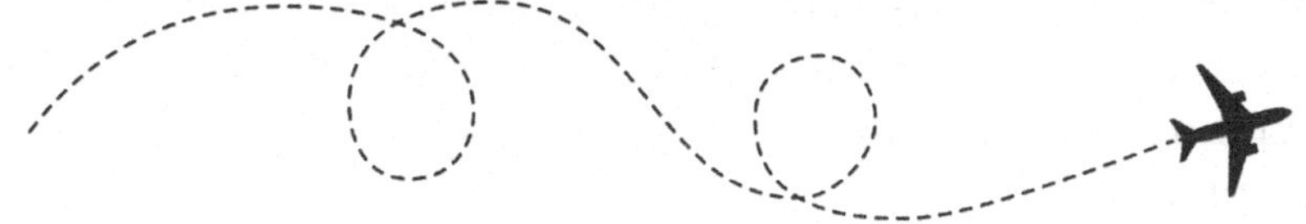

With the Wichita Falls (SPS) VORTAC off the air, FOXY94 requested direct SPS.

Pete Moss: "FOXY94, cleared as requested."

FOXY94 (A deeper voice, obviously the instructor's): "Center, disregard. SPS is off the air. Requesting direct Sheppard."

PM: "Cleared as requested. I knew it was off the air. I thought you might know a trick I don't."

FOXY94 (same voice): "Negative. Training in progress."

PM: "We have that problem, too."

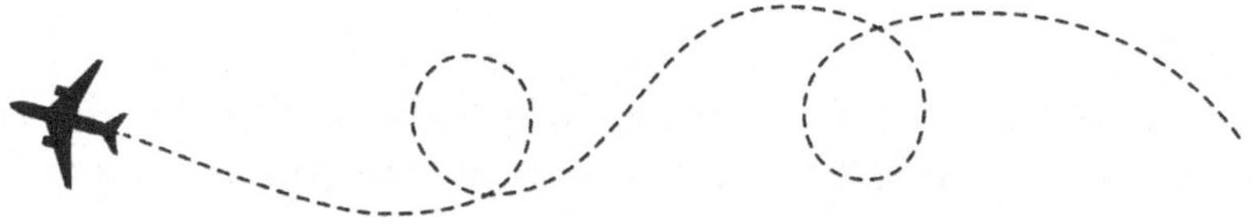

There's a fellow on Frisco (Jerry Stephens) who says, "tree" instead of "three." Pete Moss relieved him one day on ADM-hi. On hearing the new voice, one pilot asked, "Is the controller on the previous sector a tree-hugger? 'Cause he's doing his best to save the whole forest."

ATC Tales 37

There's an old expression referring to someone who curses that goes, ". . . swears like a sailor." The sailor that phrase refers to is named Cindy, a controller works at Fort Worth Center. (Curiously enough, she was in the navy.) One day she was working a sector when a group of "99s" came through the facility for a tour. (The '99s' are a group of female pilots and aviation enthusiasts.) Wanting a break and not realizing they were standing immediately behind her, she shouted, "Who do you have to f----g blow to get a f----g break around this place?"

The woman conducting the tour hustled the group on down to the next specialty.

Doug Plume was working an American with a female pilot who sounded a lot like the aforementioned Cindy. At that moment he was being relieved by the very same Cindy and said as much to the female pilot, saying, "I think you sound a lot like the woman relieving me. Why don't you say a few words?"

They exchanged a few words until a male pilot on the frequency said, "I think it sounds like the controller's taller."

Cindy said, "I think it sounds like the pilot has bigger tits."

Silence after that.

Dave Ritchie was plugged in on Frisco-lo, a DFW north departure sector, when a tour group came through the Center on a tour. An older woman (who had been a pilot in her younger days) plugged in with Dave just as they ran a DC-10 out behind an old DC-9, overtaking DC-9 like he was sitting still. Dave had not yet realized the woman was plugged in with him and not liking what was happening on his screen, started shouting at the supervisor, "They're fucking me! They're fucking me!"

The supe came over, saw the situation and quickly DFW Approach to tell them to turn the DC-10 out as Dave was shouting the same thing on the landline. The -10 turned out and the supe came over to introduce Dave to the woman, who had been standing behind Dave this whole time. She sat with Dave for another ten minutes, sharing an uneasy conversation, then she unplugged to continue on with the tour. As she unplugged, she leaned over and whispered in Dave's ear, "I thought they were fucking you, too."

ATC Tales 38

Larry Foreman (LF) was working a VFR Mooney this week that departed H45 going to TUL. He got about halfway there when MLC Radio called up and said someone at Seminole called and said he left his car keys there and should return for them.

LF: "Mooney 72 delta, Fort Worth."

72D: "Mooney 72 delta, go ahead."

LF: "Ya got your car keys?"

72D (silence then): "Uhhhhhhhhhhhhhhhhhhhhhh—no."

Larry thought about saying: "Radar indicates they may be at Seminole," but he didn't want the pilot to keep going away from Seminole while trying to think of something really witty. Besides, the tone of the pilot's voice was really good when he realized Larry knew he didn't have his keys and he didn't know how Larry knew it.

I was working MLC-lo when a KingAir 300 at FL220, out of Olathe Industrial (in Olathe, Kansas), to Mexico, said, "Center, we have a problem and need to return to Industrial." Pete cleared him to Industrial, asking the nature of the problem and did it affect the aircraft? "No," he said, "We just need to return to Olathe." I cleared them to Industrial and shipped them to SWO-lo.

Five hours later here he came again and curious about his earlier problem, I inquired about the same. With an ironic tone in his voice, he said, "We were flying along just fine when we realized that our passports were still at home on the kitchen table."

Lisa Simonds was working Ardmore-hi. Janet Landman was working OKC-hi next to her while Tom Thorpe was working McAlester Low.

THE STORY . . .

Lisa switched a Tulsa inbound to Tom on MLC-lo and the pilot asked him what Lisa looked like. Tom said, "She's across between Dolly Parton and Marilyn Monroe." Then Tom started laughing about this and Lisa and Janet heard him and, after being told what he'd said, started laughing about it, too.

A moment later Janet switched a Continental to Lisa, saying:

"COA 841, contact Fort Worth Center's answer to Marilyn Monroe and Dolly Parton on 132.97."

The Continental went over to Lisa's freq laughing and Lisa was laughing, but she just rogered him and didn't say anything else. When she switched him to DECOD, he said, "Okay, which is it?"

"Which is what?" Lisa asked innocently.

"Is it Marilyn or Dolly?" he said.

She said, "Dolly." Then keyed up again before he left saying, "Well, there are a couple of things Dolly and I don't have in common."

The COA laughed and said, "Your hair's brown, right?"

Lisa said, "Yeah, and I can't sing."

ATC Tales 39

Dwan Stregles was on a fam trip on DAL422 inside DFW Approach, inbound for landing when he heard a worried DFW Approach controller say, "Delta 422, turn 90 degrees left immediately!"

Hardly a moment later he heard the same controller say, "American 268, turn 90 degrees right immediately!"

Then the controller said, "Delta, tighten up your turn. This is gonna be tight."

With the 90-degree left turn and the word "immediately," the Delta captain already had it cranked pretty far over. The first officer and Dwan both strained against their seatbelts as they craned their necks over the window's bottom to hunt for the traffic.

They didn't have to look far.

The American was yards away, maybe just feet away, the 727's dirty bottom close enough to see everything, rivets, oil, and nicks in the metal. The first officer, startled at the nearness of the aircraft, started shouting, "Harder, Captain, harder!"

Slowly, ever so slowly, the two aircraft pulled apart and the crew, and Dwan, settled back into their seats, with all hands still shaking, and sweating, at the gate.

Dwan, who is a US National Judo Champion, boarded one American for a fam back from Hawaii. As he stood in the 1st Class galley waiting for admittance to the flight deck, a flight attendant came up from the back and whispered in his ear, "If you're interested, there's a flight attendant in the back who would love to give you a strip search."

Dwan smiled gratefully but allowed as how his wife, also in the back somewhere, wouldn't think that was a good idea.

One Mother's Day a FLIB at FL210 said, "I'd like to take this opportunity to wish everyone a Happy Mother's Day." After the controller offered his thanks, the pilot continued, "Just how are all you mothers anyway?"

ATC Tales 40

I'd been at work about an hour today when a fellow stopped me in the hall to relate something that happened this morning. Seems there had been some pretty bad wind shear and air turbulence. It, the wind shear, was bad enough to where there were two Southwest Airlines jets holding above it as they waited to land at Oklahoma City. If Southwest won't go through it, it must have been bad.

Jim was on McAlester-low, working a Twin Beech Baron, one of the "Indians" that mill about in the low-altitude structure. This fellow was inbound to Norman Westheimer and he was hot to get there. Jim told him about the wind shear and turbulence, told him three times, the tapes showed later, and told him that other aircraft were holding until the wind shear stopped.

This information didn't stop the pilot and he pressed on to Norman. Jim told Oklahoma City Approach Control that he had warned the pilot about all the bad stuff and then shipped him.

The pilot got to Norman but on approach to that airport, the wind shear reached out and smacked him to the ground, killing him. Now Jimmy has been walking around asking himself and others if there was anything else he could have done. He's trying to reassure himself that he did everything possible. He did, but he has to convince himself of that

It's tough, working a crash. I've been a D-side on two and worked one. It's a helpless feeling sitting there, listening to events develop, events that are way beyond your control. You want to help, you try, you might say a word or two of encouragement, but that's about all you can do. Oh, you might say a silent prayer as you get the machinery in gear to find the wreckage but there's not much else you can do.

Hopefully Jim will be OK. I'm sure he will. He wasn't working the guy when he crashed, and he didn't have to hear the screams of the pilot and passengers on the way down. He's just concerned that maybe he could have done more. He couldn't have but he has to come to that conclusion himself.

Some years ago, there was a young man out there who had been checked out as a radar controller less than two hours when an airplane he was working crashed. He was working a holding stack at Texarkana when a Bonanza at 6,000 said he had run out of gas and was going down. The pilot hadn't said anything about being low on fuel, nothing about an emergency. He just announced he was out of gas, then crashed, killing all on board. The crash destroyed the young man's confidence and he eventually transferred out to flight service.

Considering Jimmy's dilemma, I've been asking people if they've ever worked a crash. Surprisingly enough, very few have. That's good, too, because there's no benefit from working them, none at all. Just a feeling of helplessness and desperation that sometimes takes a few days to go away.

ATC Tales 41

On MLC-lo Larry Jones forced an American dash 80 down to 9,000 (the Tulsa Approach inbound altitude). At the pilot's query, "Is that at pilot's discretion?" Larry snapped – negative – and down the American went. Larry handed the track off to "K" as he would any Tulsa inbound. Someone took the handoff and Larry switched him to Tulsa Approach

The next voice Larry heard was Tulsa on the Five line wanting to know who this American was. The pilot was really hacked being forced down to 9,000, considering he was going to Kansas City.

Dave Stewart called "Fort Sill Approach on the 86 line, inbound." Dave then gave them an overflight estimate on a FLIB going to Wichita Falls. The word "inbound," however, rang clear in the receiving controller's ears and he vectored the aircraft to the Lawton airport. On landing, the pilot was seriously torqued because she was supposed to be going to Wichita Falls.

Pete Moss assigned FL240 to an American at FL350 that he thought was going to DFW. Approaching FL280 the pilot asked if he could stop there "since we're going to San Antonio." He'd been trying to get a lower for 300 miles, but no one would give it to him.

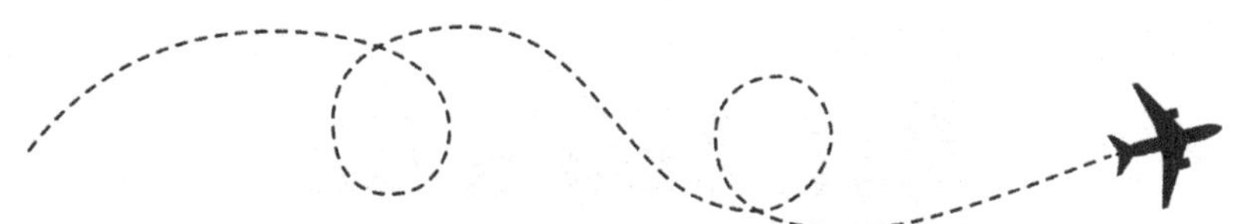

N7066G was off T32, Collinsville, Texas, to Enid, Oklahoma. The flight plan's remarks were rather curious, "DEPTG COLLINSVILLE SUDDEN STOP." Wondering what might have precipitated a sudden stop, Pete Moss inquired of the pilot to that end, "Did you have to make a sudden stop?" The pilot started to explain why he landed there and then realized what Pete was getting at. Turns out the Collinsville airport's name is "Sudden Stop."

ATC Tales 42

In Albuquerque Center a Delta was deviating for weather and was told he HAD TO GO over Socorro, that the White Sands missile range was hot.

When the aircraft was 30 miles southwest of Socorro with no apparent intention of turning northeast, the controller once more told him that he HAD TO GO over Socorro because of the missile range.

The pilot said, "There's weather up that way," adding that he wasn't going to turn.

The controller replied, "Roger. Radar services terminated. If you're still flying in 75 miles, your next center frequency will be 135.25."

The pilot said, tentatively, "How much of a turn will that be?" And he took it.

Landing Austin, an American MD-80 was slowed for a company FK-100. His laconic comment came, "We have the 'Fokker' in sight," with a lot of emphasis on "Fokker."

Dutch Daugherty told an American, "Lay your ears back [go fast]; descend and maintain FL240."

AAL: "We don't know what you mean by 'lay your ears back.'"

Dutch: "Southwest, do you know what 'lay your ears back' means?"

SWA: "Affirmative" came SWA's reply.

Dutch: "American, disregard. You're number two. SWA, lay your ears back. Descend and maintain FL240."

N391RR, a B350 at FL290, had the words "2 DOGS" in the flight plan's remarks. Pete Moss asked if there was any significance to them. The pilot replied that there was. Flight Service added those in case there was a crash and parts had to be pulled out of the wreckage, that searchers would know there were two dogs on board and some of those parts were dog parts.

A voice asked, "Are they two-legged or four-legged?"

Another chipped in, "That's pretty optimistic, isn't it?"

And, of course, there was a chorus of "Woof, woof, woof."

Jason Canton, a Waco specialty controller who was a big-time fisherman, was transferring to Memphis Center. He was a quiet, laid back guy who was well-liked by all hands. It was decided to give him a farewell party and that something special needed to be done so a big chocolate cake was ordered from a local grocery store. From the same store the perpetrator of the foul evil deed purchased a frozen fish, taking the same and inserting it in the now cut-in-half cake.

The cake was put back together, the icing smoothed over and brought to the appointed place where Jason was to dish up pieces therefrom. Everything went fine until he reached the middle of the cake . . . and the frozen fish. It took him a minute before he figured out what was going on. It didn't matter though. He cut around the fish and the guests all ate the cake, and that was that.

ATC Tales 43

Pete Moss was working Ardmore-low when JUD113 came out of OKC climbing into high southeast bound. (JUD is the US Department of Justice callsign.) Always the curious type, PM asked how many "non-rev" guests they could accommodate, "100 on the 727-100, 125 on the 727-200, and the Falcons are used for special need prisoners," the pilot said.

"Does your 'airline' have a motto?" Pete asked.

"Sure does," the pilot replied. "If you're indicted, you're invited." Then he said, "And, 'if your prisoner absolutely positively has to be there, we'll get him there sooner or later.'"

Pete thanked him for the information and shipped him to high altitude. A moment later the pilot was back. Pete repeated the frequency thinking the pilot had taken the wrong one. "No," he said, "We're talking to them on the other radio. Since you're interested, we wanted to give you the cabin announcement we give when our 'guests' are strapped in "

"The Department of Justice US Marshall's Service Oklahoma City Flight Base would like to welcome you aboard ConAir flight One, the number one choice of incarcerated prisoners worldwide."

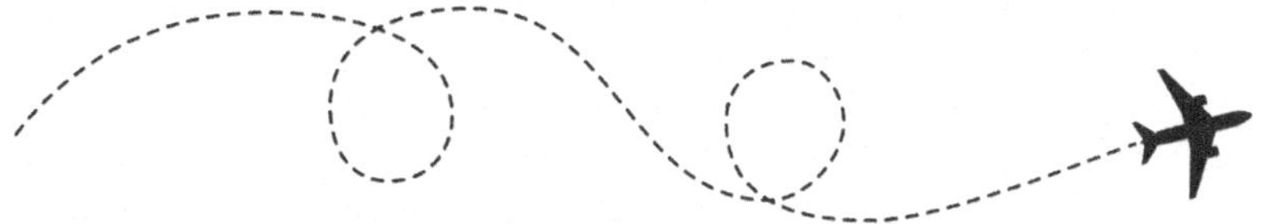

Jim Elkins was working MLC-high one stormy day with his sector saturated with bad weather, a seemingly impenetrable line of weather covering the entire sector. He had no traffic, only lots of "remove strips" messages, when here came a JUD inbound to Oklahoma City out of Memphis Center. Jimmy told him about the weather, but the pilot said he was going through it, and he did, right through the worst of it.

With the plane on the back side of the line, Jimmy asked the pilot, "How was your ride?"

"The guys in the back were really acting up. The ride was not half as bad as I wanted it to be," came the reply.

ATC Tales 44

Air Canada flight 42F came through one night on its way from DFW to Houston Intercontinental. The flight I.D. showed ACAF042 for the flight identifier, so Pete Moss asked the pilot if it was a ferry flight.

"I suppose we should be called 'Air Canada ferry 42,'" he said, "but we just get tired of being called a ferry."

Pete asked AAL9520, DFW to Tulsa, "Are you a ferry flight?" The pilot replied, in a very deep voice, "The plane is; the crew isn't."

One day on Ardmore high Pete was working BIKE91, a North American Super Sabre F-100, out of Sheppard AFB to Tyndall AFB, climbing to FL290. Not having worked an F-100 for many years, he asked the pilot what was the purpose of the flight.

"I'm ferrying this down to Tyndall where it'll be converted to a QF-100 drone," he said.

Pete asked, "What company is doing the work?"

"Sperry Corporation," the pilot replied.

"So you work for Sperry?" said Pete.

"Affirmative," said BIKE91.

"And you're a ferry flight," Pete inquired.

"Affirmative," came the reply.

Pete closed with, "So that would make you a . . . Sperry ferry?"

A short pause, then BIKE91 said, "Well, I've . . . never thought of it quite that way before."

ATC Tales 45

A friend of Pete Moss's flies for American. He was the captain on a dash 80 from Seattle to Chicago one day when somewhere over Montana a flight attendant popped into the cabin saying an old lady in the blue hair brigade wanted to know what was the name of the lake over which they were flying at that very moment. Dave replied he had no clue but why let that stand in his way.

He grabbed the PA mike and began, "Ladies and gentlemen, we're overflying Lake Fugawi which is in the middle of the Fugawi Indian Reservation in eastern Montana." He added a few details about the Fugawis and the area and let it go.

At Chicago he did his usual bit for the company, standing at the door saying farewell to the passengers, the announcement having slipped from his mind. It had caught the attention of a few passengers however, as several gave him a thumbs up, saying, "Fugawi."

(For those of you who don't know, the "Fugawi" Indians are one of the "lost" Indian tribes. They're always saying, "Wherda Fugawi?" It comes from an old joke that evidently some passengers had heard.)

Remembering the above story, one day Pete was working Dallas-hi, working a southbound American who inquired about the big lake off to the west. (It was Lake Whitney.) Pete went through the same story his friend had told and sent them off to the next frequency, happily so.

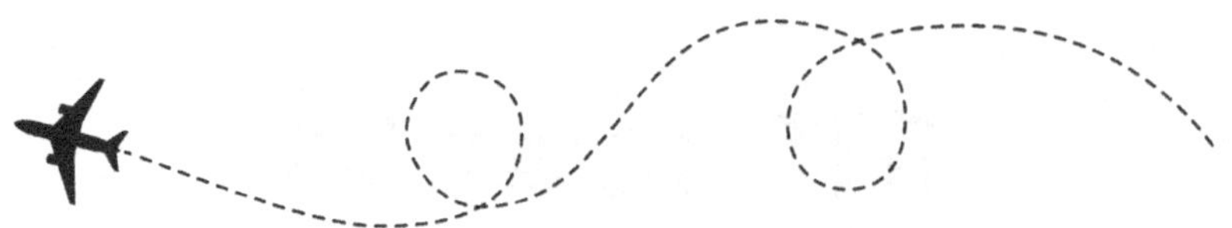

On a mid-shift KE started down an Austin lander, AAL1795, to FL220. Came the reply, "We were just talking about asking for a lower."

"Was it the captain or the first officer who initiated the conversation?" Pete asked.

"I'm afraid I'll have to defer to the captain," said the F/O.

"That's why he's the captain and you're not."

Margaret Rendon was at DFW Tower working a Mexicana in, working him from "Cleared to land," to "Off frequency approved." Every time she said anything to the Mexicana he responded with, "T'ank you, lady."

On "cleared to land," came "T'ank you, lady."

With "cleared to taxi" came "T'ank you, lady." It was "T'ank you, lady" this and "T'ank you, lady" that.

She finally got him off frequency and gone when every other airplane on frequency began, "T'ank you, lady." "T'ank you, lady." "T'ank you, lady." She was very glad when they were all gone.

ATC Tales 46

These next few stories might be called "The IFR section . . . I follow roads."

Pete Moss was on MLC-lo one afternoon, busy busy busy, when TANGO38 checked on, Fort Smith J6 to Will Rogers VORTAC direct Tinker AFB at FL220. It wasn't long before TANGO38's navigation equipment failed and he started wandering all over the sky. After stopping the wandering, TANG038 requested a no-gyro vector to Tinker. Pete didn't have time for it but what can you do?

He asked TANGO38 if he was in visual contact with the ground.

"Affirmative."

"See the interstate down there?" asked Pete. (I-40 runs east-west through Oklahoma, neatly bisecting the state north and south.)

"Affirmative."

"TANGO38, roger. Keep the interstate off your left wing and follow it on into town. When you hit the outskirts of Oklahoma City, you'll see Tinker off to the south. Cleared direct Tinker when able."

And it worked just fine.

One mid-shift about two in the morning a C-172's nav equipment failed ten miles northeast of Ardmore, Oklahoma. The pilot was a bit distressed but once again the compass provided the solution.

PM asked the pilot, "Are you familiar with the interstate system in Oklahoma and northern Texas?"

"Affirmative."

Pete went on. "Can you see the lights of the cars on I-35 over west of you about ten miles?"

"Affirmative."

"Roger," said Pete. "That's I-35. Cleared to the Fort Worth Meacham airport via radar vectors to the interstate. Fly H240, intercept I-35. Cleared I-35 Denton, I-35 West to the Interstate 820 interchange direct Meacham."

Frisco and DFW bought it and the pilot flew it. It may not have been a strictly legal clearance, but it got the job done and the pilot safely to Meacham.

One afternoon a student pilot was lost "somewhere northeast of Mcalester, Oklahoma," MLC FSS kept telling PM on ADM-Io. Why they called ADM-Io, I'm not sure but they did and now PM was trying to find her. Turns out she was southwest of MLC, having given FSS the radial's reciprocal, and she eventually came up on 128.1.

Pete could hear the frustration and even fear in her voice. She was lost, no clue as to where she was, and a long way from Tulsa, her home base, on her first solo cross-country, originally trying to go to Dallas Addison. She was ready to go back to Tulsa and requested a heading for that but then Pete asked her if she was familiar with the highway system in Oklahoma. This time she grabbed the ball and ran with it.

"Affirmative," and though heading northeast her brain must have been in overdrive because she quickly turned around saying she was going to follow the roadways to Dallas and on to Addison. Her confidence growing with each transmission, by the time Pete switched her to Frisco all her confidence was back, and she had a new lease on life, or at least a new lease on her life as a pilot.

The OKC Approach Control (OKC Z) Letter of Agreement calls for aircraft to be through the arrival gate, on a certain radial, and even when the Will Rogers Vortac is down OKC Z wants them through the gate. Ascertaining that the aircraft is in visual contact with the ground, one controller tells the aircraft "Keep the interstate off your left wing and proceed direct Will Rogers Airport when able." That puts them through the west side of the gate, keeps OKC Z happy and they can do their own navigation. "Today," said one ASE DFW to OKC, "I guess IFR means, 'I follow roads.'" And it did.

ATC Tales 47

Jim Elkins was working LOBO213, a Marine Corps C-9, offering him direct destination, Navy Jacksonville (NIP), if the pilot would provide the lat/longs. The pilot rattled off a series of numbers, Jimmy cleared him direct and then tried putting it in the computer using the numbers the pilot had given. Wouldn't work. Jimmy asked about the coordinates and now came a slightly different but similar set of numbers. Jimmy tried again and again it didn't work. Now Jimmy requested the pilot specifically check NIP's coordinates.

Turns out the pilot had been giving the present location lat/longs and had done so twice! Jimmy had to check a retort, remembering that the key words here are MARINE CORPS C-9.

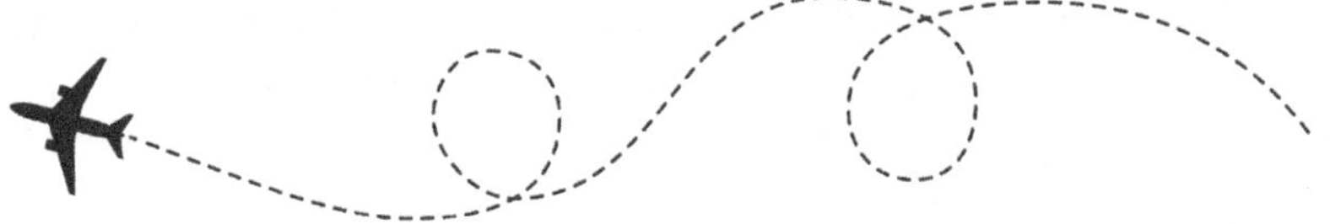

Pete Moss was on OKC-hi when a Delta cracker checked on . . .

"Foat Wuth, Del-ta wun sex-ty fo' wich yew et flat level three fahv ze-ro."

Pete, who has been known to imitate a pilot or two, came right back with, "Del-ta wun sex-ty fo', Foat Wuth Centuh, roguh."

The Delta came back with, "Awr yew mekkin fun o' me, boah?"

Pete replied "No suh!" and had to talk like that until the Delta left the frequency going to Albuquerque Center. It was a long time before he did that again.

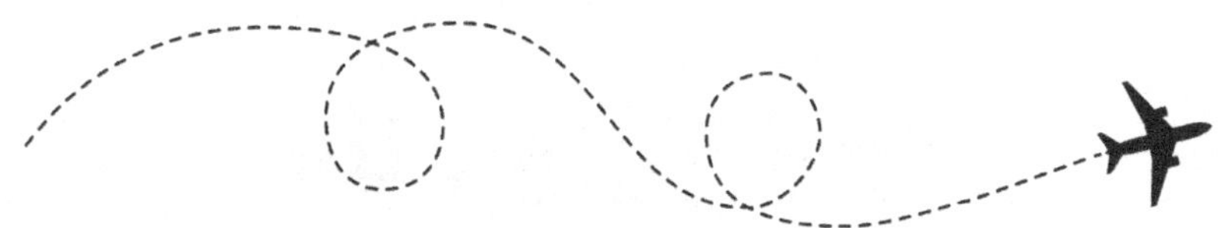

Similar sounding callsigns are always a problem and particularly so one day on MLC-hi when PM had five callsigns ending in "69." There was American's 169, 369, and 569, and a United 369 and Delta 369. Always mindful to keep pilots aware of similar sounding callsigns, Pete advised each pilot of all the others' sound-alike numbers. At the end of the routine out of the frequency netherworld, "Wow! '69' must be a popular number."

ATC Tales 48

Larry Foreman was climbing a Continental to FL350 when he noticed a limited data block 350 in the next sector that would definitely, positively be traffic for the COA.

LF: "COA821, descend and maintain FL 330."

The pilot, with whom Larry had exchanged a few words already and now not happy about going back down to an altitude he had already left, and one knew was choppy, replied in an irritated tone.

COA821: "Center, it's pretty choppy down there and we're not going to like it."

LF: "COA821, you're going to like 3-5-0 a lot less when you run into that 727 at 36, 2 o'clock, 12 miles westbound."

The COA took the descent.

The difference between pilots and controllers is that we call each "sir," and the pilots mean it.

CDL9163 checked on frequency mumbling the callsign but with "9163" clear.

Taking a wild guess and trying to approximate what he heard, Pete Moss replied, "Tailhunter 9163, Fort Worth Center, roger."

CDL9163 answered, "Negative! Carolina 9163," but after a pause came, "But I like 'Tailhunter' better."

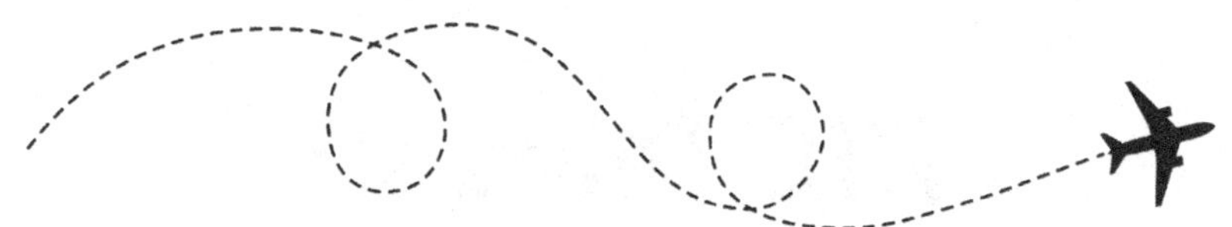

Wayne Coley (LR) was working OKC-hi on the mid right after UPS changed their callsign from "Upsco" to "Browntail." An inquisitive sort, he asked a FEDEX . . .

LR: "FEDEX1274, did you hear U-P-S changed their callsign to 'Browntail'?"

A bored female voice replied, "Negative."

LR: "I was just curious; what color is your tail?"

A long pause ensued and then a snappy "Orange!"

ATC Tales 49

Some years ago, a book came out by a well-known Air Force test pilot. I had been reading the book for a few days when I came to the World War II part. Somewhere in there the author made the point that a fighter pilot's job is to fly and fight and that nothing comes between the true man, the true fighter pilot, the true warrior, and his mission. If the aircraft is out for the count, the pilot gets out so he can live to fight another day, regardless of what will happen to the aircraft or the people on the ground wherever it might fall.

A day or two after reading that particular section I was at work, heading out on a break (I am a controller, after all), ready to read some more. Bob Benton was just down the aisle on OKC-low working Navy403, an A-7 out of Denver's Buckley Field inbound to Tinker AFB. I was shooting the breeze at the supe's desk when Benton started screaming, "I need help! I need a D-side," and me being the devoted troop I am, grabbed my headset and rushed over to him out in his moment of need.

Plugging into the D-side, I learned that Navy403 had just left FL290 southwest of Gage, descending to FL240 when he had a flameout and couldn't get it restarted. Heretofore Bob hadn't been busy but Navy403 was changing all that. Bob started working him alone, devoting all his attention to problem, with me telling Bob when he needed to do something else, switch someone, taking care of the minor stuff. There weren't many airplanes, three or four at the most, which was a good thing.

The other airplanes on frequency soon realized there was a definite problem and soon they began to fall silent, listening as the drama began to play out. I had plugged in right after the flameout, when Navy403 was out of 2-7-0. Between talking to the supe, Flight Service and Clinton-Sherman Approach, I could hear Benton talking to the pilot.

By this time the pilot had given up on Tinker and had turned the A-7 south toward Clinton-Sherman (CSM), 10,000 feet of concrete in western Oklahoma. A former SAC base, all that concrete was a great big target for Navy403, if only he could glide that far. It was obvious there wasn't going to be a restart, at least any time soon. The pilot, a Navy Lieutenant, allowed as much through FL210, saying things didn't look good and if he couldn't get it going by 13,000, he would punch out then.

Now Navy403, "Navy Rock," the latest in glider fashion, A-7 style, was through 1-8-0 and Benton started asking the pilot, "Are you still planning to get out at thirteen?"

A quiet "Affirmative, if I can't make the runway," was the only reply.

But thirteen came and went and the pilot stayed with the aircraft. He was just north of Clinton, Oklahoma, heading south as he strained for CSM. Now Benton was getting nervous, literally on the edge of his seat, face just inches from the scope as he talked to the pilot. "You need to get out," he said. "Get out now."

"Still trying," he said, but it was clear to all hands, him and us, that he couldn't make the runway, wouldn't get anywhere close.

Navy403 was now down through 8,000 over the outskirts of Clinton and Benton was all but pleading as he implored the pilot, "Bale out! Bale out!"

And then that man, that fighter pilot, that man with a mission, whose mission it was to live to fly and fight another day, uttered a line I will always remember, in a voice that was so cool, so calm, so clear, "I'm just looking for a place to put it; I wouldn't want it to hit a school."

With that, Benton sat back. The pilot was obviously in charge and no matter what Bob said, this guy would get out when he wanted to. And at 5,000 feet came a simple, "I'm out of here," and then silence.

The cleanup work began as we started the Search-and-Rescue effort. Benton had already vectored VANDY04, a T-37, in CSM's direction. CSM Tower called to say they had the chute in sight, seven miles north of the airport, just north of the lake." Radio called to say the highway patrol was in the area, so Bob had the T-37 circle the pilot until they got there.

The highway patrol picked him 20 minutes after he ejected, sitting alongside a highway on his chute waiting for a ride. Taken to a local hospital for observation, the pilot was released the next day with some bruises and minor injuries, nothing serious.

Thinking back on it, from start to finish it was over in less than 30 minutes, 30 pretty exciting minutes for us but no doubt much more so for the pilot of Navy403. The thing that has that has stuck with me though, the thing that stands out over the years, is that simple statement coming from this man in desperate straits, his comment, "I'm just looking for a place to put it; I wouldn't want it to hit a school."

What a guy.

[This story appeared in the Naval Aviation Museum's magazine, "Foundation," under the title, "Navy Rock."]

ATC Tales 50

Pete Moss asked a Continental, "Does your computer know BAFFY intersection?"

"No," said the pilot, "but if you can hum a few bars, we'll type it in."

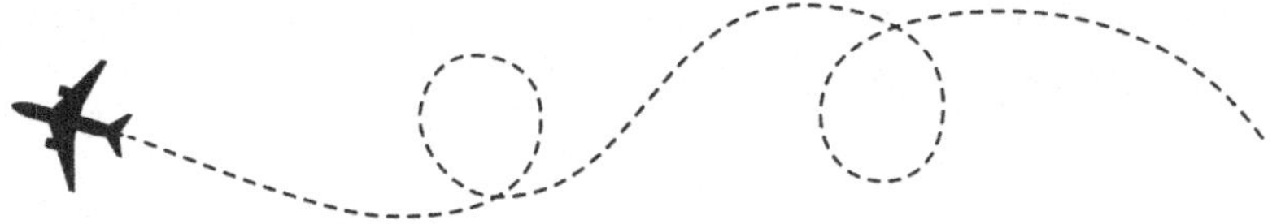

Brian Throop asked a LogAir pilot if he could test some new equipment on him.

"Sure," the pilot said, so Brian told him, have the first officer hold something shiny up to the window; and don't look outside for the next two minutes because this may cause temporary blindness.

A few years ago, there was a late-evening flight that went into Tyler sometime after ten p.m. Some nights the controller working the flight would ask how many passengers were on board. Finally, curiosity got the better of one pilot who had been asked this question several times, so he asked why the interest in the passenger load.

Turns out there was a pool going. Each controller still on duty kicked in a dollar the person who came closest to the passenger load without going over the number of passengers won the pot.

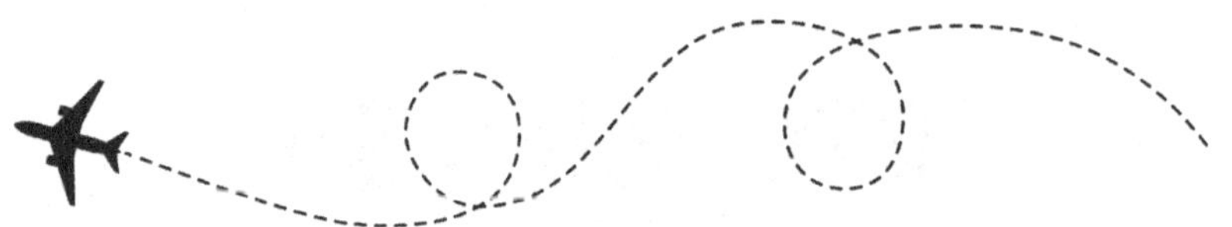

At Travis AFB, CA, there was a sign hanging on the tower that said: PRIDE.

The tower controllers said it stood for: "Pilots Remain Ignorant Despite Education."

Pilots countered, saying, "SHAME! SHAME!" (Staff harasses and mistreats everyone.)

ATC Tales 51

Bill Shea was working AQN/EDNAS when he gave a B727 the crossing restriction. The 727 looked pretty high so Bill asked if he would make the restriction. The pilot replied, "We look pretty high, don't we?"

"Affirmative," said Bill.

"You know what, Center? You're never too f------g high in a seven- twenty-seven."

Mike Copp was working Ardmore-high when a United came through that wanted to know if there was an AM station on which he could listen to the Dallas Cowboys football game.

"KESS, 1270 AM," said Mike with an evil grin.

A moment the pilot came back, "Real funny, Center." KESS is a Spanish language station.

A UPT (Undergraduate Pilot Training) T-38 student at DLF ignored all of DLF Approach's calls. Finally, his instructor asked, "Do you hear those calls?"

The student replied, "Don't talk to me, sir. I'm trying to fly the airplane."

A UPT T-38 out of Sheppard AFB was given traffic. He replied, "Searching."

A moment later came the instructor's tail-chewing as he obviously wasn't happy with the student's search technique.

"When you say, 'searching,' get your f-----g head on a f-----g swivel, you dumb-f-----g son-of-a-bitch!"

Then a moment of silence, followed by, "We know where he thinks the intercom switch is."

ATC Tales 52

SWA209 off OKC made a PA announcement on Ardmore-low's frequency, closing with: "And if you have to get it up, be sure to look out for our three great flight attendants."

A controller who had a reputation for being late called in one more time, this time saying he was in the doctor's office and would be late. Mark Gordon, the supervisor on duty, was overheard to say, "You'll have to come up with something better than that. You've used that excuse three times in the last three weeks."

A young lady whose name escapes me was working a FLIB of Mexican registry, all five letters worth. She called and called and called to no avail. After one last desperate try, he finally responded, "Whatcha want, lady?"

Looking for a ride report, I asked a FEDEX, "How's your ride?" Obviously bored, he replied, "Long—but smooth."

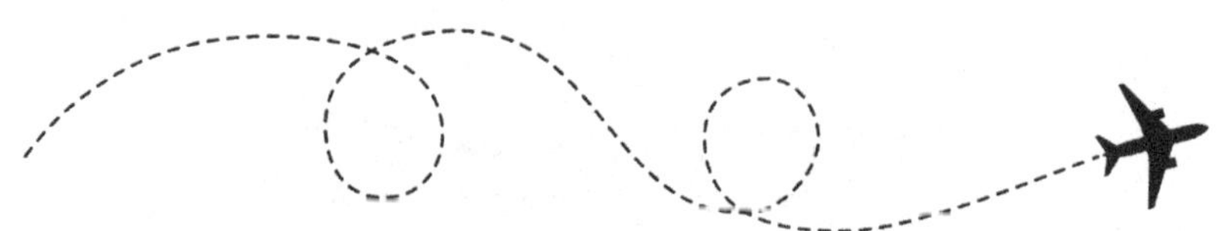

Larry Foreman wasn't very busy when an American commented on the obvious, "Sure is quiet tonight."

Larry: "It was."

AAL: "Sorry."

ATC Tales 53

On Memorial Day Pete Moss was working ADM-high with only a couple airplanes on frequency and few transmissions. AAL1433, the one inbound, was somewhat disconcerted by the quiet, and asked, "Fort Worth, AAL1433, radio check."

Pete keyed his mike, cleared him direct Bowie, gave him the crossing restriction and added that he was "loud and clear."

AAL1433 read the clearance back, then added that he thought we might be outside holding the holiday bar-be-cue.

Pete said, "Yeah, and I had to run back in here to answer YOUR call!"

With one airplane on my frequency, a Delta ATL to LAX, it was very quiet. He checked on and 120 miles later I was just getting ready to switch him to ABQ Center when he said, "Fort Worth, DAL160, radio check."

I keyed up and switched him. He read back the frequency, then added "Gee Center, we didn't mean to piss you off."

A Japan Airlines 747 and an American Airlines MD-80 were opposite direction and given traffic. The JAL replied, "Traffic in sight." The AAL shouted, "Banzai!"

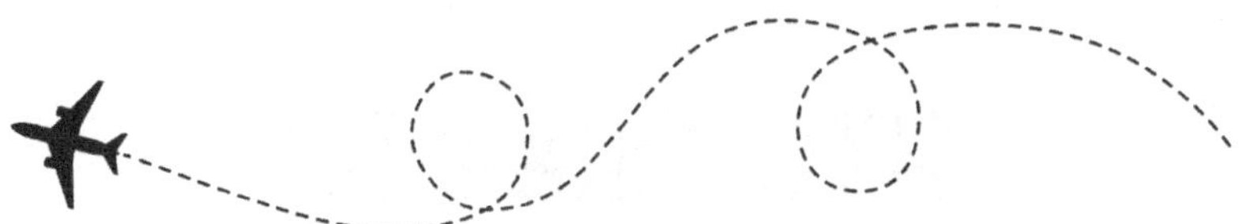

While in the Air Force, Tim Gravens was stationed at Pease AFB, NH. Based there was an F-111 wing. One day their call-sign was "BIRTH" and when they called the Wing Control Office, they would say, "BIRTH CONTROL, BIRTH," chuckling as they did so. The duty officer was a female captain, and she didn't chuckle at all.

ATC Tales 54

What a day. This was one of those days at work where if one airplane showed up a particular altitude, two more showed with him, head on, in a corner of the sector, no red "W's" on the strips, no warning, no heads up, no nothing. It was one of those days most everybody has once in a while and today it was my turn. I got on Ardmore-high early and then the fun started. There was an inbound rush with three, count 'em, three bizjets climbing out right through the middle of them. What a pain in the teeth. I had inbounds scattered everywhere . . . though eventually all of them found their way to Bowie.

Ardmore-low later with the Washita area in full swing. The NATO people up at Sheppard AFB have their own callsigns, usually something to reflect their personality, demeanor, that sort of thing. One is OTTO, another is BEAVIS, another one is BLOODY and yet another's SATAN. I don't think I'd like using that last one.

The head-ons didn't stop when I got to low altitude. Guys were headed up V77 and those fellows would come screaming out of the WASHITA area right into them. Sheppard Approach had a T-38 (SHOOTR11) going to Tinker AFB (at Oklahoma City) that they were supposed to run out to the east over Ardmore. Instead, they run him up to the north with BLOODY right in his face. I told OKC-lo to dump BLOODY to 14000 'cause SHOOTR11 was going to cream him if they didn't. They did and he didn't.

At one point on high there were three at FL310 headed for the proverbial DAT. Mike Ross, my trusty D-side of the moment, had been paying a bit of attention to the radar and not so much attention to the strips. Here comes the three and presto, instant surprise! The first transmission was, "UAL 25, turn 30 degrees right for traffic" The turn took him into another 310, fortunately a DFW lander that went to 280. And it went on like that all day.

One time I was sitting there on high and two airplanes showed up in the northeast corner, two at 350. Two airplanes total in the sector and they nearly get together. One outbound push there were airplanes all over the sky northbound and I was spreading them out as best I could, with three or four overflights mixed in for good measure, so I turned one departure just a tad to the right behind an overflight. There was another departure out there off to the east, but I didn't think this guy would get over there. He did though and there was some more yanking, cranking and banking. And so it went, all day.

I worked the BEAVIS in and out of the WASH and as I did so, I was reminded of the controller working ground control over at DFW who was being given a ration by some American dash-80 pilot. Finally, he had had enough. "Let me talk to Beavis," he said, "'cause I'm tired of talking to you."

There's another good story about DFW ground control, one I happened to hear personally. I was over there "observing" one day, on one of these "let's learn to love our brother controller" programs.

As it turned out, I plugged in on ground control with Fred Hochreiter, the brother of Mike, a controller at the Center, DFW was departing north so everyone was taxiing south, the jets to the end and the props, including the two ASEAs in question, to an intersection where they were supposed to make a 90-degree left turn. Seems they made a 135 degree to the left, heading up the high speed for 17. "Stop!" Fred yelled into the mike. "Stop right there. You're the third m-th-- f--ker that's done that today!" And then he started in on the second ASEA, who was well into the turn behind #1 "And you stop right there; don't you be an idiot like your company in front of you!"

I tell you this . . . for the next ten or fifteen minutes, everybody sat up straight and paid attention.

ATC Tales 55

FW: "Traffic's an aircraft." [Duh.]

VS: "Turn 20 degrees."

The pilot came back: "Which way?"

ZFW: "AAL2077, turn 10 degrees right, direct Omaha when able."

AAL2077: "We're going to need an initial heading."

PM asked AAL1945 his heading. AAL1945 replied, "Heading 3-6-1 . . . err, aah, 0-0-1," and then asked plaintively, "Don't pass that around, OK, center?"

Pete Moss was working Waco-lo late one night when N839CA, a LJ31/A, got off Waco for "Spirit of St. Louis Airport." The pilot, who had filed direct, was vectored north for traffic, then turned on course. Pete asked, "N839CA, how are you navigating direct Spirit with slant alpha equipment?"

The reply came back, "The captain has better homing skills than a Canadian goose."

PIREP: some interesting ones have appeared over the years. Recently one came out: "05E FSM a C402 rptd mod-sev turd at FL090 at 1245z." I figured the guy really had to go, what with the object being moderate to severe.

Another PIREP said: "3/4-inch hail reported at MLC158032 by a man."

In flight plan remarks this appeared: "No ice on board." I'll bet the passengers were ticked until they found out it meant "No de-icing equipment."

ATC Tales 56

While on a USAir fam trip through Pittsburgh, we were taxiing along when the first officer said, "See that spot? We ran off the taxiway right here one night in the pouring rain. The nose gear collapsed, and we made an emergency evacuation. After we got out, we couldn't account for four passengers."

Turns out security called the airline a short while later. They had found the four passengers in the terminal, dripping wet, hand luggage in hand, waiting for a connecting flight. One guy said that when the airplane came to a stop everybody scrambled to get out, so he stood up, opened the overhead bin, and got his hand luggage, then followed the crowd. When he got to the bottom, he could vaguely make out the terminal and knowing he had to catch a connecting flight, he walked to the terminal, crossing an active runway and several taxiways before he got there, where he found a door and entered. "I've got to catch a connecting flight," he told the police.

Kelly Maxwell, one of the old hands when I got here, was what Buddy Davis would call, "One of the unique characters of ATC." He was, too. He had a way with trainees. He once told Greg Peterson, "Boy, if I tell you it's Easter, you better start coloring your eggs."

He got off a mid-shift one morning and went home. Getting there he decided he would mow the yard before going to bed. Kelly was, at times, a pretty rugged and occasionally a ragged looking individual. Just off the mid he looked like he'd seen better days. His battered old pickup parked on the street, Kelly was mowing his front yard when a big car pulled up and stopped, and a woman got out. She stopped Kelly and asked, "How much do you charge for mowing yards?"

Kelly, realizing that she thought he was the local mowing service, pointed at his own house and said, "Well, the lady in this house lets me sleep with her." She got in her car and left.

Frank Rawls, a training instructor, asked a class of new hires if there were any ex-military controllers in the class. When there were, he would ask them if they knew the difference between military and civilian air traffic control. "When the Air Force sends out a bunch of C-130s," he said, "they expect some casualties. When American Airlines sends out a bunch of dash 80s, they expect 'em back in one piece."

Rawls taught the new hires some of the first classes upstairs in the training department. Right after the PATCO strike in 1981 the FAA hired some furloughed airline pilots, mostly American Airlines in this area, as "strip-rippers." To impress the new hires, he used to pass his paycheck around the class. That stopped permanently when a furloughed pilot looked at it and announced that he would be making that much a week within a year of getting back to work.

He also used to pass his Rolex watch around the class. That stopped when someone in the back of the class got the watch and started banging it on a table, shouting it didn't work. Turned out he had slipped his own watch off and deftly switched them, but it still gave Frank quite a start.

ATC Tales 57

Rick Mariano cranked a Delta out and the pilot asked, "What's the reason for this vector?"

Rick responded, "Because you love to fly and it shows."

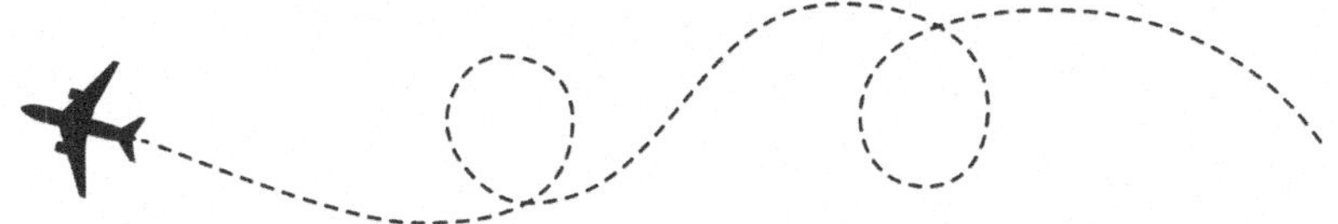

FF told an American to extend his holding pattern, saying, "I'll call your turn." He quickly added, "If you see the Pacific Ocean, I've forgotten you."

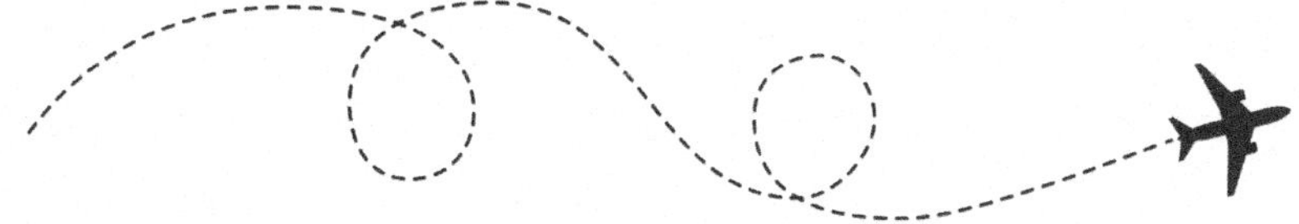

George Harris worked N6755C, a BE55, who came up on frequency to airfile. George asked him what type nav equipment he had (slant what?) but the fellow had a bit of a hard time understanding him Finally George explained in simple terms what the airplane was capable of. The pilot, still not understanding the question, started listing every type of equipment the plane had . . ."A NavStar 2000, a stormscope, VOR . . ." Somewhere in there came "GPS" so GW just entered, "slant G."

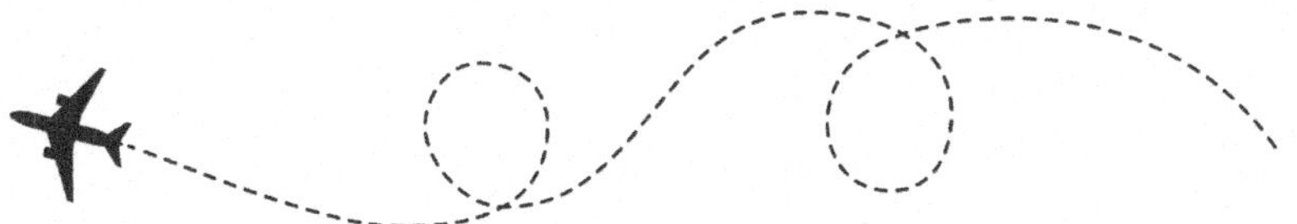

Early one morning Chad Etheridge found himself on Frisco-lo working northbound departures. UAL8179 came off DFW to DEN, a B737/E, requesting direct somewhere and Chad, unable to comply with the request, told him Pete Moss might have something for him on the next frequency.

When United checked on Pete's freq, he made the same request, adding that "the previous controller said you might be able to help us." Pete climbed him to altitude, FL350, then added, "that guy [Chad] is the biggest liar in the building."

"3-5-0," the pilot read back, then came "So we've heard."

ATC Tales 58

Pete Moss's wife is from Scotland and periodically visitors come to Texas for a wee while to enjoy this clime, a much better one all-round than Scotland's. A few years ago, Pete's brother-in-law Jackie came for the first time, leaving Glasgow, Scotland, one early late-June morning and arriving at DFW at 5pm. When he left Glasgow it was 48 degrees and raining. The 757 to Chicago was air-conditioned, as were the O'Hare terminal and the dash 80 to DFW.

When he arrived at DFW it was 95 degrees with a 15-knot wind out of the south and Pete saw Jackie visibly stagger when he hit the terminal door heading outside. Later he said, "My first thought was, 'It's a damn poor design for an airport where they'd have the jet exhaust blowing down the street.'"

One evening I had two aircraft on ADM-hi's frequency, a Delta and American, and asked the Delta (to SFO) if he wanted direct Coaldale, then added "I see you're an NRP [national route plan]. You'll have to request to come off NRP before I can give you direct."

The pilot actually said, "Let me think about this for a minute."

Minutes went by and finally I asked the Delta if he had decided. The pilot wondered if anybody really cared about him coming off NRP.

"I don't," I said.

"OK then. I don't either," said the Delta.

"I'm proud of you, Delta," came a voice out of the frequency netherworld, obviously from the American, the only other aircraft on frequency.

I was on a SF-340 DFW to SGF, a few years ago. The jump-seats are in the middle of the aisle and the flight attendant has to lean over and shout into the cockpit to be heard. With only a few passengers, this particular flight attendant wasn't too busy, and asked how one got a job as a controller. I told her, then asked if she was married or engaged, because there would be a four-month separation while the trainee went through the training at the FAA Academy in Oklahoma City

"I'm engaged to that fellow in the right seat," she said.

Later I had the same conversation with "that fellow in the right seat," asking him the same question (not telling him what the flight attendant had said).

"That girl in the back thinks we're engaged."

I didn't say another word.

ATC Tales 59

Pilots are funny people. I don't mean funny ha-ha, I mean funny as in " strange." They don't mean to be strange or funny, I'm sure. They just seem to be that way naturally. I have a lot of respect for pilots of all sorts, airline, air taxi, military, FLIB . . . well, I'm wary of the last lot, particularly wary. Heck, I'm wary of the whole bunch of 'em. I say this all the while having an airline pilot who is one of my best friends. I'd go to the ends of the earth for this guy and he'd, well, he'd sure enough go to wherever American flies!

A controller tends to see the strange ones every once in a while. Weeks go by and nothing out of the ordinary happens, then a day like today shows up and there's a whole passel of them folks on the frequency. They act normal until they get to you and then they go crazy. Today was like that for me.

I was on Waco-low this morning, working the R-side while Mr. Penguin was training on the D-side with his instructor, Jerry Stocks. The Penguin is so-called because he walks like a penguin. The "quack-quack-quack" he emits when entering a room. His instructor and I were telling him how easy Waco-low is when several things happened to belie our supposition

The sector is an easy one, that's for sure. It's so easy to camp there that KOA, Kampgrounds of America, is thinking about charging people for staying on position more than three hours. It's so easy that people think there has to be something they've missed, figuring it can't be this easy. But it is. It has its moments though, and this morning was ever so briefly one of them.

A Kittyhawk came over going to Austin. There was some weather in Austin this morning, weather that was causing aircraft to hold. I got the handoff on this guy and prepared to start him down into Austin when he said the Austin weather was below his minimums and he wanted to go to San Antonio. So we got ready to get him on the road to San Antone when he changed his mind and opted for Austin. This meant more coordination and we started on that. No, San Antonio; no, Austin. He finally opted for San Antonio, adding that Austin was on the way and he could always change mind further south. I don't know if he any options left 'cause he'd already gone through a bunch of changes on my frequency.

So Kittyhawk and all his friends left and eventually there was only one plane left, N228H, a business prop that flies from Duncan, Oklahoma, to Houston's Hobby Airport every business day. He goes down and he goes back every day and this morning he was southbound to Houston, the only airplane on frequency or even in the sector, when out of the clear blue he announced, "Center, you seem to have a stuck mike. Do you have another frequency?"

"A stuck mike?" I replied. "You're the only aircraft on frequency!"

He replied that there seemed to be a lot of interference and static, but he'd do some checking. A moment later came the announcement that "the fellow over in the other seat turned the number two radio up so I was getting interference from that."

Problem solved, but not before the fellow stepped in it.

Then came a break and Ardmore-low. In a sense it's a camping ground, too, though not nearly like Waco. Stuff actually happens on Ardmore. It can be a garbage sector and there were trashmen out there today, all of them masquerading as pilots.

AAL1028 came off Oklahoma City to DFW and was rerouted over Bonham, the northeast cornerpost, rather than staying over Bowie, the northwest cornerpost. This guy headed off in the right direction, to the southeast, but he had forgotten to take out the Bowie VOR frequency and set in the Bonham (BYP) freq. When his airplane was 70 miles north of Ardmore it seized the Bowie VOR and headed to the southwest, almost climbing into an Eagle flight above him. When I finally herded him toward Bonham his GPS nav equipment couldn't go to the BYP010030 direct BYP. I finally gave him a heading and shipped him to Frisco.

It probably wasn't half an hour later when EGF553 came out of DFW to OKC, a Saab 340 who was given direct Ardmore, then fly heading 345, vectors to the arrival gate. He got to Ardmore and turned northwest, probably a 315 heading, clearly not what he was supposed to be doing. When I quizzed him, he said he was outbound on the 3-4-5 radial. Not so, I replied, adding that he was headed northwest. Silence, then a moment later the plane swung a little to the north but not much. Finally, I gave him a H350 for the gate, asking if he got his equipment squared away. He said he had and added that they'd set "325" in the heading window instead of "345."

I let it go at that but was not surprised to hear his worried query a moment later asking if anything would come of this. I'd heard such queries before. Pilots are like anyone else when it comes to Big Brother and the FAA, of which I am part, a little Big Brother. "No, because there was no loss of separation or airspace violation nothing will come of it." Then I added, "And besides, I'm sure you're going to write up a maintenance slip on that defective heading knob."

ATC Tales 60

TWA760 was inbound to the Rome International Airport, Rome, Italy, holding at the Rome NDB, for an approach, when it was descended to 3,000 feet and told to continue holding prior to receiving an approach clearance. Bob Cannon, the First Officer, acknowledged the clearance and a moment later was surprised to hear another aircraft, the one being stepped down above them, also cleared to 3,000 feet at the Rome NDB.

Bob queried Rome Approach Control, "TWA760's holding at 3,000 over the Rome NDB and I just heard you clear another aircraft to 3,000 feet at Rome NDB. Is that correct?"

"Dat's aright," said Rome Approach, in heavily accented English, "So you watcha out!"

Dave Asbell was on a USAir flight out of Pittsburgh back to DFW and found himself on a 737, in one of those cramped little jumpseats that straddle the aisle and block anything and everything going in or out of the cockpit. Still at the gate, a young flight attendant made her presence known to Dave by leaning over him and also rubbing his back with . . . well, let's just say she was rubbing his back with her front.

Dave, who's happily married (see the next story for a bit more on that), didn't mind the extra attention too much but was surprised when, after the door shut, to find the captain and first officer laughing at some inside joke that they weren't sharing with him.

When the laughter finally subsided Dave asked the obvious question, "What's up?"

They weren't going to tell him at first but finally the captain smiled, tipped his head toward the door and said, "Last year she was a he."

The next time "she" came to the door Dave made it a point to lean as far forward as he could.

And speaking of Dave, not too long ago, Dave was on the short end of the stick with his wife. He didn't know what he had done wrong but obviously his wife did and she was letting him know about it, long and loud. She went on and on at him for ten minutes or so and he just stood there taking it, when she finally paused for breath and gather her thoughts.

Dave, sensing that this was his moment, seized it: "If that was an apology," he said, "I accept."

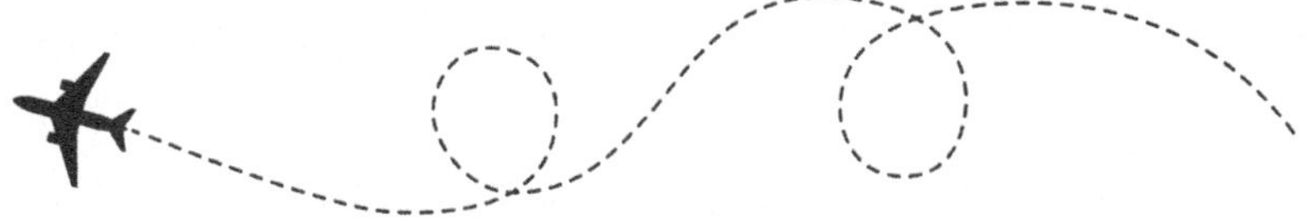

Pete Moss told AAL1993, "Say heading."

AAL1993: "Heading 3-6-2."

PM: "Roger. Fly heading 3-6-2; direct Omaha VORTAC when able. "

AAL1923 at FL310, was overflying Oklahoma City for DFW but departed IRW heading about 205, right for the Fort Sill Restricted Area, which was hot to 32,000. (He should have been outbound on the IRW165 radial for the Bowie STAR.)

"Where are you going? You're heading southwest instead of southeast," PM inquired.

"We're on the Bowie 4 arrival," came the response.

Turned out he thought he was over Tulsa instead of Oklahoma City, and was flying the Tulsa transition. (Tulsa is 105 miles to the northeast.)

Not that Pete has ever made any mistakes, but he once cleared Southwest 241 requesting FL290, to "climb and maintain flight level two-ninety."

ATC Tales 61

A Citation departed JFK for OKC and was cleared from the JFK180007 direct OKC. Pete Moss on Tulsa-hi cleared the aircraft direct Tulsa and the arrival route into OKC. The pilot went into his motorboat routine, "But but but but our previous clearance was direct Oklahoma City!"

"That's correct," Pete retorted, "and your CURRENT clearance is via direct Tulsa and the Tulsa 2-4-6 radial!"

It was a Christmas Eve morning and Pete had everything combined up on OKC-lo, setting it up with a handset and the radios in the speakers. Wanting to check the speaker volume he asked an air carrier to give him a radio check.

The air carrier said, "Eenie meenie mynie moe. How do you hear my radio?"

Pete was at a loss, but Chris Boswell wasn't. She said, "Tell him this . . ." and Pete did.

"Fe fi fo fum. Loud and clear with a little hum."

The pilot was quite surprised, saying it was the first time in many years he had heard the correct response from the FAA. He heard it quite often from military controllers but not the FAA. Pete didn't tell him Chris Boswell, a former army tower controller, had told him.

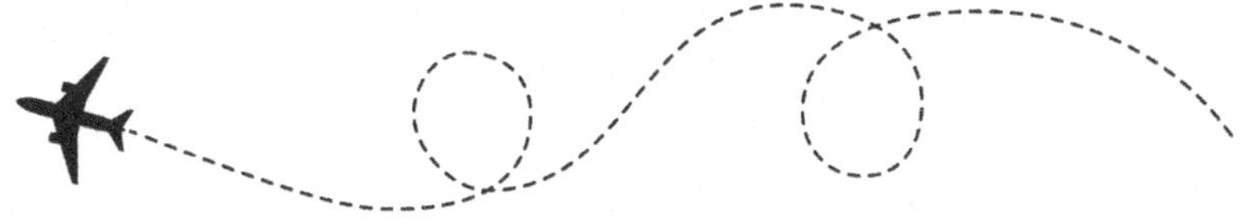

One night there was a line of weather from Kingfisher, Oklahoma, to St Louis, and nobody was getting through it. A VFR popped up at Miami, Oklahoma, on the north side of the line, looking for an IFR to Fort Smith, Arkansas, on the south side. Pete explained that no one was getting through and that maybe the pilot should consider another option.

"Got a bunch of chickens out here tonight, huh?" was the pilot's reply and then asked for the clearance.

"Roger," said Pete. How could he argue with logic like that? "Cleared to the Fort Smith airport via direct. Maintain 7,000," and then he got the SAR information.

The airplane charged in and out of the line time after time, but it was finally too much for the pilot who meekly requested a clearance to Tulsa, saying he would continue on to Fort Smith in the morning. Pete gave him the clearance, adding, "I think you've made a smart decision."

The pilot didn't say anything else until he acknowledged the frequency change to Tulsa Approach, as he added, "I'd rather be a live chicken tomorrow morning than a dead hero tonight."

ATC Tales 62

Alvie Ring had one airplane, a TWA, on his ADM-hi frequency, a DFW departure deviating around weather on his climbout toward MLC. He had already cleared the airplane to "Deviate as necessary," but the pilot insisted on telling Alvie every single thing he did.

Exasperated with the guy, Alvie finally told the pilot, "TWA574, you're the only aircraft I have on my frequency. You lead and I'll follow."

Sounded great at the time but not so funny a few days later when the report of the on-board FAA evaluator reached the front office.

N4283Q, a Comanche off Grayson County, Texas, to Albuquerque, New Mexico, departed VFR, looking to pick up an IFR. There was no flight plan in the computer, so PM started taking the basic information while Mike Ross started calling FSS looking for a flight plan

At some point the pilot started answering "Affirmative" to every question.

Do you have a flight plan on file? Affirmative.

Did you file with radio? Affirmative.

With what radio did you file? Affirmative.

What altitude are you requesting? Affirmative.

It didn't matter what PM asked, the answer was, Affirmative. Pete finally asked the question designed to weed out the malcontents and nincompoops . . ."Are you IFR rated and is your aircraft IFR equipped?" The answer? Unfortunately, you've probably it already, Affirmative.

And we never found the flight plan.

I had a klong yesterday. Klongs are, simply put, a giant rush of muck to the heart. They aren't pleasant, that's for darn sure. I had a Continental inbound to Tulsa at 27,000, with an American climbing up underneath him to 26,000. Because I get a bit antsy about situations like that, I issued the clearance a couple times, 260, and asked the pilot his altitude a couple times so he knew I was concerned about it.

I had lost the climbers altitude readout, so I asked him his altitude . . ."We're out of 2-6-6," he said. "2-6-6," I thought; "What's he doing there? He's supposed to stop at 260." Now he was climbing through his assigned altitude into the overflight. "Say again?" I queried. "We're out of 2-5-6 for 2-6-0," he said, and my heart fell back down my throat, settling into my chest. It was still beating a thousand beats a minute, but it was slowing down quickly.

You hate to hear stuff like that, pilot readbacks that are incorrect or unwanted. Richard Ard was climbing an American dash 80 off DFW, trying to jump a 310. It was getting tight and Richard, normally an unflappable sort, started asking the guy his altitude. He needed the guy to say, "Out of 330," but the fellow said, "3-2-4 . . . 3-2-5 . . . 3-2-6," etc. At this last one Richard could take no more. "Wrong answer," he said, adding "turn 30 degrees right vector for traffic."

ATC Tales 63

Greetings from the northland. I'm going to start this because that'll give me incentive to finish it later on today. We were at a burger joint up in Elk River, a pretty good place called "Daddio's" on Main Street. Good food, good atmosphere, just a likeable place. Laurie and I venture out that far every once in a while just because we like the place.

It has a '50s motif, a lot of Elvis stuff on the walls and an Elvis mannequin up in the front. It's dressed in a Santa suit now though through the course of the year, it appears in one outfit or another. A lot of '50s and early '60s music plays and most of that seems to be Elvis stuff, too, including my three favorite Elvis songs, "Are You Lonesome Tonight," "Heartbreak Hotel," and, "One Night With You."

Listening to all that Elvis music made me think of when I first hired on with the FAA. I was a lowly A-boy which meant I pretty much did nothing except rip strips and go-fer work. Finally, a job I could handle! On the mid-shift we ran strips out by hand some of the time but really, we were probably just there to keep the real controllers awake. One night I was working the mid with Big Bill Eaton, a larger-than-life character who had been a Navy seaplane pilot in WWII and had hired on with the CAA right afterwards.

As an aside, Bill had had quite a life. During the war he had been stationed down in Key West, Florida, in the Navy and still loved going down, him and his wife packing a small case each, then jumping on their Harleys and riding down the way to Key West. That came to a stop when a truck hit his wife on one of those long bridges out toward Key West and she was thrown into the water where she was swept out to sea. Not good. Bill later remarried and had a great second marriage. Doris calmed him down to the point where he took up crochet

– and was good at it.

Anyway, one mid-shift about three in the morning we're sitting there working Oklahoma on the high side, 24,000 feet and up, when Elvis Presley's airplane, a Convair 880 with the registration N880EP, came through. The strip showed the callsign, N880EP, the type aircraft, a CV880, and a route of flight from Memphis to Las Vegas. Bill thought Elvis might be going out to Vegas to work a show, so he asked, "Is the king on board tonight?"

A deep-throated, "I sure am," came the reply.

Elvis had been known to sit in the right seat from time-to-time and there he was that night. Amazing! Me listening to Elvis Presley! Could an A-boy have it any better? Doubtful.

That wasn't my first connection with Elvis Presley. I had had another, albeit an ever so remote one. When I was a 10-year-old kid in Germany, Elvis was over there as a buck sergeant, a tank commander in the 2/32nd Armor in the 3rd Armored Division. The 3rd AD went on maneuvers against the 24th Infantry Division and the 24th ID commanding general was hot to put the 3rd AD to shame. He promised a $100 and a 3-day pass to anybody who captured Elvis during the course of the war games but it wasn't collected.

Years later when I was stationed in Germany, I took a 30-day leave during which, among many other places, I went to Greece. I had gone on the trip with two Air Force medics, Tom Stanley, and Rich Gallo, from the base across town, piling all our gear into Tom's beat-up 1959 Opel sedan and cruising south through Austria and Italy, finally parking the car at the USAF station in Brindisi, Italy, and taking the ferry to Corfu, Greece, and a bus into Athens. It was a great trip.

On the boat to Greece, we ran into several other Americans, including an army lieutenant who was a tank platoon leader in the same platoon Elvis had been in some 10 years earlier. He told us that Elvis had always held a drawing for his pay since he didn't need the money, and the rule was that if you'd won the drawing before, you couldn't draw again until everybody in the platoon had had their time. Also, he said that Elvis hadn't liked mowing lawns with the push mowers the army had so he had riding mowers sent over from the States and everybody could mow the area grass with those.

One last comment on Elvis. The Air National Guard unit based at Memphis International Airport flies transport aircraft, or at least they used to when I was moving airplanes, and their call-sign is ELVIS and the flight number, such as ELVIS21. When you'd switch the aircraft to a different frequency, the pilots, instead of reading back the frequency and saying, "Roger," would read back the frequency and then, doing their best Elvis imitation, would say, "Thank ya, thank ya vehry much."

What are the five most worthless things to an airborne military pilot?

1. Runway behind you
2. Altitude above you
3. Fuel in the fuel truck
4. Charts in the car
5. A field grade navigator

ATC Tales 64

Lisa Wooten was working TXK-hi a few weeks ago and needed to coordinate something with Memphis Center. The VSCS scope showed the land line she needed was in use but when she listened in, no one was talking. The situation was pressing, pressing, pressing, as the airplane neared the boundary. Needing to speak to Conway-high, she started calling "Line in use? Line in use?" Conway finally picked up the line saying, "The only reason this line's in use is cause you're on the line shouting, "Line in use?"

I got scared today, real scared, so scared that for a moment I got tongue-tied. It was one of those situations that jump up and slap you in the face. "POW! Here I am! Ain't nothing you can do about it that is going to help very much."

There was a lot of weather down south, bad stuff, the kind Houston Center has to deal with a lot. I moan and groan about the weather here, but all things considered, it isn't near as bad as Houston. There was bad stuff over east as well and all the J180 traffic, Chicago and east to Houston, all that was shifted over DFW and southeast to Houston. That's a lot of traffic and it all had to be meshed with the normal stuff.

The sector just west of Dallas-high is HICOE-hi and the fellows over there are pretty lax and loose. They have to be really, 'cause it's a high-arrival feeder sector to a cornerpost sector and those folks need to be that way. One thing they do is cut everybody short, give airplanes direct whenever they can. So when Austin and San Antonio departures cross into their airspace, they clear them direct DFW on course instead of letting the aircraft stay on their filed route. 999 times out of 1000 it works great but there is that one time . . .

A Delta got off going to San Antonio but was deviating west because of the weather south of Waco and it was getting close to their boundary, so I had my handoff man point the Delta out to them. They had three departures opposite direction, head-on, cut short, two of them no factor but the third, a TWA off Austin, was a definite problem. The pair of them, the Delta and the TWA, were not quite head-on, maybe off-set two or three miles but the TWA was east of his course and the Delta was west of his. They were both out of 27,200 with eight- or ten-miles separation but losing it fast. I was so surprised, so startled to see the TWA out there that I was shocked speechless.

It didn't take long to regain a bit of my composure, enough of it to realize I wasn't talking to the TWA and had to do something to the Delta and quickly. So I turned him southeast and descended him back to 27,000. It worked and the pair of them went on their respective ways, separation threatened but never lost and everything settling down somewhat.

The problem with a situation like that, one of them, is that one tends to get tunnel vision. You want to focus every single bit of energy you have into dealing with the pending situation, but you can't. You have to deal with every other aspect of the sector, the other seven points of the sector compass, not just the southwest corner. There were airplanes all over the sky this morning and all of them potential threats to other airplanes. You have to do what needs to be done and then, while you're waiting for it to work, you have to get on to other stuff that needs doing, and there was a lot of it today.

I should have known bad stuff was about to happen when the D-side started saying, too gleefully I thought, "You're gonna get busy!"

After this low point things got better. I kept chiding myself for missing it and for messing up but after thinking about it all day, I've come to the conclusion that there was little or nothing I could have done except what I did. I feel better about it now. Maybe it's a defense mechanism, convincing myself that there was nothing that could have been done except what was, but if it's a defense mechanism, it's a good one 'cause it's working.

Later on, I worked Ardmore-high and got just as busy and did just fine. There was as much traffic or more as Dallas-high this morning, but I'm used to Ardmore-high. I've worked it for 18 years while I've worked Dallas-high six months. This was the first time I've ever worked the "J180 shift west" and now know firsthand its complexity and the additional problems it presents. I know a few other things, too, like telling HICOE to leave the departures on their route. Their giving an airplane a shortcut into my traffic when mine's deviating into theirs just won't cut it.

A few days ago, I had a "klong," a giant rush of muck to the heart. I mentioned it in another missive. This one wasn't quite a klong but it was there and gone in a flash. I'd say the whole thing didn't last longer than 30 seconds before it was resolved . . . but those 30 seconds seemed so long, almost an ATC lifetime.

ATC Tales 65

A few of us were sitting around a few days ago talking about retirement, plans for the future and when and how we plan to retire and what we'll do afterwards. I mentioned that I'd like to go out like Stretch Norman did. He and a guy named Jim Wacker were sitting on ADM-lo, the sector next to me on Frisco at the start of a day shift some years ago and I could hear them talking about breaks and how they'd "one in, one out," all day long. Wacker went first and came back an hour later, according to plan, then Stretch went. An hour and fifteen minutes later he still hadn't come back into the control room and Wacker was getting antsy. This was, after all, cutting into his second hour-long break and he wanted to get that part of the program rolling.

So Jim started complaining to the supervisor, Don Faram, that Stretch had been gone too long and would the supe page him back? Which Don did.

After ten minutes of fruitless paging for "Stretch Norman, return to the specialty," a secretary in personnel called up the desk asking if the person the supe was looking for was really named "Bill or William Norman?"

On the supe's affirmative response, the woman said, "Why, he retired an hour ago!" He had told Wacker he'd see him in an hour, turned in his headset and badge and then left the building, never to return again.

ATC Tales 66

Some years ago Jim Wacker was working an Air Force F-4 over western Oklahoma that went, in less than a split second, from a flying airplane to a glider—and not a very good glider. The pilot tried for an airstart but it wasn't happening. Finally the pilot advised that the crew would have to eject and would be going out shortly.

"Roger," said Jim. "Advise just before you go."

A moment the pilot said, "We're bailing out now," to which Jim replied, "Roger, have a good day."

The pilot wrote a letter to the Center later, saying that he had broken a vertebra during the ejection but in spite of the pain, he laughed all the way down, thinking about Jim's last comment, the admonition to ". . . have a good day."

And speaking of airplanes that become gliders . . .

Bill Cooper was working Midland-low when a Navy S-2 declared an emergency due to an engine failure.

Bill inquired, "What are your intentions?"

Came the laconic reply, "I guess we'll ride it on down and crash."

I got quite a shock a few days ago when a T-38 checked on Dallas-high's frequency saying, "Fort Worth Center, FOXY46, EMERGENCY."

I was surprised and even turned to Merv Newman, my D-side, and asked, "Did he say 'emergency'?"

Merv thought he had so I asked the pilot, "Did you say 'emergency'?"

He had, due to a partial engine failure. Fortunately he made it back to Sheppard safely and all was well. Still, that word isn't one you particularly want to hear first thing when an airplane checks on frequency.

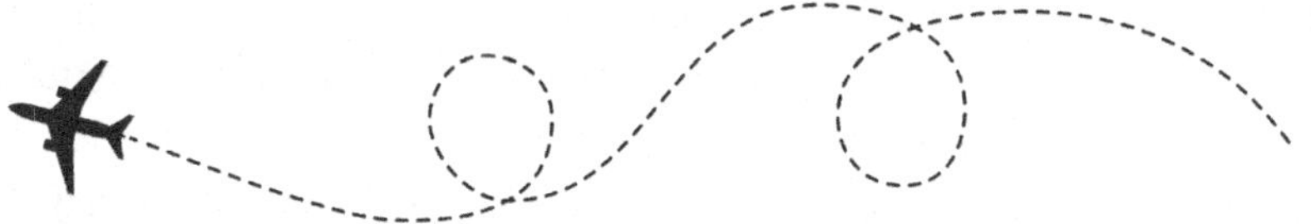

One last story about airplanes and their problems . . .

Greg Garcia and Don Frenya were working Dallas-high, R and D respectively, when a Learjet climbing off Dallas Love southbound was through 370 going up when he had an engine failure, gave his callsign and said, "Mayday, Mayday, Mayday."

Before Greg could key his mike to reply, Don leaned over and asked, "Did he say 'Mayday' or 'have a good day'?"

Greg couldn't stop laughing and that came out when he started talking. The Lear made it safely into Marlin and Garcia made it safely out of the control room, laughing all the way.

ATC Tales 67

Bill Eaton was a gruff, crusty old fellow whose language was salted with epithets of many sorts. He was a virtual artiste when it came to blue language. It was as blue as the Pacific where he'd served in the Navy in World War II, and where he had learned the various terms he used so often.

One night, on the mid we were sitting around shooting the breeze when Bill started telling a story about a hunting dog he had that just wouldn't hunt worth a hoot. Well into the story he realized, his horror, that the handset he was using, that was sitting just a few inches away, was keyed and that every word had gone out over the air. Quickly unkeying the handset's mike, he didn't say another word until it came time to switch the TWA, the one aircraft that was on frequency.

The TWA read the freq back, then added, ". . . and what that hunting dog needs is a good swift kick in the ass."

SWA1 departs Dallas Love every day for Houston's Hobby Airport. Pete Moss asked the pilot, "Does this being Southwest's flight number one mean that you're the senior or the smartest captain in the Southwest fleet?"

"Yes," came the only reply.

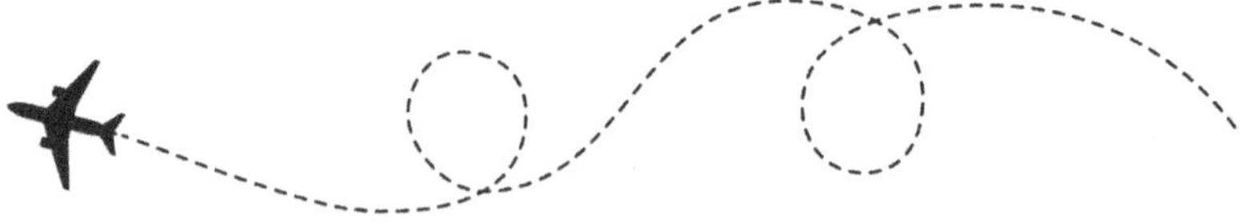

A few days ago, I split off Dallas-high first thing after getting to work. I'd been on the sector maybe a minute with one airplane, a Continental inbound to Houston Intercontinental at FL350. I was sitting there minding my own business, just getting ready to switch him when conflict alert went off. There was another 350, an Airborne Express, just south of my boundary, maybe 15 miles from my Continental, and converging.

It didn't look good. I could tell the other airplane was landing Austin and he should have started down but I wasn't talking to him, just mine, and something had to be done in a hurry.

So I cranked mine 30 right and dumped him to 310, telling him to expedite all the way. He started down and then the ABX did too.

"We're going to plan B," I said. "Climb and maintain FL350 and expedite back up there!" He did, and it all worked out but what a way to start the day!

ATC Tales 68

Earlier today we had a little bit of excitement on the specialty. Seems Mcalester Radio called to report that an aircraft had crashed near Caney, Oklahoma, and could we have an airplane fly over the supposed site and look for the wreckage? "Sure thing." So Mike Ross drafted an Eagle Flight for the first couple hours and flew back and forth along US69, the main north-south parts of the state, and didn't see anything. He then went back.

I had a VFR BE35, N1856Z, out of Lee Summit, Missouri, to Ardmore Downtown, who said he'd go on over for a look. He went maybe 50 miles out of his way, cruised up and down the highway in both directions before pressing on to Downtown. He didn't find anything and there was no ELT either, a good sign that maybe there hadn't been a crash after all.

Controllers never derive any pleasure out of working with crashes. There is some satisfaction in finding a crash site so that the survivors can be rescued, if there are any to be rescued—and you always hope there are.

One of the hardest things I've ever had to do out there was get information from an air taxi pilot about another pilot from the same company. On a mid-shift some years ago, I was working a Bankcheck out of Kansas City to Dallas Love when Kansas City Center called to say that a company flight had crashed north of Bartlesville, Oklahoma, and could I get some information from the pilot I was working, the victim's name, the chief pilot's name, phone number and all that.

It was difficult asking the questions. The fellow knew something was wrong when the questions started and it didn't take him long to figure it out.

One time Ardmore Tower called to ask if I'd run an aircraft over the Red River to find a VFR aircraft that had supposedly crashed there. I did and the pilot found the aircraft which led to a rescue of the plane's occupants. That was a great ending to what could have been a tragedy.

It has always amazed me that some people go through their entire ATC careers never working even an emergency, much less something worse, I've been the D-side on two serious crashes, one fatal and one where the Navy pilot ejected safely. If I never work another one, that'll be soon enough for me.

One morning, the VFR pilot didn't have to go over there so that he did go over reflected well on him, his willingness to spend his time—and gasoline, to search for a downed aircraft. They'd do the same for him.

ATC Tales 69

I was on Ardmore-low today, working a sector below Ardmore-high when our little ATC world went to hell in a hand basket, as the old expression goes. There was a training session going on, a young trainee was getting some OJT on Ardmore-high, which is our specialty's busiest sector. Her instructor had been working with her for a few months, checking her out on her first five sectors and now on the last. He wasn't worried about her because heretofore she had done pretty well. She had proven herself, to a degree, by giving as good as she got, from other controllers and pilots as well.

Today, however, the story was a bit different. The normal inbound rush, busy enough on its own, was complicated by a stream of Air Force student pilots on cross-country flights, the route of which cut right across the inbounds.

Generally, the big thing about getting arrivals in is to get them down below any departures and/or overflights. Ardmore-high gets the handoffs early from the sector to the north in plenty of time to start them down but today she didn't. Instead, she let them ride until they were mixed in with all the Air Force overflights and then realized she couldn't get them down.

She had worked arrival rushes before, busy ones, but none of them had the added complication of the military overflights—and this threw her for a loop. So, rather than adjusting to the new traffic picture, as she should have, she froze. She sat there watching it all develop, making routine calls to airplanes until she stopped making, or answering, calls altogether.

It didn't register with him right away. Her transmissions dropped off but it took him a moment to put two and two together. Even the handoff man, who had plugged in a few minutes before to work the handoff position, didn't see it coming. Her transmissions slowed, then stopped. After a silent moment, the instructor realized nothing was going out so he leaped out of his chair to stand behind her, looking over her shoulder at the scope.

In Ardmore-low, the next sector over, I could see the drama unfold. "I've got it," her instructor said, and he started talking a mile a minute, giving instructions for turns, descents, whatever was needed to maintain separation, first, and gain control of the sector, second. At one point he even used the word "immediate" when he issued a turn, that word indicating "immediate" action is required and the pilot needs to get with the program.

After a bit, he had everything under control and she took it once more. They didn't stay long though, just long enough to let her "get back on the bicycle" so she wouldn't be afraid the next time she worked the sector. They unplugged a few minutes later and went out on a break. He was going on leave, something he was now looking forward to more than ever. Stepping away from the sector, he allowed as how this was the first time he had ever used the word, "immediately."

Did he need to use it? He turned an aircraft 30 degrees right "immediately." You can argue it back and forth. Some might say it was unnecessary, saying a 30 degree turn hardly called for the use of that word. Others would say that if he felt the word was called for, then he should have used it. It's obvious that he doesn't overuse the word, considering that it's his first time ever to use it in ATC. On the other hand, was it warranted here?

I've used the word twice, that I recall, twice in 25 years. The first time I was working OKC-high with a B-52 on frequency, the B-52 at FL330, still in Albuquerque Center's

Amarillo-high's airspace. The Kansas City Center Gage-high sector called, the man speaking in a high-pitched, almost panicky voice saying to descend the B-52 "to FL310 immediately!" I dumped him as the D-side called AMA-high to tell them what was going on.

It turned out that GAG-high was concerned about an inbound to Oklahoma City, also at FL330, but which was 60 miles away! They should have started the inbound down, not the B-52, and their irresponsible action was totally unnecessary.

I used it a few years later, also on OKC-high, when an Eastern Star at FL310 wandered off course into the path of an Airlines DC-9, also at FL310. I dumped the NWA to FL290, an altitude the pilot read back twice. Unfortunately FL280 where he came within three miles of TWA altitude. Then I used the word "immediately" to climb to FL290 altitude.

As for freezing on a sector, I've seen that happen a couple times. It isn't very pretty, either.

About 12:15 one day a few years ago a controller was going down the tubes. The supervisor sent Bryan Warnica to plug in as handoff because the controller was so busy. When Bryan got there, he was surprised to see the controller sitting there not saying a word. The D-side, Chuck Andrews, was doing all the talking, running the D-side and the R-side both, and getting further behind all the time.

Bryan plugged into the handoff position and found the controller doing nothing, just sitting there staring at the scope. He took over the R-side as he stood behind the controller, doing everything the controller should have been doing. This went on for maybe ten minutes when all of a sudden, the controller looked at her watch, and said, "It's 12:30 and I'm going on blood leave," then stood up and left!

Nothing was ever said to the controller.

I've seen two other times where people have lost the picture, once in a mid-shift when Jimmy Arnold was so busy that it overwhelmed him. He lost it altogether and came off the sector. Fortunately Janet Landman, his D-side, had the picture and took over, doing a great job.

The fourth time was when a supervisor got in over his head on Ardmore-high. I was sent over to take the sector from him. When I plugged in he pointed to a place just northwest of Ardmore, a place on the scope that was literally covered with targets and data blocks, and said, "I've got ten airplanes in here and I don't know what any of them are doing." Most of them were going to FL240, right through a pair of Air Force aircraft on a refueling track in a block of FL250B270. Not good. It all worked out though Don never worked Ardmore-high again.

ATC Tales 70

I heard a good story at work today. On the old 300 system, an intra-communication system, your microphone could be keyed when someone else plugged in with you—if they plugged their headset into the jack all the way. That meant whatever you said, or mumbled, went out, even if you didn't want it to.

Craig Whitwell, a pretty good controller, was working Dallas-high when Dwan Streggles plugged in, almost all the way, to give Craig a break. Craig had been working one eastbound aircraft 20 miles west of DFW, supposedly heading direct to DFW. His heading, however, was taking to a point 20 miles NORTH of DFW instead of over it. Quizzing the pilot about it, the pilot insisted he would pass right over DFW.

Craig, not realizing he had a hot mike, muttered, "Yeah, you're gonna be missing it by a hell of a lot to be that f---ing close." Hearing himself talk (you can hear outgoing transmissions in your earpiece), he suddenly knew that what he said had probably gone out. Hesitantly he asked, "That didn't go out, did it?"

"Sure did," came the laconic reply

Craig apologized and let it go at that, hoping, for the next 15 days, that the pilot wasn't hacked enough to call in.

CT Schroeder got so busy one day last week that he started babbling about his family. He kept hollering, "Uncle! Uncle!"

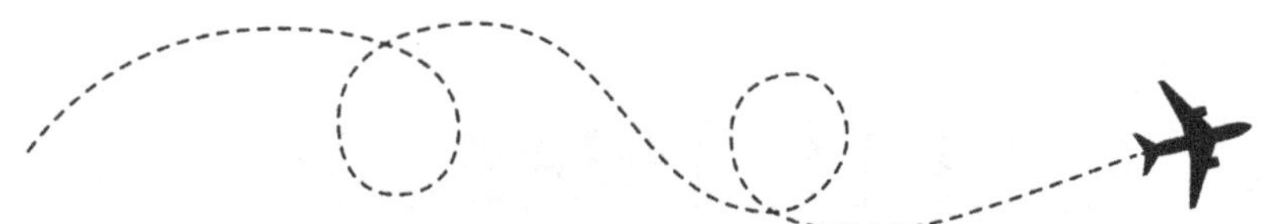

Heard a good story at work yesterday. There's a guy out there named Dave Asbell. His uncle worked for the Texas Department of Public Safety. He was pretty high up, high enough to where he got to travel to places to represent the state at meetings, functions and whatever else might be called for.

One time he found himself on a 727 down in the interior of Mexico somewhere, him and one other guy the only two Americans on the plane. They were also the only two who didn't speak Spanish. They'd gone along for a while when the pilot made an announcement after which a low wail passed through the cabin. He looked around and found everybody crossing themselves and starting to pray. Bad news!

Turns out the plane had run out of gas and they were "gliding," as best a 727 can, to a controlled crash landing in the desert below. The pilot got it down in one piece though the gear collapsed. No serious injuries and everybody walked away. They didn't walk far though, 'cause they were so far away from everything. It was five hours before buses got to the scene to haul people away.

ATC Tales 71

Robert Jenkins had a system deviation today. He was working Dallas-high R-side and the sector was down the tubes. Busy, busy, busy. Somewhere in there he ran a guy into Houston Center's Austin -high's airspace. Bad news. That's a no-no in air traffic control, running a guy into someone else's airspace without a handoff.

At least the system we work with, is notorious. You get on the landline and start shouting at the handoff, but they don't answer, they don't take the call because a lot of consternation, trouble, and, in this case, paperwork.

A system deviation is a bad thing. It causes a lot of grief for all hands. The controller usually has to go through remedial training of some sort and then be recertified on that position. In today's case there was a supervisor standing right behind him watching all this happen. This particular supervisor is checked out on that very sector Robert was working so he knew what to look for, what problems Robert was encountering and what difficulties he was facing. At one point Robert called for a "handoff man" which is really an extra set of eyes to watch what's going on but in this case the request came too late.

The idea is that if a handoff cannot be made, the aircraft must be contained in your own airspace. Robert waited too long to spin the aircraft and it got down in Austin-high about five miles before it turned back northbound. About the time it turned northwards Austin-high finally took the handoff but by then it was too late, the violation had occurred.

Sometimes the receiving controller, Austin-high would say something like, "I've been watching him all the time," or "I thought I took the handoff." That would clear the offending controller, keeping everything legal and almost above board.

Today, however, with a supervisor watching, there was no choice but to turn it in.

So it was turned in. Robert got pulled off the boards and the paperwork process started. Tapes are pulled, statements are taken and eventually something will happen, a decision made as to what sort of "rehabilitation" the controller, in this case, Robert, will have to go through before being recertified.

One problem here is that these incidents are fairly traumatic to the average controller, especially the older ones. For years management harped and harped about avoiding system errors and deviations, telling of the dire consequences that would befall any unfortunate soul who had one. Lately they haven't and the younger controllers have a different attitude toward deals and deviations. Older guys try to avoid them like the plague. Younger guys say, "what's the big deal? I'll just get recertified."

One problem with the FAA's approach to system deviations and errors is that it, management, wants to blame someone, some person, and not the ATC system or a part thereof, as being responsible for the error. Today's deviation was caused by two factors, first and foremost being Robert's failure to make sure Center took the handoff. The other factor, however, was the fact that the "automated handoff" feature didn't kick in and the computer handoff had to be manually entered in the computer. This was done very late. Had the feature, which is supposed to work all the time worked as advertised, today's deviation wouldn't have happened.

So Robert will get the blame. Contributing factors like the automated handoff feature not working, the Austin-high controller not taking the handoff or even answering the handoff line, and the supervisor's failure to get the "handoff man" in there, might be mentioned in the controllers' statements and might, might, even be listed as contributing factors but will be discarded as the primary cause, if they are mentioned at all.

Something interesting did happen at work today. Chuck

Andrews was working ALMITY1 (pronounced "Almighty One"), an eastbound F-14 on Ardmore-high. After the aircraft checked on, a voice asked, "Who is Almighty One?"

Chuck replied, "Well, in my opinion the Almighty One is God . . . but in this case he's an F-14."

A voice floated out of the ether "What other kind of airplane would God fly?"

ATC Tales 72

What's the difference between God and pilots?

God doesn't think he's a pilot.

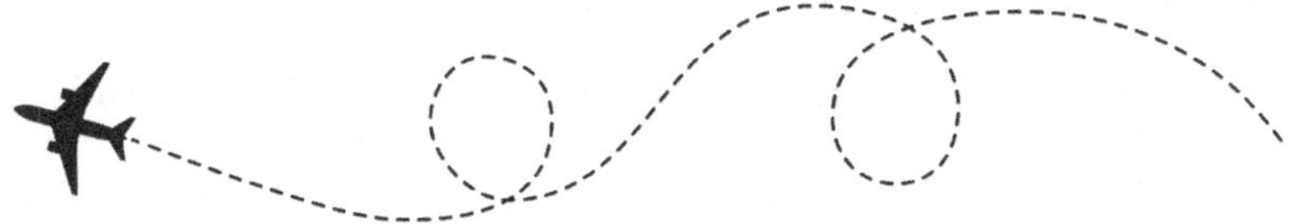

PILOT: "Good morning, Minneapolis ground. Mesaba 2342 request start up, please."

GROUND: "Mesaba 2342 expect start up in two hours."

PILOT: "Please confirm, two hours delay?"

GROUND: "Affirmative."

PILOT: "In that case, cancel the good morning!"

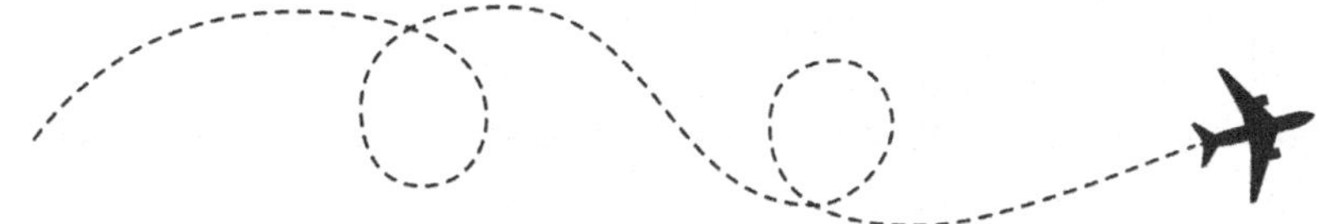

TOWER: "Mission 1234, you're are cleared to . . . via . . . and via . . . After takeoff . . . and . . . then . . . climb to . . . and further . . . and descend . . . further instructions on frequency . . . or . . . and squawk . . . Acknowledge please!"

PILOT: "Roger tower, we are cancelling IFR."

Reportedly true:

ATC: "Delta 23, cross Gainesville at and maintain flight level two seven zero."

Delta23: "Delta 23, roger."

Three minutes later, Delta 23 is five miles from GNV, still at FL 360.

ATC: "Delta 23, did you copy the crossing restriction, Gainesville at flight level two seven zero?"

Delta23: "Uhhh . . . Jax . . . we're gonna miss that, my first officer took that clearance."

ATC: "Delta 23, do you think you could borrow his notes?"

ATC: "Critter 127, maintain flight level two niner zero, traffic twelve o'clock, niner miles, opposite direction at flight level two eight zero, King Air."

Critter: "Critter 127, roger."

ATC: "Critter, correction, your traffic at flight level two eight zero is a Beech Starship."

Critter: "Critter, roger, we have the backwards King Air in sight."

[for the unfamiliar, a Starship is an aircraft with "pusher" engines, and a canard wing]

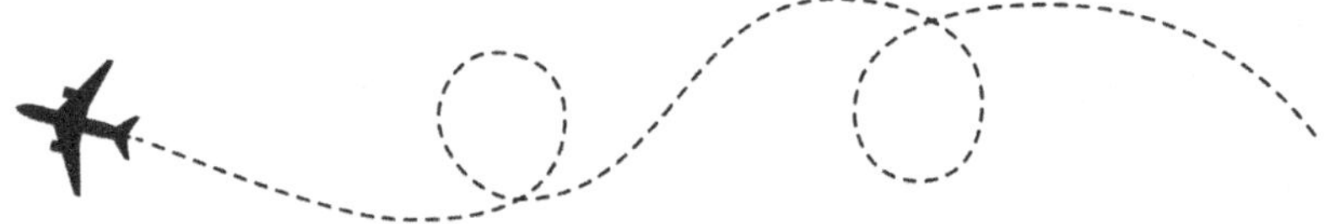

Landing Rating Scale:

5. Marvelous, ace. Couldn't do better myself.

4. I've seen better; just can't remember when.

3. Average. I could do better with my eyes closed.

2. You going to log all of those?

1. That wasn't a landing; that was an arrival.

0. Go get the trailer, boys.

Purportedly real, but I didn't hear it myself . . .

(Transmission as a DC-10 rolls out long after a fast landing . . .)

San Jose Tower: "American 751 heavy, turn right at the end if able. If not able; take the Guadalupe exit off of Highway 101 back to the airport."

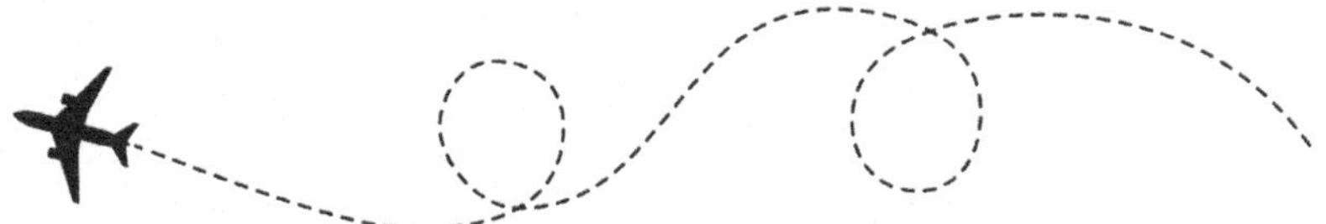

A T-38 pilot ran out of fuel and decided to put it down on a road. He managed to coast into a gas station and said to the attendant, "Fill 'er up!"

The attendant just looked at the pilot.

"Bet you don't get too many airplanes asking for a fuel," said the pilot.

The attendant replied, "True, most pilots use the airport over there."

Controller is trying to change Mooney 45Q to another controller's freq, but gets no response. Thinking that the Mooney may have already switched to the other freq accidentally, since the pilot is a local who knew it was coming, the controller contacts the other controller and asks him to check.

Controller: "Mooney 45Q, are you on this frequency?"

45Q: "Negative. But I should be any time now."

FQOZ: "Toronto Terminal, FQOZ is a Cherokee 140, Burlington skyway at 3500, VFR to Buttonville via the island, would like to get as high as possible."

ATC: "QOZ, cleared to flight level 230."

FQOZ: {sputter, gasp!} "Say again! Did you say flight level 230 for QOZ?!"

ATC: "Just kidding; I can give you up to 6500."

One of my instructors in FE school told me about this.

Apparently the loadmaster on a USAF C-130 was invited to take the engineer's seat for a while. He started jabbering away, not realizing that he was transmitting on Unicom.

LM: "Hey, this is great! I see why you engineers like this seat so much-you can see everything from here! This is just like the starship Enterprise! All ahead, Mr. Sutu, warp factor ten!"

Followed shortly afterward by:

ATC: "You wanna get back on intercom, Captain Kirk? You're transmitting on my frequency!"

A pilot called in and said he was unsure of his position but he had a town in sight. Since we didn't have him on radar, the controller told him to descend and look for the town's water tower, see what it said on the side, climb back up and tell him

Sure enough in about 3 minutes the pilot called back and said, "Approach, I found the water tower."

The controller, looking rather pleased, asked "And what did it say on the side?"

The pilot replied, "It said Seniors, 1978."

Truly happened.

PILOT: "Tower, give me a rough time check!"

TOWER: "It's Tuesday . . ."

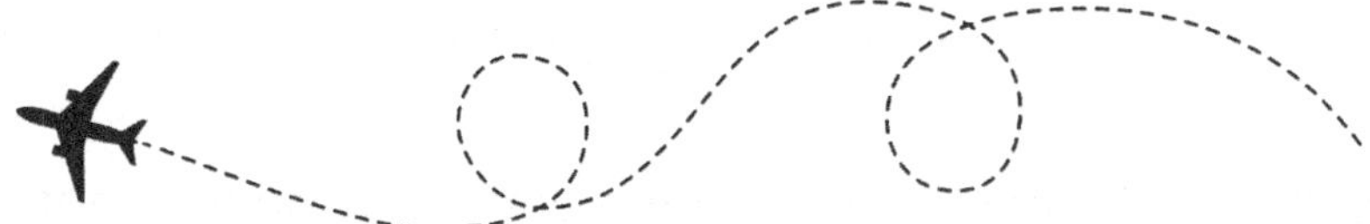

NY Ctr.: "Federal Express 235, descend, maintain three one zero, expect lower in ten miles."

FedEx 235: "Okay, outta three five for three one oh, FedEx two thirty-five."

NY Ctr: "Delta fahv twuntee, climb one ninah zeruh, dat'll be finah."

Delta 520: "Uhh . . . up to one niner zero, Delta five twenty."

NY Ctr: "Alitalia wonna sixxa, you slowa to two-a-fifty, please."

Alitalia 16: "HEY! You make-a funna Alitalia?!"

NY Ctr: "Oh, no! I make-a funna Delta anna FedEx!"

ATC: "USA353 (sic) contact Cleveland Center 135.6."

ATC: "USA353 contact Cleveland Center 135.6!"

ATC: "USA353 you're just like my wife—you never listen!"

Pilot: "Center, this is USA553, maybe if you called her by the right name you'd get a better response!"

PAO Twr: "Mooney 23D, traffic is a Cherokee just entering downwind from the left 45."

Mooney 23D: "Uhhh, tower, 23D . . . only traffic I see is a Cessna."

Pause . . .

PAO Twr: "Mooney 23D, follow your traffic directly ahead, and um, inverted Cherokee just abeam the numbers."

ATC Tales 73

Dave Dowd was working Dallas-high when a pilot mentioned that "yesterday a controller gave us direct Chanute," hinting for direct. Dave grumbled, "Today he's working the next sector."

I was waiting for a friend at lunch the other day. He was late because he was at his company's (he flies for American) quack shack taking a physical. Evidently their physical is a little better than the FAA's. In ours they check for two eyes, two ears, (can you see/hear?), a look down the throat and the blood pressure check. At his physical they actually look for things that might be wrong

American's probably concerned that something might lead to a lawsuit if the fellow isn't in good shape. I work for the feds and they just want to make sure you don't explode on the sector. Messy cleanup, that.

There was an incident a few years ago where a tour group was coming through and a fellow took the opportunity to have some good fun with it. He had concealed one of those rubber puke things, mats, whatever you call them, in his shirt and as the tour group arrived he seemed to retch all over the scope, pulling this thing out of its hiding place and laying it on the scope. The group was shocked and moved quickly away while others ran to see what was wrong. He did receive some blue-chair time but didn't mind, considering the good fun he had.

There was another tour group that came through one time, a group of "99s," women pilots who are interested in furthering women's interests in aviation. They were being given the grand tour when something happened to cause their tour to be hustled away as well.

There's a woman who works out there who swears worse than any man I've ever heard. She was a controller in the Navy and when you hear the expression, "swears like a sailor," she's the sailor they're talking about. She has a mouth on her that makes me blush—and that's her in everyday conversation. When she gets wound up, she really swears.

She was working a sector when the "99s" tour group came to a stop near her position (unbeknownst to her). Not having had a break in a while, she shouted, "Who do you have to f-----g blow to get a break around here?"

The tour moved on quickly.

One more tour story and I'll move on.

One night I was giving a tour to five USAF pilots and navigators, and their wives. The AF types were from Carswell AFB and they'd brought their wives along for the tour. I was giving them the nickel tour and we had come to NWS aviation weather desk where I proceeded to pass out some satellite pictures.

I gave them the standard spiel, these pictures were taken from a satellite in geosynchronous orbit 22,500 miles above the earth, so on and so forth. You see these pictures on TV weather spots all the time. The state lines are computer-generated onto them, common knowledge (I thought) so I didn't even mention that as I passed them out.

One woman, a navigator's wife, looked at her picture and gasped, "You can see the state lines from all the way up there."

A moment of silence fell over the little group, broken when the young lieutenant took his wife's arm and escorted her all the way to the other end of the control room. The rest of us just stood there tittering, not really saying anything about her comment, all of us just sort of embarrassed for her more than anything. They finally came back and we finished the tour. She didn't say another word, not even goodbye.

ATC Tales 74

I was working OKC-high this morning and it was busy when I first sat down. Wes Wygle was going home—I'd probably be more accurate in saying he was going to play golf—and he wanted to get out of there so in I went. The briefing wasn't much and it took me a few minutes to catch up. There was some weather out there and a little deviation though nothing spectacular that anybody had to go way out of their way for.

For a while in there I had a D-side, a young guy named Jimmy Elkins who will, in the long run, be a good controller. Right now he needs to learn to talk to his R-side. We beat the sector down to a pulp and he went to chow.

Over the years various panels, study groups, and other bodies of interest to ATC have met to discuss and debate the system error situation. Their goal has been to determine just what might be done to avert and avoid system errors. One conclusion every such group has come up with is that most system errors happen not during but after busy periods, during that "letdown" period when the controller thinks the situation is well in hand.

Such was this noon when all but a handful of airplanes had disappeared and I had three (and soon four) airplanes on frequency.

One of the main players was AAL61, heading over ADM onto the great circle route going to Japan, level at FL310. Today's flight was an MD-11, one of those "stretch-10s" with a shrunken crew. Actually the overseas flights have several extra people on board to spell the primary crew.

There were two other planes on frequency, neither of them a factor, and there was MANIAC1, an F-16 out of Tinker climbing to FL230 on a heading of 260. He was looking for direct Gage and FL350, going to Hill AFB. Before MANIAC1 checked on I asked the American if he had TCAS and when he answered affirmative, I told him there was an F-16 ten o'clock, six miles, doing a rocket climb and he might get a TCAS alert but the guy was only going to FL290

When MANIAC1 checked on I climbed him to FL270 and he read it back, "2-7-0." He was going to clear the bizjet I'd stopped at 280 (thinking I'd be able to top him with the F-16) so I climbed MANIAC1 to FL290, stopping him for the American. The F-16's heading would take him just behind the American and I'd be able to get him up that much quicker.

MANIAC1 didn't read back the first clearance to FL290 so I reissued the clearance and this time he read back "2-9-0." When I heard C show "2-8-7" I said, "MANIAC1, verify level overshot." I saw his Mode C at FL300 with the wing (3.907 miles according to the sheet). I heard a Manager's computer beeping up front as I turned to the supervisor and I knew the two had printed. Not a pretty picture.

The F-16 leveled at FL290 as the American proceeded north. As the F-16 cleared the MD-11 I turned him northwest and climbed him to FL350, his requested altitude. I asked MANIAC how high he overshot and he said "300 feet." No way. I don't blame him for saying it and I suppose he'd best stick to it.

Before I shipped him to Kansas City Center, I read him his rights, "Mirandized" him, telling him there had been a possible pilot deviation and giving him the Center phone number and that he needed in.

The supervisor and area manager were there over my shoulder asking what had happened. I told them, hoping they'd let it go without pulling the tapes but once they were so close, they decided they'd best be pulled.

Up to that point there was no doubt in my military mind what had happened. I gave the guy 2-9-0 and he read back 2-9-0. When I asked him to verify level 2-9-0, he said, "I overshot." If

I'd assigned him anything else, he'd have said, "You assigned me—" but he didn't; he said, "I overshot." I was relieved from the position shortly after it happened and was told to go to chow, that the tapes would be pulled in short order and we'd listen to them later.

Then the doubts set in. "Did I give him 2-9-0 and he read back 3-5-0? Did I do something else and miss it altogether? All sorts of things go through your mind and they all went through mine. The supervisor asked if I wanted a NATCA representative present in the tape room. No, I said, if I screwed up, I screwed up. I must admit, when the tapes were set up and started to roll, I felt the butterflies start flying in my stomach

There it was, clear as a bell, MANIAC1's readback of "2-9-0" and then, "I overshot." That cleared me and while I feel sorry for the pilot, I am relieved to know I'm in the clear.

ATC Tales 75

I got real busy at work today. I took Dallas-high from Chad Etheridge so he could go to briefing and sat down to confront a real shitpile of airplanes. (Pardon my French but that word fits the bill "to a T.") There were 350s and 310s everywhere and two airplanes at 350 that had to descend through a whole wad of other airplanes so they could get down into Austin and Killeen. And there was a guy off San Antonio, AAL1244, that the next sector wanted stopped at 310 for some traffic in their sector so we stopped him there at their request.

I've been talking to airplanes for quite a while, 25 years or so, almost 26, and while I'm not the best controller in the world (Larry Foreman is—he told me so) I'm far from the worst. When you've been doing this for as long as I have, you develop a "feel" for what's going on in the sector.

It's a feeling you get that prickles the hairs on the back of your neck and says, "Something's not right here. Look around." You learn to pay attention to that feeling and start to scan, scan, scan, checking and rechecking every data block in your sector. Generally there is something wrong, something "off," something that's not quite right and needs fixing, so you take care of it by doing whatever's necessary to resolve the situation.

Sometimes the feeling pops up and nothing's wrong. That happens occasionally but more often than not there is something wrong and you'd best heed that feeling by finding and fixing the problem.

Today the feeling was almost burning the short hairs on the neck (and with as little hair as I have, I can't afford to burn too many) so I started looking. Sure enough, after a moment I found a westbound 310, DAL391, that was headed right for AAL1244. A 20 degree right turn on AAL1244 took him behind the Delta and everything was just fine.

I'm not sure if it was my natural smarts [;-)] or just pure luck but a few years of experience sure helped . . . and the burning hairs helped, too.

A Navy A-4 with engine trouble diverted to a nearby Air Force Base for landing. On final landing, he was told to "Go around because there's a B-52 with an engine out on his way in."

"Oh no," replied the A-4 pilot, sitting on top of his single-engine attack fighter, "the dreaded seven-engine approach!"

ATC Tales 76

EGF503 never checked on Pete Moss's freq, no matter how many times he called. Finally getting the pilot's attention, the pilot said, "I guess our radios haven't woken up this morning. We're here at 12,000."

The plane was almost in the next sector by this time so Pete bid him farewell by saying, "Well, that being the case, you might want to slap 'em a couple times 'cause it's time to contact Center on 128.1."

Ever had something really embarrassing show up on a tape talk? Pete Moss did one time and it didn't come out good for any of the parties concerned. Moss was on Ardmore-lo one day, not busy at all, and was preparing a lesson plan for the radar class he would start teaching the following week, a class that would include, among others, Earl Schmidt, who was, this day, working Larry Foreman's D-side on MLC-lo.

Pete approached something with Earl who checked with Larry who in turn said, "Unable." Pete switched the aircraft to MLC-lo's freq and was a bit surprised when, just a few seconds later, Earl called Pete on ADM-lo, saying Larry wanted control for the same thing he had told Pete, "Unable," just a moment before. Pete told Earl, and I quote, "Tell Larry to bite a big one."

A few seconds later Larry called Pete, saying, "Does the supervisor know you're writing on the sector?"

"It's all ATC cra . . . stuff," said Pete.

Unbeknownst to all three of them, the supervisor was doing

a tape talk on Moss, as he had done one on Schmidt earlier in the day. Moss was surprised but not concerned about the remark. Schmidt on the other hand, whose ATC fate would soon be in Moss's hands, was concerned that his remarks would get Moss in trouble, and in turn cause trouble for him in radar class. Nothing of the sort happened, of course, and Schmidt is still out there today.

Speaking of Schmidt, there's an area newspaper named "DFW People" that floats around the facility. In a recent issue there was an advertisement for single guys to meet Russian women. Using a scanner, some wag substituted a picture of Earl for the young lovely's photo and then showed the ad to Earl. "That's one ugly looking woman," Earl said, never noticing the "woman's" mustache or even that it was himself. As he started to throw the ad away, someone told him he wanted to take a closer look. He did and a good laugh was had by all but one in the room (him).

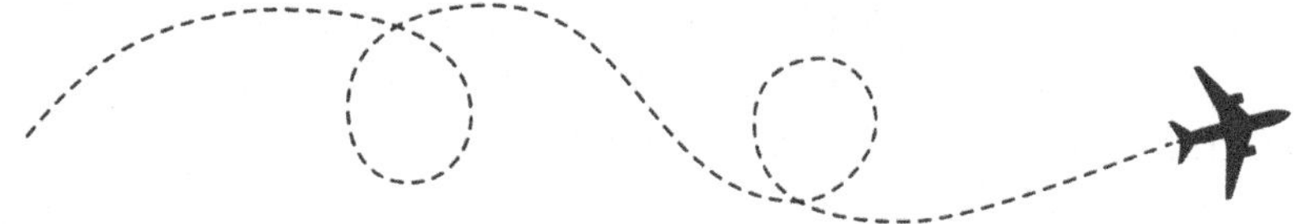

Larry Foreman, who is, as we all know ('cause he keeps telling everyone), is the facility's best controller, hardly ever works mid-shifts. In fact, he avoids them like the plague. They are hideous, ugly, and revolting in every sense of the words, as far as he's concerned. With that in mind, imagine the watch supervisor's surprise when another controller on the mid reported him for being "a weak stick," because he wasn't familiar with mid-shift procedures.

ATC Tales 77

N900DM, FA20 DFW to UGN, requesting FL330, checked on ADM-hi and was climbed to FL290, stopped there for traffic. When the traffic finally cleared PM climbed him to FL330. The pilot must have had 290 on the brain because he immediately began protesting, "But we're already climbing to 2-9-0!"

Ronny Rose told an FLIB, "I have a clearance when you're ready to copy."

FLIB: "Do I need a pencil or can I remember this?"

RY: "I don't know. How good's your memory?"

FLIB: "I can't remember; I'll get a pencil."

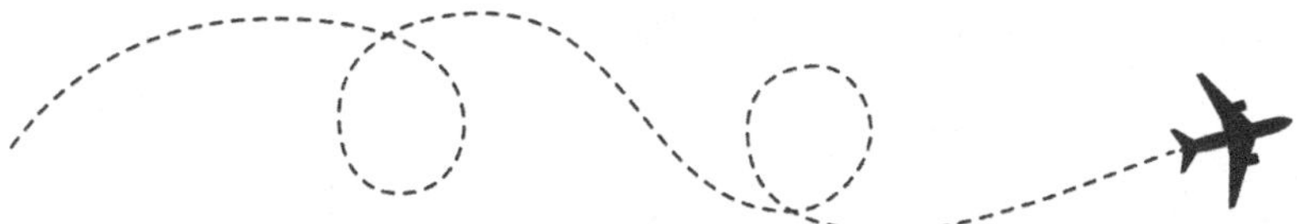

There was a flight of four F-16s playing around in the Brownwood MOA as they waited to refuel with an Air Force KC-10. There was an American Airlines DC-10 overflying the area, level at FL240 as he waited to clear the MOA before descending into DFW. One of the F-16s, seeing the DC-10, swooped up to it and tucked itself into the refueling position as he searched for the refueling boom. Overhearing the pilot's mystified queries on the discrete frequency's speaker, he told F-16 pilot to break off, that he was trying to hook up to an American DC-10 and as the F-16 broke away, he told the DC-10 not to descend, that an F-16 below him had been looking for the "Mother Ship."

A day or so after 1999 departed the fix and the year 2000 arrived, N4148L made the remark, "Our aircraft is Y2K compliant. It just doesn't work very well anymore."

On ADM-lo Pete Moss took a handoff on SWA755 (DAL to OKC) and then heard Jerry Stephens (on ADM-hi) switch him to ADM-Io's freq.

A moment later PM heard: "Fort Worth, SWA37 with you at FL240."

PM: "Is that SWA37 or SWA755?"

SWA: "SWA37."

PM: "I have a SWA755, not a SWA37."

SWA: "We're SWA37."

Pete told him to ident and sure enough, the ident showed up right with SWA755. He then asked the SWA to say his position, which also coincided with SWA755's position.

PM: "I have a SWA755 at that position, no SWA37."

There was a long pause, then a new and deeper voice came on: "Now we're SWA755."

ATC Tales 78

John Davis was an Air Force controller at Little Rock Air Force Base. One day he was working a PAR approach when a women's tour group came through, headed (he found out later when called on the carpet for his remark) by the colonel's wife. She asked him, "What's your job?"

He pointed to the targets on his scope, saying his job was to collect all these targets as they fall off the scope, put them in a bucket, take it to the other end of the row of scopes and pour them back in the far scope so they could work their way back down to his.

She didn't see any problem with it but her husband didn't think it too funny—and later on, neither did he.

A plane landed at LRF and was taxiing down the runway when another pilot started goosestepping around the tower while saying, in his best accent, "making yo tok; ve haf ways of making yo tok."

An A-4 approached touchdown the pilot realized he had a problem and began shouting, "Cable! Cable! Cable!"

John's reply? "Unable. Unable. Unable."

"Roger. Overrun," said the pilot, and off the runway's end he went.

TWA563 didn't acknowledge a frequency change but showed up on the next sector's frequency.

Asked if he answered the frequency change, the pilot replied, "Yes, but I did it on the intercom."

Roy Newsom told an aircraft he wanted "A big S-turn."

The pilot said, "I'll give you a big-ass turn."

ATC Tales 79

Mike Ross, Sr., was working an Eagle Flight north out of DFW. It wasn't too busy so the EGF said he had a question when Mike had the time.

"Go ahead," said Mike.

The pilot remarked that, to the best of his knowledge, he had never ever been assigned a transponder code that had an "8" or a "9" in it. Why is that?

Mike was, to say the least, surprised. 4096 transponders don't have now, nor have ever had 8's or 9's. He explained to the pilot the how and why of 4096 transponders (something he thought was basic information and that the pilot should have known).

Then Mike asked, "Just out of curiosity, does your transponder have an 8 or a 9 in it?"

There was a long pause, then, "I think we'll just take the 5th amendment on that, Center."

A pilot asked George Harris for direct Lamar, a route that George explained, take him right through the army's Fort Sill restricted area with its live artillery fire.

"No problem," the pilot said. "Big sky, little bullets."

Because of a line of weather that went through yesterday, the rides for pilots (and their passengers) today were pretty bad. There were a lot of people changing altitudes as they looked for a smoother ride (which most of the time couldn't be found). Controllers ask pilots "How's your ride?" expecting them to say something like, "Light chop," etc. Today a pilot at twelve thousand, a commuter from DFW to OKC, made his point very clearly when he said, "The ride at twelve's absolutely crappy! How 'bout going to ten?" Talk about an accurate description of flight conditions. That fellow got right to the heart of the matter.

ATC Tales 80

Rick Baugh was an enterprising young man, bright, sharp, keen, and always looking for a way to better . . . and beat, the ATC system. One particular day he came up with an ingenious way to do just that.

Rick was on the Waco specialty and thus, ran inbounds, many of them, into DFW Approach. DFW Approach owned 17,000 feet and below. One of the many airports in DFW Approach was Navy Dallas (NBE). It had an approach penetration procedure that began at the BINNY intersection and began at 15,000 feet. This particular day Rick had two Navy F-14s, Navy 123 and a separate flight, Navy 789, both going to BINNY for the penetration, Navy 123 at 15,000 and Navy 789 at 16,000. So far so good.

The aircraft were heading to the cornerpost for a handoff to DFW Approach when Navy789 declared "minimum fuel" and said he needed to go in ahead of Navy123, if at all possible. What to do? The aircraft were not MARSA and were pretty much stacked. How to get Navy 789 in first?

Rick's no slouch when it comes to quick thinking. He knew that the Center radar did five sweeps a minute, once every 12 seconds. He told Navy123 that 789 needed to go in first and why, and 123 said he'd be glad to trade places. He then asked both aircraft how long it would take to get to the new altitude, once given the go-ahead. Both said, five seconds.

That was perfect, he thought. The radar sweep is 12 seconds, so he had seven seconds to spare. He told the two aircraft that he was going to assign them the new altitudes and when he said, NOW, they were to proceed to the new altitude and do it quickly, in the five seconds they had promised. Now he had to wait for the right moment.

Here came the radar sweep and as it passed the trailing aircraft, Rick said, NOW! The two aircraft swapped altitudes in the promised five seconds and were level, showing the computer the (new) correct altitudes when the radar sweep came by again. Navy789 went in first and landed safely, followed on the penetration by Navy123.

It was a good day at the office. No paperwork.

ATC Tales 81

A good week this past week, that's always good, at least for the next two years, two months and two weeks. I did have an American MD-80 that gave me a bit of a bother at work—or maybe he was just giving me some fodder for ATC Tales.

I had a C-130 over Waco southeast bound at FL210 with the American climbing south out of DFW requesting FL350. He was not the world's best climbing MD-80 so I asked if he could cross 15 north of Waco above FL220 to jump the C-130. Otherwise I would stop him below and let him go under before climbing him.

"Affirmative, we can do that," he replied, so I gave him the specific restriction, "Cross 1-5 north of the Waco VORTAC at or above FL220, maintain FL350."

He read it back but said ". . . AT FL220 . . ."

I issued it again, clarifying the "at or above" but once again he read back ". . . AT FL220."

This might not sound like much but I didn't want the guy leveling off at FL220 to that point and then climbing so, wanting to make sure he was getting it but at the same time a little frustrated that he wasn't, I told him, "I feel like I'm beating a dead horse here. You keep saying AT when it's AT OR ABOVE FL220."

"OK, we've got it, finally," he said, and he was right . . . finally.

Readbacks are an important part of our job. Yesterday I had a Continental descending into Oklahoma City, so I gave him the standard, "Cross 3-0 south of Will Rogers at or below one-five thousand, descend and maintain one-zero thousand." It took him three tries to get and read back the one-zero thousand part—and then, when he went over to OKC Approach he told them he was assigned one-five thousand.

One problem we're having with pilots of late, a BIG problem, is that they just are not listening. It's all of them, air carriers, VFRs, FLIBs, all of them. These seem to be getting worse exponentially compared to air carriers but it's really all of them.

Another thing that bugs me about VFR FLIBs (funny little itinerant buggers) is their tendency to ask for a clearance for descent or climb (especially a descent). They are VFR and we cannot legally exercise any sort of air traffic control over them. When some FLIB asks me for a descent clearance, I tell them to "comply with the appropriate FARs governing VFR flight." They all start right down after that earful of gobbledygook. Sometimes I suggest that they turn or maintain a certain altitude for traffic but only twice in 28 years have I ever issued a "do this" clearance to a VFR, both times for traffic when I felt there was imminent danger of a lot of paperwork.

One of the times was to a Bonanza at 4500, flown by Ron Smith, a neighbor of mine. I recognized the voice and the callsign and shot the breeze with him until I saw another VFR at his altitude, 4,500 feet, heading right for him. I turned Ron all over the sky, climbed him, descended him, and all the while the other aircraft kept a boresight on him. It was like the other aircraft wanted to ram him. No matter what I did the other aircraft kept pressing in for what I thought was going to be a long paperwork session. Ron finally saw the other aircraft and was able to evade successfully. Thank goodness.

And speaking of VFRs, one afternoon on MLC-lo I saw two VFRs at 10,500 feet, neither of which I was talking to, coming together about 25 miles north of MLC. One was southbound, one westbound. In just a few minutes one or both of them were going to get a big scare, or worse. I keyed up the mike, "Attention all aircraft on this frequency. There are two VFRs at ten-five coming together 2-5 miles north of MLC, one southbound, one westbound. If either aircraft is on frequency, if you're southbound, I suggest you turn left at least 45 degrees to go by the westbound. If you're westbound I suggest you turn 30 degrees right to go behind the southbound."

A voice came out of the frequency netherworld, "We're westbound turning 30 right." He saw the traffic a moment later, just as he passed across his nose.

The pilot's sigh of relief was audible in his "Thank you, Center, that was close."

ATC Tales 82

Donnie Starnes retired last Thursday. There was no band, no crowd of people down at the front door to watch him leave, wave goodbye, and make empty promises about getting together later. There was no supervisor or anybody else from management down there to thank him for 28 years of faithful service with the FAA or his three years in the army. There was just Donnie and me and one other guy on the lobby phone, and I just happened to be passing through when he was going out.

It was kind of sad, really. This guy had given most all his working life to the agency and here he was, passing out the door as had many before him, leaving without so much of a "by your leave."

Donnie was on another specialty. He hired on a couple years after me so, while we had the same days off, we were never on the same crew or worked much with each other. Still, seeing him for some twenty odd years, I got to know him fairly well. As we stood there in the little lobby talking, I could sense a reluctance on his part to actually go, to pass through the door to the parking lot. It would be, in a sense, the door shutting on one part of his life and opening into the next, an uncertain part where there was little or no sense of immediacy, of necessity, of purpose.

To be sure, those will develop. There are always tinges of those present though perhaps not of the intensity heretofore experienced. He will, no doubt, learn to adapt. He has to, as do we all upon reaching that point in our life. Goodness knows I will have to, in about four months when I walk through those same doors.

Some people have left that place in interesting ways. One fellow literally went on a break and never came back. He had filled out all his retirement paperwork over at the Regional Office some weeks before and it would be effective on a particular day. On that day he came to work as usual and even worked for a while. Then on his second break he went down to the personnel office, turned in his headset and badge, and left. It was only when the supervisor started paging him back from his break that they discovered something was amiss. Someone in the personnel office heard the page, then called the control-room desk to say that Bill Norman had retired an hour ago.

Occasionally people will go out of there and be missed big time. There will be a great party for them with not enough room for the assembled multitude. Other times people won't be missed so much. There was a retirement dinner for one supervisor, Joe Bumbles, with space for several hundred; 12 people were there, including the guest of honor and his wife. The only reason I went was because I was asked to speak.

We had a guy on our crew retire a couple years ago. This fellow was, how can I say this and be diplomatic? Let's just say he was well-known for coming back late for every break he ever took. So at his retirement dinner very few people were surprised when he showed up 30 minutes late.

Most people leave out of there and are never really missed. It is a 24-hour facility that is, in a way, like the mightiest of rivers, it just keeps rolling on and doesn't stop. Air traffic goes on whether a particular individual is there or not. I worked out there 11 years before I missed someone who left, old Shorty Bush. He was a heck of a guy; and I've missed a few since then but not many. Schroeder, Merv, a couple others. I stay in touch with some of them and wonder what happened to the rest.

As for me, when that day comes, as it will soon enough, I want to slip out the side door, not the front. I already have an idea of what's on the other side and am ready to get on with it. I am staying through year's end for mercenary reasons, no other. Will I miss it? The people? Most of them. Airplanes? Maybe. Weather? Heck no!

ATC Tales 83

Today was the first day in two weeks that the sun was out, ceilings were high and VFRs and FLIBs were out in force. Up north in Oklahoma the ceilings were just low enough that aircraft had to shoot instrument approaches to get under the stuff before they could cancel IFR. Add to that mix a flock of T-37s out of Alliance into and out of Ardmore (ADM), all of them mixed in with a fleet of FLIBs trying to get in and out of the Ardmore area.

I left ADM-Io and curiously enough, found myself going right back in there to help Carter Evans as the T-37 flock arrived. The Tweets (so called because of the sound their engines make) were arriving, four of them, just close enough that a lot of vectors and 360-degree turns were required for the trailing aircraft while the first, then second, etc., shot their approaches. What a pain. He handled it pretty well though, and between the two of us, the situation calmed down enough to where he could take a break.

It was quiet for a while and I mused as to how wonderful ATC life can be. I should have passed on those musings because pretty soon the ATC world turned to muck.

Somewhere in here the chow run returned and my three tacos were plopped onto the table behind me. It was about then that another FLIB fleet began arriving, five of them, including a C130, a Beechjet, two single-engine Cessnas and a Mooney. It was also the time that ADM Tower started calling for release on the T-37s, Radio started calling for clearance on a guy on the ground at Ardmore Downtown, going over to ADM, while I had a guy on approach to Downtown with a VFR departing in his face, climbing to 700 feet AGL and screaming for an IFR clearance to Breckenridge, Texas. The rub here was that all of this was a mix of radar and non-radar coverage with both types of rules being applied to the same airplanes within, say, a five-minute period.

Back on the old Oklahoma City system we used to run a lot of non-radar stuff out at Clinton-Sherman. I enjoyed it. I got to where I could have three aircraft on the CANTO penetration all at the same time, the first turning final, one turning onto the 10-mile arc and one starting out on the BFV056 radial toward the 10-mile arc. It took some doing but if you understood it, it worked, and it was all legal. Today I used some of those same rules, procedures, and principles to get this lot where they were going.

These days a lot of controllers are uncomfortable with non-radar procedures, degree divergence and all that. Most of the facility is in radar coverage now but it has not always been this way. There are a few people still out there who have worked a lot of non-radar, me included, and who feel comfortable doing it. All that stuff came to the fore today.

I will let it go at that because some things, even as legal as you think they might be, do not bear talking about for at least 15 days.

One more thing . . . speaking of Tweets, I gave traffic to a Candler on a T-37 that was so slow the Candler could not descend. When the Candler spotted the Tweet he replied, "I have the Sample Jet in sight."

ATC Tales 84

When I showed up at work this morning, Dwan Stregles was not a happy camper, but he was a darned good detective, first learning the facts and then pressing for an indictment of the controller who had caused the problem.

Seems he worked a Learjet out of Dallas to Chicago who was curious about something that had happened when she was inbound from California earlier. She was arriving about two in the early morning when every approach control in the country (including DFW Approach) is "direct and descending," direct to the airport and descending to the assigned altitude. Cleared "direct Dallas" from the west coast, she was surprised to be vectored for "airspace avoidance" as she neared the DFW Terminal area.

When I showed up Dwan had some time to investigate the matter and investigate he did. Dwan is generally a pretty easy-going guy, fairly laid back, not much bothers him, but this did and away he went, making forays to several specialties in order to uncover the truth.

There are, it develops, several people on the POSSM specialty who don't particularly like to work traffic, even on the mid-shift, and who will go out of their way, even on the mid-shift, to route traffic out of their specialty's area. They are careful to stay within the letter of the law but their own interpretation of the law, the ATP manual, and the various letters-of-agreement, are not a particular interpretation but a peculiar one.

At night, with no traffic in the area, NO traffic, they will reroute an aircraft over the cornerpost and put him on the arrival route rather than let him go direct to the airport, an airport he has been looking at for a hundred miles.

One night a Delta asked this particular individual why he, the controller, was re-routing the Delta over the cornerpost. The response? "Because I can."

Arrogance like this has no place in ATC.

ATC Tales 85

AAL1988, a Fokker 100 out of DFW to OMA, had his climb held down for a Citation, N323LJ.

AAL1988: "I read they were going to put props on the Citation but that would only make it faster." Then he realized what he was saying . . . "I shouldn't talk," he said, "me being in a Fokker."

Before the snitch patch, Glen Floyd was working two aircraft non-radar over Fort Stockton at 8,000. The D-side said there was no manual separation. Glen said not to worry, that he'd take care of it. The first aircraft reported over FST and the second reported over FST just one minute later. Glen asked the second one his flight conditions.

"We're IMC now but we're in and out of the clouds.

Glen replied, "Next time you get out, stay out, 'cause there's another one at 8,000 in there with you."

A PAYE, already in the middle of the world's worst line of thunderstorms, asked for vectors around them. The controller, not realizing he was keyed up, said, "You damn stupid motherf—er."

The pilot didn't say a word—and he didn't request any more vectors either.

Every flight plan in the computer has a CID, computer identification number. When AAL455 declared a medical emergency and requested to return to DFW, it was interesting to note the flight plan's CID, 9-1-1.

AAL1776 declared a medical emergency one day, requesting direct DFW. Jason Judy, a trainee now working his first medical emergency, said, "I have your request." Brian Rountree, his instructor, quickly took over.

ATC Tales 86

ABX191, inbound to Waco's TSTC airport on a mid-shift, reported on frequency saying:

ABX191: "Descending to one three thousand. We have the TSTC weather."

FW: "What is the TSTC weather?"

ABX191: "I don't know; we don't have it yet."

FW: "I thought you said you had the weather."

ABX191: "Oh yeah, I did say that. Let me find it . . ."

At Salt Lake City a Delta 737 in line for takeoff said they were going to do a long takeoff roll.

SLC tower: "That's approved as long as you don't use any more than 12,000 feet."

DAL: "Why not more than 12,000 feet?"

SLC tower: "That's the length of the runway."

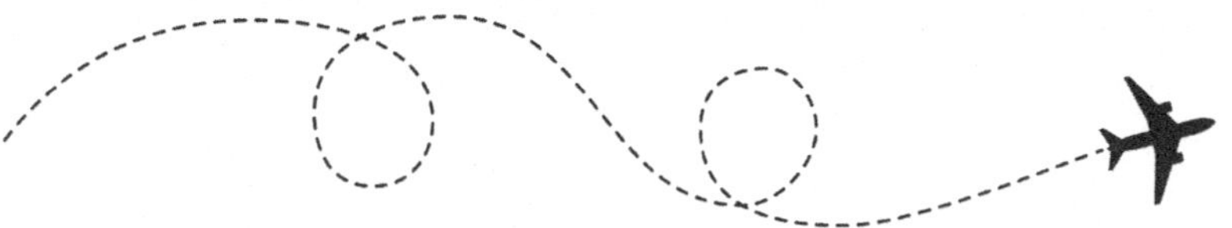

Wayne Coley on MLC-hi was supposed to be working VVRAM21 (Navy RAM21). Wayne kept calling him "Vee RAM21," and later complained, ". . . the SOB never answered!"

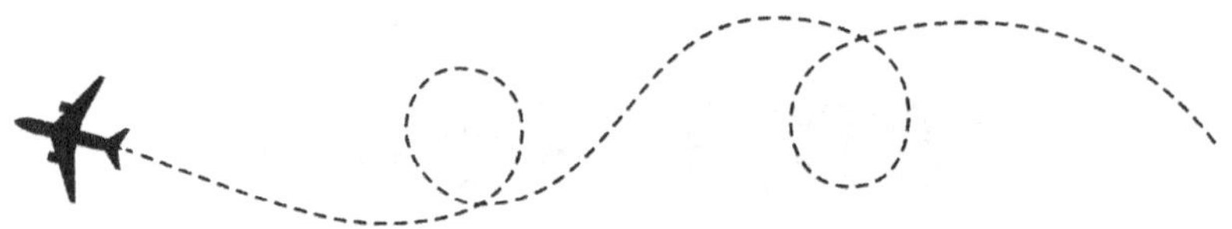

Rick Mariano (NO) was working KANZA51 on OKC-hi.

NO: "Contact Kansas City Center on 133.2."

KANZA51: "Do you have a uniform?"

Rick, who served four years as an Air Force controller, said: "Yes, but it doesn't fit anymore."

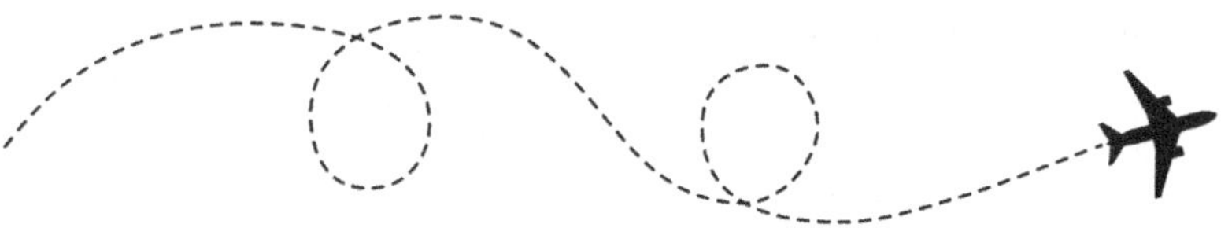

USC552, a northwest-bound C402, was moved from 6,000 to 5,000 for traffic.

Wanting to stay at six and knowing he was wrong for direction, asked, "Isn't this going against the grain?"

ATC Tales 87

CAA894 at 12,000, started complaining about chop south of ADM. "The ride here at twelve is absolutely crappy. How about ten?"

Pete Moss was working STAVE51, an F-15 near Waco at FL390, was drifting south of his direct Holloman AFB route.

PM: "Are you direct Holloman?"

STAVE51: "Affirmative, but we're flying this heading for winds."

PM: "Roger, cleared direct Waco direct Abilene direct Holloman."

STAVE51: "Roger, we're direct Holloman now."

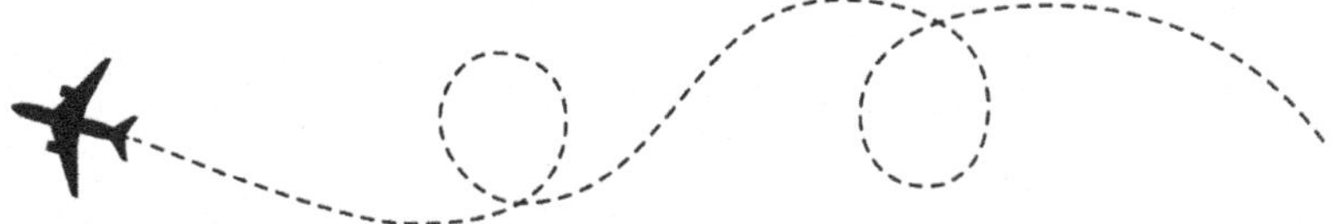

MDCAT5 was recleared "direct Ranger" [FUZ is the three-letter identifier] and outbound on the required re-route.

MDCAT5: "Roger, direct fuzz, and the rest."

ADM-hi sequences inbounds to DFW over UKW. One day I was told by Phil Enis, a UKW controller, that "ADM-hi screwed me so bad I was thinking about filing rape charges."

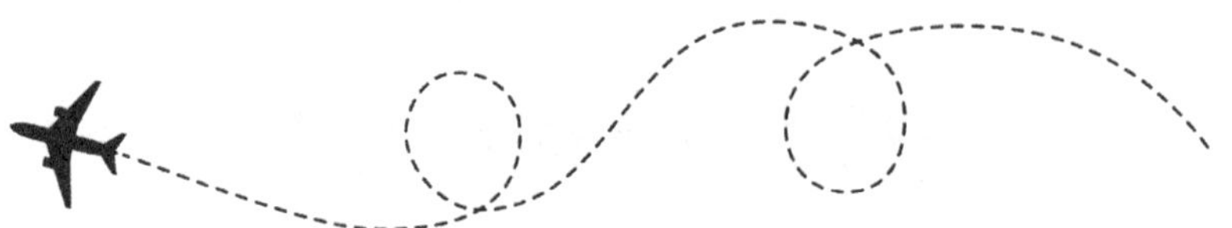

George Harris was pretty busy on ADM-hi R with Alan Neace on the D-side. Alan told John Frey on MLC-hi to have a south-bound 350 at 310. John exclaimed, "What about those two converging at 330 that you're giving me that the 350 will have to get down through?"

Nonplussed, Alan calmly replied, "I suggest you separate 'em."

49R called Merv Newman on 48D with three handoffs. "Hand-offs?" Merv inquired, ever so calmly. "I suggest you call the handoff man."

ATC Tales 88

Dave Asbell heard a retiring American Airlines chief pilot speak at a retirement luncheon. The pilot started off with: "When I started this job, my hair was brown and my underwear was white."

FW: "AAL145, what's your mach speed?"

AAL145: "It's an indication of how fast this aircraft flies through the air. But that's not important now. It's eight-oh."

Wanting to turn ABX205 direct Waco . . .

FW: "ABX205, say heading."

ABX205: "Heading."

FW: "Roger, fly H205 direct Waco when able."

Gary Laws (GL) need a Learjet descending into Waco for an approach and needed him below 8000 quickly.

GL: "Say altitude."

Lear: "Altitude."

GL: "Say cancel IFR."

Lear: "We're out of 8,000."

N900DM, requesting FL330, was assigned FL290 for traffic. Reassigned FL330, the pilot exclaimed, "But we're already climbing to 2-9-0!"

ATC Tales 89

Some years ago, there was an ALTRV coming through of eight flights of four A7s in each flight, the flights being maybe 20 miles in trail. Their route took them from over Amarillo to OKC northeast over Tulsa on to the east coast. There were some clouds out there but no real weather. At one point one of the flights reported they had lost contact with the #4 member of their flight. Just a moment later the flight behind them reported they had picked up a fifth member and wanted to know, "Where did he come from?!"

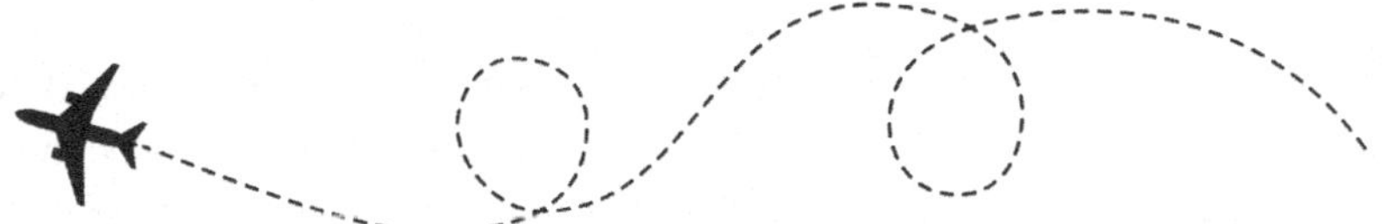

Coming from the west, VANDY27 (a T-37 on a training flight) overshot IRW to the east whereas he should have turned south down V77. Instead he was proceeding southeast. The aircraft then turned west in an effort to correct. Pete Moss queried the pilot . . .

PM: "VANDY27, you're heading west instead of southwest to join. Any particular reason?"

There was a pause, then the response came in that tone instructors use to express their disgust, boredom, and expectancy all together, "Training in progress, sir."

George Harris asked a Citation, a NearJet his mach speed.

"Mach speed?" Came the reply. "We use a calendar to calculate mach speed."

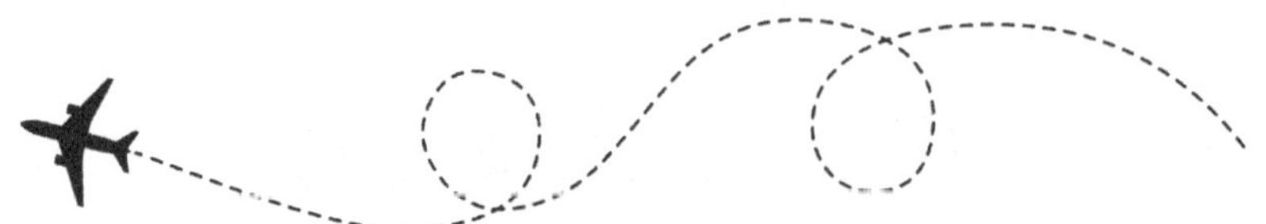

During a recent Center evaluation, Ed Hulsey had Lisa Simonds, an evaluator, plugged in with him on ADM-hi. To show his grasp of ATC coordination, Ed kept calling Rick Baugh on DECOD. Rick finally said, "Ed, if you don't stop calling me, I'm gonna unplug, come around there and kick you in the ass."

Dana Alexander was carrying a full box of popcorn down the aisle in the old control room. He tripped and the box went sailing, coming to rest upside down on Dave Kuykendall's head, popcorn falling out everywhere and the box covering his head completely. Talk about losing the picture.

ATC Tales 90

There are few things more inherently disconcerting to open your locker at work and be greeted by a smell that is sickeningly sweet to the point of (almost) being nauseating. Over the last few days I have been greeted by such a smell, a scent growing stronger by the day, growing stronger to the point where today I actually had to do something about it.

Bearing in mind that I am a federal employee, and ain't all us feds supposed to be lazy critters? I shouldn't be expected to do much more than talk to airplanes and take breaks in between. But there is also a thing called "public health" and my health and everything else that goes with that. What goes with that, the public health thing, is that such a smell, the sweet, almost rancid smell of whatever it was that was decomposing in my locker, such a smell does not bode well for me.

Among other things I did in the army, I used to inspect mess halls, food lockers, kitchens, and the like. I was pretty good at it, doing for a year or so in sunny Zweibrucken over in Germany. It was called "Preventative Medicine" then but nowadays, at least in my locker, would be called "Preventing Smells." This morning I had to break out the old skill bag and out some of those rarely used skills to work.

I have been in that locker 30 years and there was, oh, maybe 15 years' worth of junk piled up in the bottom part. A few years ago, 15 or 20 years ago, I cleaned out some of the locker but never to this extent, never having had the need for it. This morning though, the need for a field day right there in the locker was evident and so it began. First break I was out there and started emptying out some of the assorted junk.

Cleaning out a locker that has been in use this many years is akin to an archeological excavation. In archeology you scrape off the dirt in layers to find out what is on the next-lower level. Once that is done, you move on to the next layer of dirt so as to excavate the next-lower level and so on.

When you are cleaning out a locker you need three things . . . Two hands and a trash can. The good thing about it is that you can go down through many years at a time. To heck with the sanctity of archeological history, you reach in and grab as much as you can, glancing through it briefly to ascertain that there are no checks or money hidden there (never is), and then you chuck it all in the trash can. You reach in for the next couple handfuls of stuff and then the process repeats itself, over and over. In today's case I repeated the process until I got to the offending, and offensive, items in question.

It was a banana. By the time I found it, it wasn't much of a banana, either. There was the banana peel and the rotten remains of what had, at one time, been within the peel. Now the peel was split wide open and the contents were all over the bottom half of the locker. It didn't look good, didn't feel good, and believe me, it was not a good experience either cleaning out the rest of the locker or cleaning up the mess, but it needed doing.

Everything I needed for such a task was under the kitchen sink at the house. I did manage to get handfuls of wet paper towels to wash it down and dry ones to dry it up. Someone knew where some disinfectant was and brought it around. Later on, the head janitor brought along his super-disinfectant and washed the locker in it, which was a good thing. I let it dry out a while and hopefully it is good to go now.

What's the lesson here? Two things . . . First, never leave old bananas (or any banana) in your locker, and two, always stay on good terms with the head janitor.

ATC Tales 91

There was another little bit of excitement at work earlier this week, one that had very serious overtones but, so is the general feeling, will have not have any serious repercussions—though, according to that same general feeling, it should have.

Without going into a lot of detailed explanation, there's a sector on the Frisco specialty named Ardmore-high (ADM-hi). It is, at times, one of the busiest sectors in the house, with DFW arrivals from the north and northeast, and OKC and TUL arrivals and departures to and from the south, as well as a large mix of overflight traffic at all altitudes between FL240 and above. A busy sector at times though fortunately it wasn't too busy one day last week when something very serious happened.

There's a woman on Frisco specialty named, well, let's call her Julie. She is six or seven months pregnant, due sometime in February. She had a 4-12 shift a few days ago but thinking she had a 3-11, she showed up at 3 pm. Realizing she had a 4 o'clock, not a 3, she asked if she could go to work an hour early, leaving an hour early at the end of eight hours.

The supervisor told her, no, she couldn't, that she could work an hour's credit time on the front end of the shift, between 3 and 4, and could go home if the staffing warranted it at the end of the shift. If she was needed, she'd have to stay the extra hour as part of her regular time.

Fine with her, she said, and she went to work on ADM-hi. Plugged in by herself, she wasn't busy, working just five airplanes. In the meantime (about 3:15), the same supervisor who had approved the hour's credit earlier, now went to the facility stand-up briefing (where all system supervisors and managers get a daily briefing on weather, air traffic conditions, and anything special that might affect their shift). The supe left another controller in charge (CIC), who would be in charge until the supe returned in ten or so minutes.

The CIC, a young man named Tom Dodge, is a young man who can get a bit loud at times, kidding a lot and becoming somewhat obnoxious in short order. Such was the case this particular day.

Tom realized that Julie was there earlier than her assigned shift (the 4-12) and, not knowing what the supervisor had said, started razzing Julie about coming in early, saying she was going to get in a lot of trouble, etc. He then turned back to the supe's desk to answer a phone call. Julie, whose patience with a lot of stuff tends to wear thin quickly even at the best of times, waited just a moment, then unplugged from the sector (with its five aircraft) and left the area, saying something about going to find the supervisor, intending to square Tom away.

When there's no controller plugged into a sector, all transmissions on that sector come out of a speaker above the position. Those calls were the first clue that something was wrong, when airplanes started "Fort Worth Center . . . Fort Worth Center . . ." and they came out on the speaker.

Tom, looking around to see why the calls were on the speaker, was shocked but grabbed a handset, ran over, and plugged into the sector to start working the traffic. Another controller, one plugged into yet another sector, stretched his headset's cord across the room, then dialed up the facility intercom and started paging controllers back to man the sector. The supe came back with Julie in tow, made her plug back into the sector, then, right there on the floor, chewed out Tom for razzing Julie. Was anything said to her about unplugging from a sector where there was LIVE TRAFFIC? No one knows and nothing's being said to the controller workforce because the matter is "under investigation."

The same aforementioned general feeling runs that nothing will happen to her because she's, one: a she, and two: a pregnant she. The feeling is that she should get time off because this a SAFETY violation, leaving a sector without telling anyone, a sector in which five airplanes were flying. When Wendell Bryant did that, he got a month off (there were some other circumstances that caused him to get the full 30 days off but one of the biggest was leaving the sector unmanned without telling anyone).

What will happen? Who knows? Something was floating around this afternoon before we left that the time off would be served while she was on maternity leave. Personally, I don't think that's right. If this happened as I believe it did, the way I've been told and have described it here, the time off should come now, not later. There should be no double standard in this issue, as there should be no double standard in the separation matter mentioned above.

The controller-in-question received a two weeks suspension for abandoning the position. This were served in conjunction with her maternity leave, taking the place of the Leave-without pay she would have been forced to use because she doesn't have the annual or sick leave to cover the entire maternity leave.

ATC Tales 92

A few days ago, a "Lifeguard" Learjet, LN18LH, departed Addison southbound to Corpus Christi, climbing high into the skies over central Texas on its mission of mercy when the phone rang at the supervisor's desk. The supervisor, Dave Asbell, took the call, then moved to Dallas-hi where Randy Harvey was working the Lifeguard, which was leaving FL210 climbing.

Dave: "Are you working Lifeguard 1-8-lima hotel?"

Randy: "Yes."

Dave: "Tell him Jeff from his office just called. He needs to return to Addison to pick up the two surgeons he's supposed to carrying in the back. "

Jason Judy (JY) needed a southwest to turn direct Cowboy Vortac but somewhere the need for the turn got lost . . .

JY: "SWA—, if you don't turn 10 degrees left, you'll be 10 degrees right of where you need to be if you turn 10 degrees left."

I was working ADM-hi today. Pretty busy at times. Right in the middle of the busiest spell there came a TWA up from the south, San Antonio to St Louis, that should have been over DFW direct Mcalester, maybe a H010 out of DFW. Instead, at

DFW he turned east, H080, toward SHV. He obviously had the wrong Vortac dialed in. I caught him in short order, probably 'cause he had been wired with a couple 370s out there and had been watching him. The turn caught me by surprise, and I got on his case pretty quick. Had there been another 370 down there just east of him, he could have turned right into him. Pretty dangerous stuff. But I caught it, had Jerry Stephens do some quick coordination and then turned him up to the north toward Mcalester.

Turns out the turn helped us with the other two 370s, which was good. Thing is, this stuff happens every day, airplanes turning ways they aren't supposed to, going where they shouldn't, and every day someone catches it and turns them on their way. It's rarely seen, rarely noted, rarely mentioned, this and the other little things that make the ATC system work. One fellow's busy and inadvertently runs an airplane toward another sector with no PVD where that controller sees a limited data block, so he hits the line and says, "Pointout approved, Delta 990." That makes it legal, having it on tape. Saves the busy guy from a lot of paperwork, too.

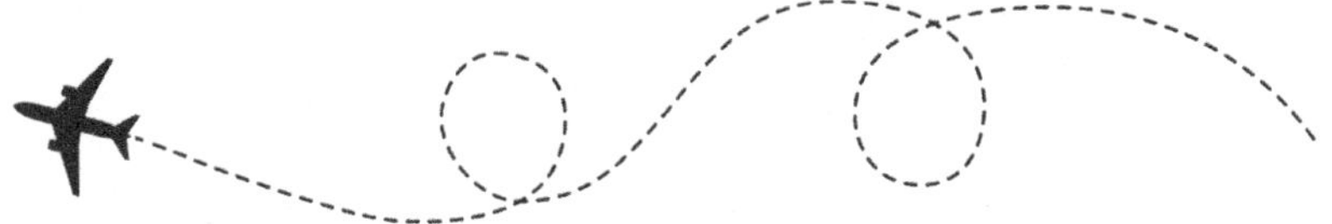

And the next day I worked ADM-hi again, early on in the morning for the first big push. We were working away, shoveling airplanes out of DFW like they were on sale. Approach must have launched 10 or 12 of them right off the bat and I managed to spread them out just so. I felt pretty good about it because we were real busy . . . but I didn't have time to pat myself on the back too long. I had five airplanes bumping the Mcalester-hi boundary, all flashing handoff, but MLC wasn't taking them. I hit the hot line but couldn't get a word in edgewise because the controller was in the panic mode. Kansas City Center had run a plane over Tulsa to the southeast, when the MLC-hi controller thought he'd be heading southwest.

This fellow is a marginal controller, one who puts a show on for everybody in the room—and he doesn't even know he's the star. Today was no exception. I had to turn all five airplanes away because he got so wrapped up in the two conflicting airplanes that he ignored everything else, putting all the sectors around him down the tubes, or at least heading them that way. Beyond that, just another day at the office.

ATC Tales 93

There used to be a fix named BINNY, a penetration fix for military aircraft inbound to Navy Dallas. Aircraft would go there to shoot a high-altitude penetration procedure to Navy Dallas. The penetration altitude was 15,000 feet.

One day there came a flight of two F-14s, NAVY01 and NAVY02, inbound to the fix, staggered at 150 and 160. NAVY01, flight lead, told ACT-Io that he needed to go in first. NAVY01 was at 160 and two miles in front of NAVY02, who was at 150 and in trail. The problem was, how to get NAVY01 down to 150 and NAVY02 up to 160 without, 1) having a deal and 2) taking a lot of time and work, neither of which the controller had.

It struck the controller that Center radar turns five sweeps a minute, once every twelve seconds. He asked NAVY01 (at 160) if he could be level at 150 in ten seconds or less. "Affirmative," came the reply.

He asked NAVY02, at 150, if he could be level at 160 in ten seconds or less . . . another "Affirmative."

He briefly explained the situation to the two pilots, saying that when he said "NOW," that NAVY01 would descend to 150 and NAVY02 would climb to 160, both of them getting there as fast as possible and definitely within 10 seconds.

He waited until the radar's sweep had passed, said "NOW" and within ten seconds both F 14s were then level at the new altitude. He had already made the necessary computer entries so now the computer showed the new altitudes as the assigned altitudes. How clever, one, to get it done but also, even to think of it!

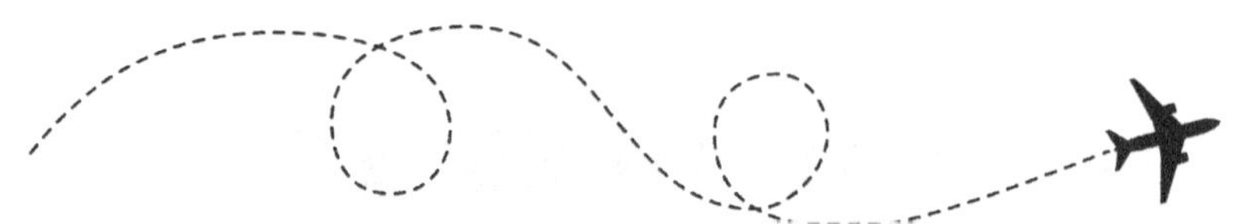

A while back there was a fellow on the Dallas specialty, let's call him, "Killer," who wasn't well-liked at all. No one liked working with him and sometimes he seemed not even to like himself.

Killer was running the break list when he got to Dallas-high where Steve Baird was working the R-side. There was a comely young female working the D-side who didn't like Killer to start with and especially didn't like working with him.

Steve was pretty busy, running several airplanes pretty close when Killer asked him if he wanted a break. Before Steve could reply, the young lovely leaned over close, rubbing herself on his arm, at the same time whispering, "I'll give you a blow job if you stay and don't let Killer come in here."

As Steve was debating this, POW! two airplanes came within five miles and he had an operational error. The machine printed, the paperwork package was started and Steve was hauled off to write a statement, omitting, as any gentleman would, any reference to the young woman and her generous offer. But she felt bad about it, feeling she might have contributed in some way to the error. So an hour or so later she asked to be relieved and went to the front desk where she turned herself in, saying there might be some additional information that the Quality Assurance office might want to know about.

They listened and with mouths agape, decided that maybe they'd just drop everything but the bare facts. And that was that.

I recently worked an AAL9684, a B767 maintenance test out-and-back out of Alliance. I switched him to 132.97, He acknowledged the freq, saying, "32-97. We'll see you shortly."

I thought, "You ain't gonna see me; you'll see 28-1 when you start back down." But almost as soon as I finished the thought, here he came up on my frequency (34-15), "Fort Worth, AAL9684 climbing to FL230."

"AAL9684, you were right when you said you'd me shortly. You're still on 34-15. Contact Fort Worth Center 132.97."

"Uh, that was my practice call! 32-97."

ATC Tales 94

In Bloomington, Illinois, a young flight instructor was instructing two students at the same time. With one of the students flying, they were descending through the clouds and hadn't yet broken through the bases for landing, so the instructor took over the controls. It was thick as pea soup, or maybe potato soup; they were all a bit nervous. One of the students started laughing uncontrollably. The other must have eaten beans the night before because he started passing wind like a hurricane was coming, not pleasant in the cramped little cockpit. Finally, the instructor started yelling at them, "I can't see a thing! [Of course, he was on instruments.] One of you is laughing and the other is stinking up the cockpit. If you don't stop, I'm going to open the door and throw you both out!" Silence soon reigned though stench remained . . . until they landed uneventfully and were able to air out the aircraft.

Chuck Andrews was on the back porch smoking a cigarette and shooting with the breeze with several people, including Pat Adams, who works out there as the chief of the facility, and whose husband, Hughey Adams, is a retired controller. She was talking about him and saying how he liked being retired. She liked him being retired but the one thing she didn't like was every Sunday night he'd say, "I glad I don't have to go to work tomorrow."

Chuck, obviously without thinking this through, said, "I'll tell you what I'd say the next time he says that . . . I'd tell him to bite my big fat ass!" It was at that moment that Chuck realized 1) who he was talking to and 2) the size of the aforementioned anatomy.

A Southwest pilot (who happened to be female) was told by ZFW:

ZFW: "I need to change your altitude. Do you want to go up or down?"

And then came, in a very sultry voice:

SWA: "I want to go d-oooowwww-nnnn."

A lot of chop in the area, an American was asked: "How's your ride?"

AAL: "As smooth as the thighs of a high school cheerleader."

Last week Pete Moss was working ELVIS31, a C-141 at FL290 out of the Air National Guard based at Memphis. (Their unit callsign is "ELVIS.") COA1551 at FL310 was just west of DFW, northwest bound to Denver at FL310. As the two aircraft approached each other, Pete told the COA that he had proof that Elvis was still around and if he looked for "Traffic, 12 o'clock, 3 miles, you'll see Elvis eastbound to Memphis at FL290."

The pilots, both of them, picked up on it and for the next minute or so there were continuous Elvis imitations, including, on frequency change, the obligatory "Thank you; thank you very much."

ATC Tales 95

There are times in ATC when you have to pay attention to a gut feeling . . . Something doesn't feel right or sound right or just plain isn't right. That's when you have to sit up and pay attention. Today was such a time.

Mike Nuest was on Ardmore-high-R with Jimmy Arnold on the D-side. Tank Asbell was working Frisco-low, the DFW north departure sector, when, needing a higher altitude on CAL315 (Dynasty 315, a Boeing 747), a north departure, he called Arnold. Arnold took a quick glance at the crowded scope and replied, "Flight Level 2-8-0."

"2-8-0," Tank replied, and issued the climb clearance.

When the B747 cleared his traffic, Tank shipped the aircraft to high, coming up on Mike's frequency "climbing to flight level 2-8-0."

Mike thought he heard the pilot wrong because he had traffic, an Army KingAir, immediately overhead the 747 at FL250. "Dynasty 315, say again altitude climbing to?"

"Flight level 2-8-0," the pilot replied

Mike didn't hesitate. "Dynasty 315, amend your altitude, maintain flight level 2-4-0."

The pilot responded, acknowledging the amended clearance. The 747 leveled at FL240, passed behind the KingAir by the required five miles and then Mike climbed him on up. The pilots of neither aircraft knew anything about the other and a loss of separation was avoided.

Mike got a "way-to-go" award for the save and that was a good thing. Arnold felt bad about it and that was OK because he screwed up and it didn't cause a system error. All in all, it was a good day at the ATC office, no paperwork.

I don't hate much but I hate sarcastic pilots. There have been a few on frequency lately and I've had my fill of them. A couple days ago SWA714, inbound to Oklahoma City, asked, "Is there any chance of direct Will Rogers?" (Will Rogers is the OKC airport navaid.)

"Not a single one," I said lightly, because there was a SWA53 outbound, pretty much right in his face.

"Oh, I see," he said. "Oke City has that much traffic that they can't allow us to go direct?" said SWA714, the sarcasm dripping like sweat off a cold coke bottle.

Like I said, I hate sarcastic pilots, and this particular pilot was one of those people you just love to hate. "Is your TCAS working?" I inquired.

"Affirmative," came his inquisitive response, probably wondering where I was going with the question.

I started issuing that guy traffic on SWA53, who was going to pass off his left wing maybe six, seven, miles at the most, and kept it up until they passed, then finally gave the guy direct. I thought about not giving it to him, but I didn't want to lower myself to his level.

Dwan Stregles cleared COA1662 from FL310 to FL330 for chop. When the ride didn't improve Dwan offered him FL350. The pilot declined saying, "I don't want to go any higher because I'm afraid of heights."

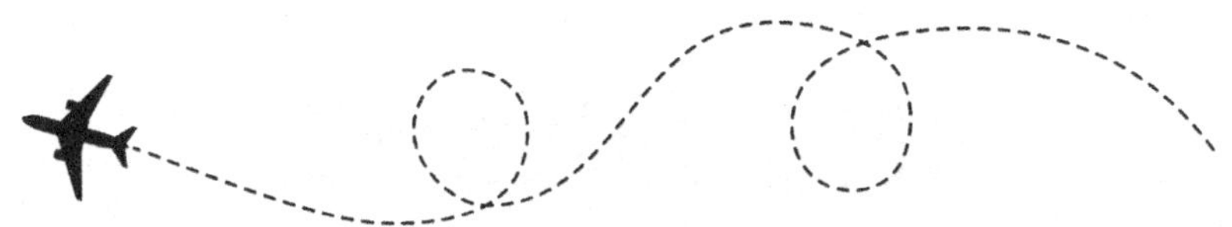

"SWA111, are you on the Maverick 166 radial?"

"We're smack right down the middle of that sucker!"

SWA121 finally, after five or six tries, took a frequency change to 135.32.

"135.32. It was operator error. Good day!"

ATC Tales 96

Chop, turbulence, it's a real pain in the teeth 'cause airplanes are changing altitudes, requesting reroutes to avoid the stuff (if, by chance, they even know it's there) and then those incessant questions.

In Albuquerque Center, Gary Ashert was working N100WN, Willie Nelson's airplane, and it seemed Willie was talking. He asked, "Albuquerque Center, N100WN, you got time for a song?"

"Sure do," Willie said. "What do you wanna hear?"

Chad Etheridge was working CON100, a G4 at FL390 landing Ponca City, Oklahoma. He was head on with two other 390s so Chad started him down to FL370.

"Any chance of staying at 390 'cause the chop's bad at 370," asked the pilot, so Chad explained about the two aircraft head on at that altitude. When the aircraft got down to 370 the pilot started moaning about the ride, saying "the ride is markedly worse than 390."

Now nobody likes it when someone starts throwing five-dollar words at them and when "markedly" hit airwaves, Chad had had enough, replying, "The ride would have been 'markedly' worse at 390 if you had hit either one of the two aircraft at that altitude!"

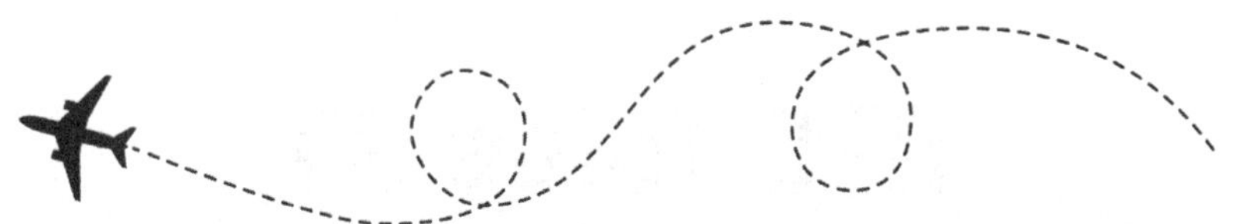

On Dallas-high there was a lot of chop when a COA said his ride was "a little jiggly up here."

Another COA commented, "I don't see 'jiggly' anywhere in my dictionary of aeronautical terms."

The first pilot said, "I said, it feels jiggly up here; I've never seen jiggly up here."

ATC Tales 97

In Jacksonville Center a VFR was looking for VFR advisories in an area with limited radar coverage and extremely low ceilings. The exasperated controller finally told the pilot, "I am unable to provide VFR advisories. I suggest you contact the highway patrol."

Mike Ross, Jr, had the bad habit of taking his shoes off at the sector, usually athletic shoes, and when they came off, the smell came out. There was a lot of the smell, too, and it didn't make those working around him happy. One day at the sector his shoes came off and then someone made off with one of them, spiriting it off to the bathroom where it was filled with water and put in a freezer where it sat until Mike went looking for it.

He didn't take his shoes off after that, at least not at the sector.

In Albuquerque Center the NAS system failed one day and as the controllers were trying to get the DARC up and running, a pilot requested direct Twenty-Nine Palms.

The controller advised the pilot that the radar system had failed and he would get back to the pilot's request.

"Does this mean," the pilot inquired, "that you can't do your job without a computer?"

"No," said the controller. "It means I can't do my job and yours, too!"

TALON59, a T-45 out of Roswell, NM, to Navy Meridian, MS, came through tonight. He was supposed to keep going but didn't. He started off at FL410 but when his altimeter froze and his other instruments became unreliable, he had no idea what his altitude was. He diverted to Sheppard AFB in Wichita Falls but when he learned that base was closed, he diverted again, this time to Tinker AFB near Oklahoma City. At 41,000 feet he was above everything but when he started a descent, he lost track of his altitude. Even with a standard rate of descent his altitude could be off by several thousand feet, thus endangering any other aircraft that crossed his flight path

And because his altitude was unknown, every aircraft at every altitude along his route of flight had to be turned out of his flight path. Five miles out of his path so as to maintain standard separation.

So Nick Richardson on Ardmore-high and later Carter Evans on Ardmore-low started moving airplanes away from him, clearing a path straight to Tinker for him. They did a great job and eventually the airplane landed safely at Tinker, a great outcome to a potentially dangerous situation.

This has happened at least one time before that r know of. A Navy T-39 supposedly at FL350 was actually at 13,000, driving through probably half a dozen low altitude sectors and DFW Approach, all without any coordination—and without any knowledge of those controllers. A quick study was done to figure out if the aircraft had gotten with any other aircraft. It was quickly decided that some things are better left undone. At 13,000 the T-39's instruments thawed out and he proceeded to Tinker where he, too, landed safely.

ATC Tales 98

Life in the ATC world is not always about airplanes . . .

Every week at work we have a briefing, always the last hour on the 4th day of the workweek, at which time management runs through a gamut of information that, for one reason or another, needs to be imparted to controllers. Today was such a day, several people from the airspace office yammering about one thing or another, very little of which applied to me or the Frisco specialty. Still, being the good little boys all of us are, we sat there with our eyes and ears open and mouths shut, absorbing all of it, then discounting and discarding the unnecessary stuff. (It was all but gone within 15 minutes of walking out.)

After it finished, I was sitting there talking to some people when a fellow named Ted Millson stopped by for a visit. Ted is an old hand, actually the most senior person in the facility, having been in the FAA since 1968. I hired on in 1974 and met Ted shortly thereafter. He and I have worked either on the same crew or near each other ever since. We even carpooled for several years, him living in Granbury and me exactly half-way the Center for him. He would chip in two bucks for gas every day he rode with me and he would still save a dollar. But I digress . . .

When Ted slid into the chair, I knew he had something on his mind. We were the only people in the room and he was taking the chair right next to me, a pretty good indication he wanted to talk with me specifically, and then when he said, I wanted to talk with you . . . I knew he wanted to talk with me.

Ted said he was getting older (the wrinkles and gray hair were pretty good indicators of that), he knew he was slowing down out on the floor, and that he was not as sharp as he used to be. He wanted to ask me a question and he knew I would be honest with him, answering a direct question.

He was, he said, thinking about bidding on a job in the flow control section (TMU - Traffic Management Unit) rather than staying on the floor talking to airplanes. He had to decide pretty quick, especially since the bid closes in a few days and all the paperwork has to be in before then. He plans to retire on September 1st, 2003, and might, depending on my answer, try to finish his last year with the FAA in TMU.

He knew he was being carried by the people he worked with and did not like the idea. He did not want to become another James Deride, a Frisco specialty controller who should have retired several years ago but finally went out late last year.

Was he or had he, he wanted to know, become a drain on the people around him? They were carrying him, sure, but did they mind it or did they dislike working with him?

I looked at him, not wanting to hurt his feelings because to answer truthfully might do just that. But he wanted an honest answer and expected me to give him one. Hesitating a bit, I looked him square in the eyes and said that people did not like working with him, either on his specialty or the specialties around him, because they felt he was stow, bordering on unsafe.

He sat there a moment, then said he appreciated the honest answer, and we talked about his options, particularly the TMU job and what it meant. For financial reasons he feels he needs to stay until his planned retirement date so he does not want to go early. His decision is whether or not to stay on the boards or try for some sort of a staff job.

It was a tough question to answer even though the answer was an obvious one. It was hard to look the man in the face and tell him what he didn't want to hear. I did it because he wanted honesty. For some time I have thought he needed to be told this . . . but I didn't think I'd be the one doing it.

ATC Tales 99

Something happened at work today that made me think of how nice a vacation will be. I was on Ardmore-low, a "trash" sector in south central Oklahoma, when I had two departures southeast bound off Oklahoma City and Tinker AFB. The Hawker jet got out there first and started climbing with the E-3 climbing up six o'clock in a big way. Business jets, even Hawkers, are supposed to perform fairly well (except Citations—you don't expect them to climb for muck) but this guy wasn't climbing worth a darn. Then there was the E-3. These guys don't usually climb worth a hoot, but this guy today must have been in a hurry to get up to the cool air up top because he went up like a screamer.

Ardmore-low is a fairly easy sector. A lot of guys don't like it because of the "trash" but I grew up on it. It was my first sector lo those MANY years ago, so I have been working it 25 years or more. Generally, I like it but today about noon these two airplanes decided to invite two more airplanes to the party and it got mighty crowded in the skies over southeastern Oklahoma.

I sped up the Hawker to 250K (he was doing 230K and the E-3 was chewing him up) and climbed him to FL230. Speeds weren't working so I resumed them both and step-climbed the E-3 under the Hawker. Then I pointed out this dynamic duo to Mcalester- and Frisco-lows, both sectors popping up a data block on my scope, an Eagle Flight (EGF) slow-climbing into high northeast bound and a Southwest (SWA) southbound at FL220.

The E-3 was no factor but the Hawker was determined to get with both of them. He was working hard at not climbing well while the EGF, still climbing, was doing a remarkable job of zooming into the wild blue.

Now the coordination started between me and Ardmore-high, the sector working the EGF. It started on the interphone at first but quickly went to a loud conversation over the heads of the people seated in-between the two sectors. Sometimes that is the quicker way of doing things and so it was today.

Data blocks were flashing, the conflict alert patch telling all hands that something was about to happen that might not be a good thing. Yet there were three of us working on it, me and my boy, the halting Hawker, and Luis Paret and Dwan Stregles on ADM-hi. Between the three of us, we managed to work something out to where the EGF stopped his climb, the Hawker continued his, and, most importantly, there was no paperwork. Another successful day at the office.

ATC Tales 100

There was a shouting match, of sorts, on ADM-hi yesterday. There were three 390s coming together about 100 miles southeast of OKC. There was a Northwest (NWA) out of Houston Intercontinental going Wichita to Minneapolis, a Frontier (FFT) out of New Orleans to Denver and a Continental (COA) out of Minneapolis to Houston Intercontinental.

Jerry Stephens was on ADM-hi R with Chuck Andrews on the D-side. They saw the problem and started taking action to separate the three by vectoring the two they were working, the NWA and FFT, behind the COA, which was being worked by MLC-hi, the sector just to the north.

MLC was working the COA and watching the other two, the NWA and the COA. ADM was predicating its vector of the FFT on the COA's route as shown in the computer, which showed it going direct Ardmore. Jerry got the NWA behind the COA and then turned the FFT some 20 degrees right to go behind the COA and sat back to make sure it worked. Jerry was pretty busy elsewhere, too, so he had the other 20 airplanes in his sector to worry about, in addition to three mentioned.

All of a sudden, the conflict alert patch went off, the data blocks of the FFT and COA starting to flash. MLC had turned the COA about 15 degrees left to go direct to Dallas which was turning it right into the FFT.

Knowing something had to be done immediately, and that MLC wasn't doing anything to help the situation, Jerry hit the line to MLC, telling them to "descend COA743 to FL370."

For some reason unbeknownst to anybody, the MLC-hi controller started arguing about it. Jerry repeated himself several times and finally wound up shouting for them to dump the

COA to 370 which, after a minute of arguing on their part and shouting on Jerry's, they did.

It should never have come to that. When a controller tells you to do something with an aircraft, you should do it first and ask questions later, not argue about it. None of it sounds good when they pull the tapes later.

Jim Wacker was working an F-4 out in western Oklahoma one fine day when all of a sudden, the F-4 pilot allowed as how he had an emergency, the engines had quit, they would not restart and they, he and his backseater, were going to eject in short order. All this, as well you might expect, took Jim somewhat by surprise. Jim offered all the assistance he could, getting the search-and-rescue procedures going, clearing traffic, etc., and everything else he could think of to help the now rapidly descending aircraft.

Finally the pilot uttered the words, "We're going now," just prior to punching out. Jim responded in kind, "Have a good day."

That was it, nothing more was heard from the crew until OKC FSS called to say they had been picked up. One further bit of information did come in, sometime later, when the pilot wrote in to thank Jim for his help. He added that he had hurt his back in the ejection but all the down, through the pain and worry and everything else, he said he could not help but laugh at Jim's parting words . . . "Have a good day."

ATC Tales 101

I had occasion to work Waco-lo today, usually a quiet little sector, today a monster, a devil, a beast, that threatened to take us all upstairs to the Quality Assurance Office.

There's a special Military Operating Area (MOA) in Waco-lo through this month, one that runs from 14,000–17,000, that all but cuts off the arrivals into Austin from the north. The arrivals can still get in but it's a bit tricky. I got a little, no, make that a lot busy late this afternoon when four Austin arrivals showed up as well as flurry of departures, a whole flurry of 'em, maybe six or eight screaming out into the skies over central Texas.

I had a D-side, Bob, a flow controller who's checked out on two D-sides, no R-sides, and hasn't, well, let's be polite and say that this guy doesn't have much of a clue about anything, especially anything to do with live traffic. Bob means well and he does try, I'll give him that much, but he just doesn't have the flick.

So there I was, mixing and mingling this pile of airplanes, one of them being a Hawker jet named N803X. I climbed him to FL210 and sent him on down the airway, handing him off to Houston Center and Houston didn't take the handoff.

I was busy elsewhere—there was a lot going on, and Bob, as he should have done, hit the voice-line to the other facility's low-altitude sector to get them to take the handoff. Unfortunately, he called the WRONG sector, killing a minute of valuable time as they tried to figure out what he was talking about and then telling him that he needed to call the right sector. It was at this point I saw the Hawker screaming up on the Center boundary, still not handed off, flashing away.

There are few things more disconcerting than this in the everyday world of air traffic control. The heart rate goes UP, the hands move without thinking, first to the microphone, keying it so I could tell the airplane to make a 360-degree turn, then to the voice line to shout for them to TAKE THE HANDOFF!

Bob had finally found the right line to the right sector, but his voice was weak, ineffectual, like he was asking them to "Please consider taking the handoff as soon as you can." I hit that line shouting, "HANDOFF! TAKE THE HANDOFF!" a couple times and they got the message, finally taking it when the aircraft was three or four miles north of their airspace. About time!

All this time the pilot was calling me, "Was that call for N803X?" He never took the turn. Just as well.

I wasn't happy with Bob, but I didn't say anything to him other than to say that, in the future, he needed to yell at them. Controllers, and people in general, don't respond to timidity; they do respond to confidence, assurance, and self-control. And if those don't work, they also respond to someone's voice screaming out the speaker, if for no other reason than to shut him up.

ATC Tales 102

Years ago, a Continental DC-3 was heading toward Amarillo. High overhead there a TWA B707 about to encounter some serious weather and the pilot (or co-pilot, whoever was doing the talking) sounded as though he were on the verge of a panic attack about it, not shutting up, going on about the weather, wondering what he was going to do, all the time his voice getting higher and higher.

The Continental captain, a crusty old salt, picked up his mike saying, in a deep baritone voice, "TWA, this Saint Peter. How can I help you?" There was a long silence, then a much calmer TWA voice said, "Thank you. I needed that."

Talk about a brain fart. One of the dangers in this job is becoming too complacent. Because of that, complacency, bad things happen. Earlier today I got wrapped up in some stuff up at the north end of Waco-lo and didn't see some stuff happening down to the south. There was a Lear descending to FL220, out of 290, with a Southwest (SWA) maybe three or four miles in front of him, already at FL220. It wasn't going to work (in terms of the "no paperwork" minimum) but I caught it, fortunately, and it worked out. A little turn, the SWA going down to 200 and giving it the gas (a SWA will do almost anything for you to keep the #1 spot in a trail of airplanes). It was a big lesson in complacency though. You have to pay attention to the whole sector, not just one part of it.

Then came ROMAN1, an F-18 out of Huntsville, Alabama, destination Navy Fort Worth, a NORDO (no radio contact with anybody). He had no clearance below 280 which meant he would follow comm-loss procedures, go the airport at 280 and descend overhead the airport for a landing.

That's the theory. In reality, when an airplane loses comm with ATC he's supposed to do the aforementioned. What really happens is anybody's guess. I have seen civilian airplanes start down with no clearance but generally military aircraft like ROMAN1 do what they should. Still, it is a big coordination nightmare and today was no exception.

One thing about NORDOs, almost all of them call somebody when they want to start down. In 28 years, I've seen three true NORDOs, one civilian and two military. Even ROMAN1 got a hold of somebody's frequency today.

Then came . . .

"Fort Worth, United 372. We're declaring a medical emergency. We need to go to DFW right now." Those are words you never want to hear in any case, much less when you're busy. John-Boy Sheddens was busy earlier tonight, "Down the mucker," one might say, when he heard those words crackling across the sound waves of radio netherworld.

Fresh out of radar training, he has been training on his first two radar positions, including Dallas-hi where he was working tonight. He was, as I said, going down the mucker when the United (at FL370) announced to the world that things were bad in the back and getting worse. John had two other situations going on, including two wired at 370 with no place to go with either when the United chirped up. He turned the United north, dumped him to FL240 and shipped him to Pete Moss on Waco-lo.

Pete was a mite busy himself, maybe a dozen airplanes climbing and descending, two head-on situations and some other stuff when the United showed up. No one had called to give Pete a heads-up on the situation referencing the United but it didn't take long to figure out when he saw the route in the computer.

Ed Gleason slid into the D-side to take care of coordination and paperwork which was a big help. The United was head-on with three airplanes heading south out of the DFW terminal area but he had priority so Pete started yanking, banking, and cranking all three of them.

When you tell an airplane he is being vectored out for a medical emergency, nobody squawks. Sequencing? Yeah, they squawk, moan and groan, but a medical problem, no. Nobody complains, nobody talks any more than they have to, and everybody tries to cooperate.

DFW Approach wanted to know what was the nature of the emergency and did the pilot want equipment standing by?

"I want the paramedics. We have a passenger expiring in the back; an elderly man in his 70s," said the pilot.

Now, for just a split second, there was utter quiet on the frequency. Gleason told Approach and they got the ball rolling at the airport and then back into the fray. With everybody out of his way the United went to DFW's frequency where he had to make a 360 degree turn to lose altitude. Half a dozen airplanes turned out on vectors for the United had to be turned back, climbed, and sent on their way . . . and so it went. Another good day at the office . . . no paperwork.

ATC Tales 103

Some days are bad ATC days and some days are good ATC days. This was a good ATC day, definitely. It was a "feel good" day of ATC, the sort of day you think of as the "after" picture in the before/after advertisements. It was a day chalked full of adventure, the kind of day a lot of folks would like to have every day, not just one day every once in a while.

I was sitting on Ardmore (ADM)-low for a while when a Flight Check KingAir (FLC78) came off Oklahoma City at 11,000 feet, going to Ada for a flight check of the GPS35 approach. The pilot, a young woman, wanted to go direct DAVEE to set up for the approach so I gave the standard clearance . . .

FW: "FLC78, cleared direct DAVEE, descend at pilot's discretion, maintain 3,000."

FLC78: "Direct DAVEE, descend and maintain, uh . . . one-one thousand."

I waited for her to catch it . . . and then (with a wee grin on me mug),

FW: "No ma'am, you're at one-one thousand. Descend and maintain 3,000."

She realized what she'd said and just laughed, saying, "You're right. Down to 3,000."

Very gracious about it, she was, and we all got a good chuckle.

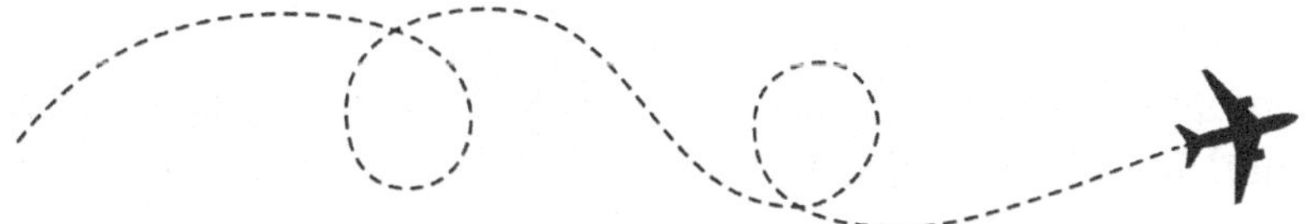

Then came JAVET34 tearing out of Tinker AFB in Oklahoma City, going back to Sheppard AFB in Wichita Falls. This is about as routine as a military training flight can get. It's a

canned route, something these USAF student pilots fly several times a day, several days a week. The T38 comes out of Tinker climbing to 15,000. We climb him to 20,000 and eventually descend him into Sheppard.

When I gave him the clearance to FL200 he refused it, saying he needed to stay at 15,000, that he had a problem and might even declare an in-flight emergency. And so he did . . .

JAVET34: "Center, we're declaring an in-flight emergency. The #1 engine nozzle is stuck. We're requesting a straight-in approach and landing to runway 1-5 Right at Sheppard with emergency equipment standing by."

I told him we'd make sure Sheppard had that information and asked Tim Gravens, my trusty-dusty D-side, to pass it along, which he did.

Aircraft emergencies are pretty serious things and they generally take priority over darn near everything else going on. This goes for FAA, military, and contract controllers, all of us.

Imagine Tim's surprise when the young woman working Sheppard's north MOAs said, "He can expect an ILS approach to runway 1-5 Center."

Tim immediately replied, "He's an emergency!" and then heard another voice on the line, obviously an instructor, come on saying, "Training in progress. He can expect a straight-in to 1-5 Right."

She wasn't the only trainee ever to tell an emergency aircraft something like that. Jason Judy was training on ADM-hi when an American Fokker declared a medical emergency, saying he needed to go direct DFW immediately if not sooner.

Jason's reply? "I have your request."

His instructor took over, the American went direct and the passenger made it.

Today's last little bit was an old army Chinook, G70116, out of Lexington, Oklahoma. This guy went up for some practice approaches at Ardmore and Paul's Valley and a bit of runway banging before going back to Lexington. Almost to Paul's Valley for the NDB35 approach there, a VFR FLIB took off southbound climbing right in to him. I started issuing the traffic, "12 o'clock, 4 miles, out of 2,500 climbing south." Finally, I couldn't stand it anymore . . .

FW: "G70116, turn right heading 3-6-0, vectors for traffic," and watched as the two targets began closing nearly to merging. The turn had been enough and in time and the two aircraft slid by each other maybe half a mile apart.

Later, after I had cleared the helicopter for the approach (cross initial at 3,000 feet) and shipped him to advisory frequency, there appeared a fast-moving aircraft at 2,000 feet that was heading right for the Chinook, at several hundred miles an hour. The Chinook was starting its descent and the two would be close.

I hit the "Guard" frequency, broadcasting an advisory to the "fast-moving military jet at 2,000 feet in south central Oklahoma to check for traffic at your 12 o'clock, an army helicopter on approach at Paul's Valley." Turned out the Chinook was monitoring Guard and he came up on my frequency asking about the traffic. It was an F-16 that went right through the approach at Paul's Valley, not exactly a safe situation. The Chinook discontinued the approach until he was clear of the F-16 and then carried on.

Another satisfactory—and satisfying—conclusion to an air traffic day.

ATC Tales 104

Today I was sitting on ADM-lo minding my own business when SWA843 out of Houston to Oklahoma City checked on, "FL350 with pilot's discretion to FL240."

Acknowledging his check-on, I gave him the standard crossing restriction into OKC, "Cross 3-0 miles south of Will Rogers at or below 1-5-thousand, maintain 1-0-thousand."

He read it back perfectly (and on the first time, too) so imagine my surprise when I later heard him report "Leveling at FL240."

An inquisitive note in my voice, I asked, "Is there a reason you're leveling at FL240?"

This was followed by a pause, an "Uh," and then, "We're having a senior moment here."

Some years ago, I was training Chad Etheridge on ADM-hi when an American checked on at FL280. He had just crossed the sector boundary, so Chad gave him, "Descend at pilot's discretion, maintain FL240," which the pilot acknowledged.

Down over ADM, the American, still at FL280, asked for a lower. With a puzzled look in his eyes, Chad reassigned him FL240 which the pilot acknowledged (again).

"Let me talk," I told Chad, and keyed up, telling the pilot I had a question if he had the time for one. "Go ahead," he responded.

I explained that I wasn't a pilot or anything like that and I was just curious. Was there any sort of device or box or anything like that in which a pilot could insert or place an altitude assignment from ATC? (There is indeed such a "window" and I full well knew it.)

There came a peal of laughter from the pilot and he said he knew what I was getting at, that he realized he had the earlier altitude assignment just as soon as he went to place it in the window the second time.

A lot of the time military aircraft, especially students, are real pains-in-the-teeth (or wherever) to work but today I was thankful to be working some of those little white rockets that can soar into the blue with little notice.

Sheppard AFB has lots of little pushes with T-38s, chucking them out into the training areas with great rapidity and then yanking them back the same way. Today there were several instances when flight after flight came roaring out of Sheppard to the Washita MOA and, after the first couple, the return flights always seemed to be headed back right in the face of the departures. Most of the time it works out but today, for some reason known only to the T-38 scheduler, the outbound and inbound flights got in each other's way every time. But with clear weather, no chop and some pilots who actually know the meaning of the word, "expedite," everything seemed to work out.

Fast-movers are good airplanes to work because they can do the rocket climbs and descents. One time I had an F-14 at FL390 landing Tinker with airplanes below him at 370, 350, 330 and a couple more between that and FL250. I told him that I'd be starting him down shortly and when I did, I need him out of FL310 in the worst way in about ten seconds and on down to FL240 shortly thereafter. Could he do that? Sure could, he said, almost with a smile in his voice.

So I dumped him . . . "Descend and maintain FL240; expedite your descent through FL310."

"Roger. Out of 3-9-0. Out of 3-1-0. Leveling FL240." It was that quick. That guy can fly on my frequency any day.

ATC Tales 105

On a Delta flight out of New York, the plane had just reached cruising altitude and the seat-belt sign had been turned off when a flight attendant came into the cockpit asking that the seat-belt sign be put on. The captain had just turned it off and was curious as to why she was adamant that it be turned back on. Tums out six Afghanis had gotten on in New York and now, once the seat belt sign had gone off, the lot of them had gotten up and spread their prayer rugs all over the aisle, blocking it to one and all as they prayed to Allah. The sign went back on.

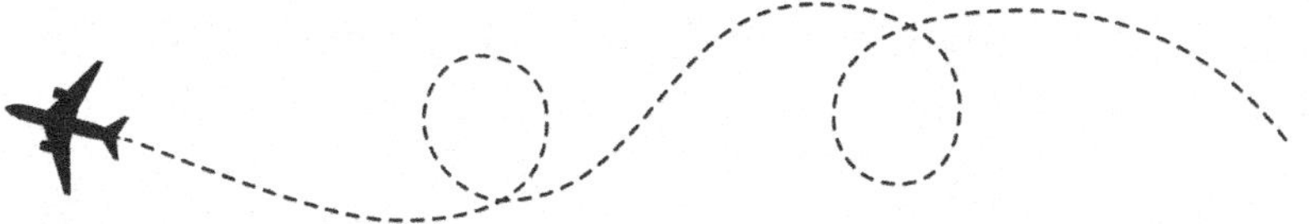

Some strange things happen at work, like today when a T-28 shooting the ILS31 approach (in instrument conditions) to Ardmore Municipal Airport got LOST and landed at a different airport. He didn't know where it was, he told Ardmore Tower when he called them on a landline to cancel his IFR, but he was down safe—which was the important thing.

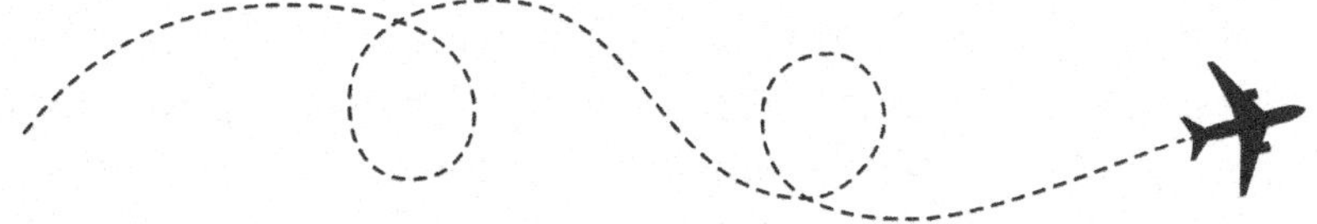

Speaking of getting lost at arrival airports . . . some years ago Dave Stewart cleared an aircraft for an approach to Mcalester, terminated his radar services and shipped him to advisory frequency. After a while the aircraft executed a missed approach . . . coming out of the Henrietta airport, 30 miles north of Mcalester.

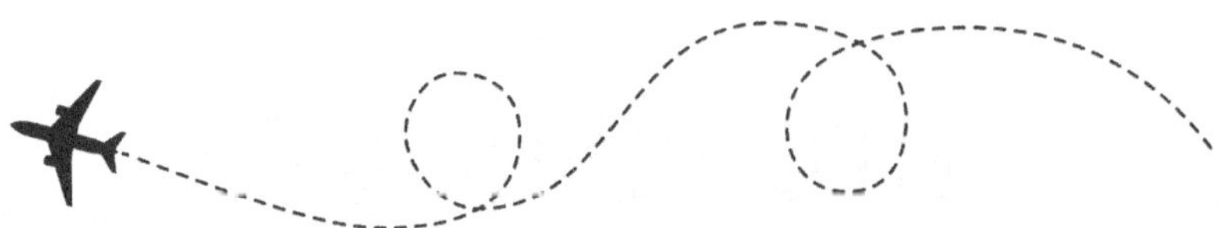

And then there was the time that a flight of four T-38s out of Vance AFB, Oklahoma, were going to Henrietta for a noon-time Armed Forces Day fly-by down Henrietta's Main Street. Out of FL180 they canceled IFR and dropped down below radar coverage. It wasn't too many minutes later when Mcalester Radio called saying the Henrietta mayor was on the phone wanting to know where the T-38s were. I advised him as to what the T-38s had done and let it go at that. Then a few minutes after that, Radio called again; this time he thought knew what had happened. Seems the Mcalester mayor was on the phone, wanting to know why four T-38s had come screaming the town's main drag, just above treetop level.

Last week I heard something on the sector that made me bubble over with pride. If such can be the case out there. Chad Etheridge was working Frisco-lo R and Jennifer McCoy was on the D-side. They had a sky full of airplanes, low ceilings and radio calling for clearance on a guy off Durant with approaches going into Grayson County and Ardmore. Jennifer was at a loss and about to tell radio to relay to the pilot that he could expect a 15-minute delay. Chad saved the day, however, telling her to clear the departure to the Durant NDB, climb to 5,000 at the NDB and then proceed on course. That cleared the arrival at Grayson, the arrival at Ardmore and it got the departure on his way.

I used to teach this little trick to all my trainees years ago, back when they would trust me with trainees. Chad remembered this little trick, it seems, so maybe there's hope for the ATC system yet.

ATC Tales 106

Some years ago, right after the movie "Airplane" came out, Mike McCully was training on Ardmore-low under the watchful eye of the World's Best Controller, Larry Foreman (just ask him), with Tom Thorpe on their D-side. Tommy T, as Thorpe is affectionately called, needed to get in touch with Ardmore Tower.

Mike, rather busy with a sector full of airplanes, had just hit a short gap in transmissions when he heard Thorpe, searching in vain for the correct landline and dial code, ask plaintively, "What's Ardmore Tower?" Meaning, what's the dial code for the landline.

Mike turned to Tom saying, "It's a tall skinny building with a cab on top that has air traffic controllers in it who tell airplanes where to go . . . but that's not important right now. It's the 3-3-4 line and dial 0-5."

There are things we run across, in the course of our daily lives, that make absolutely no sense at all. On the other hand, there are things we encounter in the course of the same day that make all the sense in the world.

Picture this . . . you're walking up a sidewalk and encounter several tightly-spaced bright orange cones blocking off part of the sidewalk. On the other side of the cones is a patch of wet cement, obviously freshly poured and troweled, obviously waiting to dry, the cones probably there to block people from walking on the new cement.

The operative word here is "probably" because it, the line of cones, while achieving its purpose for most everybody, didn't even faze one person out there yesterday.

David Asbell is a nice guy, sure enough. He's a fairly bright boy, too, making supervisor in short order after he made journeyman controller. He was one of my radar trainees and had, in my brief tenure with him, effectively learned the fine art of "scanning" for traffic. Evidently the lesson didn't transfer to sidewalks because yesterday Dave came strolling around the flagpole and up the sidewalk to the aforementioned cones where he stepped OVER the cones and into a patch of freshly-laid cement.

Am I giving him too much credit for being a bright lad? After all, this is the same guy who got his head caught in the wheel well of a golf cart as it rolled down a hill. This is the same guy who took some flowers his wife found on the dining-room table OUT of her hands, telling her they were for the neighbors (they were, too, having been left at his house earlier when the neighbors weren't home—but that didn't make his wife any happier).

His mind was no doubt elsewhere when he stepped over the cones but it, his mind, probably went straight to his ankle when they hit the cement. I say, "to his ankle," because that's where the cement went to as it closed over his brand-new shoe and started climbing up his leg.

To his credit, he does have a thing or two on his mind. His wife has a bad back that went south two days ago and they've been to most every hospital and doctor in town over the last 48 hours.

Still, you would think the orange cones might be a clue . . .

ATC Tales 107

There was a supervisor at New Orleans Approach Control who was a well-meaning but crusty old fellow. When he was notified that a tour of Girl Scouts would be coming through in a few minutes he went to each on-duty controller, admonishing them to watch their language in front of these young ladies.

When the girls came in the radar room, he gathered them around the desk and began his spiel, saying, "You have to watch these f—king guys. You never know what they'll say."

Dave Ritchey was working Frisco-low when a Raincheck group came through. Dave, not knowing they were there and in the process of being "put-to" by DFW Approach, started shouting for the supervisor, saying "They're f—king me! They're f—king me!" Evidently they were, too, and the supervisor, after introducing to Dave the woman who would be plugging in with him, squared DFW away.

Dave, a bit embarrassed about his language in front of the woman, didn't say a word about it in hopes that perhaps she hadn't heard him. The woman, somewhat older, stayed plugged in an hour or so, then got up to leave. As she unplugged, she leaned over so that only Dave could hear, whispering, "I think they f—ked you, too."

ATC Tales 108

There are some things that, in the course of an ATC career, you think you will never ever see. I saw one of them today.

Gray Approach Control (named after Robert Gray, one of Doolittle's Tokyo Raiders) is a small Department of Defense radar approach control down southwest of Waco, at Fort Hood. It serves Gray Army Air Field and Killeen Municipal, as well as providing services to a variety of other small airports in the area. Its operation seems to have a semblance to a rusty-dusty operation that is just sort of "there," if you know what I mean. It seems to be a "one-in, one-out" operation that has an airplane going in there one hour and another airplane coming out the next hour.

Today, however, was a different kettle of fish, a special day among ATC days, one of those events to be immortalized, to be chronicled in the annals of ATC history. Yes, today I actually had to, get this, sequence two army jets into Gray AAF.

Two aircraft, two, mind you, two of them, were inbound to Gray, RO1053 from Dulles and PAT287 from DFW, both of them showing up at the same time and nearly the same place, requiring all sorts of ATC swiftness, scrutiny, and dexterity.

Yes, all that attention and a quick review of every single applicable rule for separating two aircraft was called for so that a speedy issuance of a speed restriction: "PAT287, maintain 2-5-0 knots or less," saved the day for ATC.

Another good day at the ATC office . . . no paperwork.

Charlie Dugan (CC) was working Ft. Worth Center's OKC-hi sector when DAL308 checked on . . .

DAL308: "Albuquerque Center, Delta 308 with you, FL370."

CC: "American 308, Fort Worth Center, roger."

DAL308: "That's DELTA 308, not American!"

CC: "You called me Albuquerque Center, not Fort Worth."

A pause, then . . .

DAL308: "Oh, so that's the way it's gonna be, eh?"

ATC Tales 109

The world of ATC is an artificial world that becomes a reality unto itself. It is a world of radar scopes and data blocks, D-side cruds and printers, overhead charts, and a lot more right there in the control room. But there is another part of the ATC world that plays a part in the controller's life and that is the annual physical.

The physical is not what it used to be, that's for sure. Used to be an x-ray and blood work and a whole lot more. These days it is a check to make sure there's a pretty good chance you'll make it through the next year without keeling over on the scope. My physical was today and I, fortunately, made it through another one. I'm good to go for another year, needing to pass one more physical before the magic day, R-Day, Retirement Day, comes at the end of 2004.

The doctor I go to is an interesting fellow. He is a DO and an A.M.E., Aviation Medical Examiner. He also runs a winery, making and selling his own brand. He grew up on a grape farm in northern Alabama and still is very involved in the world of grapes. But before he had a winery, before he was a doctor, he was an Air Force pilot during the Korean War.

He never made it to Korea, getting as far west as Hawaii in beat-up old C-54s, airplanes that had seen better days. He was based at Travis AFB, CA, when he was flying medevac missions out to Hawaii and back to the States. They would launch into the blue and fly west for up to 12 hours as they flew (empty) to Hawaii. Then they would pick up a load of wounded and fly them to Travis where they would be put on other aircraft heading to various parts of the United States.

The flights east would take about ten hours, depending on the winds. Most of the time they were uneventful but sometimes they weren't, like the time a psychiatric patient popped open an evacuation door . . . at 6,000 feet. The door flew away from the aircraft and the patient was sucked out. The aircraft returned to Hawaii safely where another aircraft was substituted and all hands continued on to the States.

Dr. Smith has a unique understanding of the problems controllers face, particularly where weather is concerned. One time he was taking a C-54 from Travis to Warren AFB at Cheyenne, Wyoming. There was a thunderstorm between him and the field that would have taken him, he said, maybe ten minutes to go around. Ah, but the shortest distance between two points is a straight line and he pressed on, him and the empty C-54, him and the three crewmembers, entering the storm at 9,000 feet, emerging at 4,000.

As well you might imagine, the aircraft was badly shaken by the thunder-bumper, and so was the crew, to the point where they flew the aircraft by the tower for a look-see for damage. There was none and an uneventful landing ensued.

The good doctor, usually called "Sir" by the enlisted flight engineer, was doing a walk around, checking for damage when the aforementioned flight engineer sidled up to him.

"Captain Smith," he said, "are you EVER going to fly through another thunderstorm?"

The captain knew the man was serious because the fellow used "Captain Smith" on the most serious of occasions.

"Never as long as the good Lord lets me live," he replied.

"OK, I'll fly with you then."

All such incidents are reported and Smith did just that when he returned to Travis. The next day he got the worst chewing-out he ever received in the Air Force.

Only one other close call in his four years of flying but it was close enough. Flying C-47s out of McDill AFB, Florida, they had landed and refueled, then took off, launching over Tampa Bay. Unbeknownst to the crew, the flight engineer (a different fellow than the one mentioned above) had refueled the engine with jet fuel. Reciprocating engines do not like jet fuel and the two pilots were barely able to nurse the Gooney Bird back to the runway.

Another part of the ATC world.

ATC Tales 110

We have all heard of the phrase, "Truth in advertising." Not so long ago David Dowd learned firsthand that sometimes the phrase could be changed to "Truth in callsigns" because, in this case, the callsign said it all.

Dave was working Ardmore-low, often referred to as Ardmore-slow because a lot of the time not much to nothing ever happens there. Not so for Dave this one day when PAIN11, a flight of two BE-40s came up J20 to Tinker AFB. BE-40s are Beechjets, fairly reliable little pieces of equipment used by the Air Force for the advanced half of UPT, undergraduate pilot training.

This particular flight was out of Columbus AFB, MS, to Tinker AFB in the Oklahoma City area and checked on Dave's frequency at FL220. It didn't take Dave long to determine that something was wrong, particularly when the lead pilot said he had "smoke in the cockpit" and declared an emergency.

That word, "Emergency," is one of those words that causes things to happen. If nothing else, the pulse rate jumps up about ten points and the supervisor always gets up out of his chair to stroll over to behind the controller so he can see what is going on and begin the appropriate CYA procedures.

These guys were near Atoka, OK, about 15 miles southeast of the intersection of the same name, and were heading northwest to Tinker. One problem in an emergency is that the pilot doesn't have a lot of time to shoot the breeze or, sometimes, even answer questions. In this particular case the pilot, with smoke in the cockpit, couldn't see very well and so, rather than stay flight-lead, changed callsigns with his wingman. PAIN11 was now PAIN12 and PAIN12 became PAIN11, not to be confused with the original PAIN11 and PAIN12, if you get my drift. They could have just made the original PAIN12 the new flight-lead but that lesson must have been later in the course syllabus because this award-winning idea never occurred to them.

Dave started giving them all sorts of emergency-airport information about all the airports between their position and Tinker but the flight elected to press on, probably due to the fact that they are Air Force, Tinker is an Air Force base and all things Air Force go together. They remained on course right up until the time that the new flight-lead discovered a cloud layer at 3,000 feet above Tinker, a layer that would have precluded the new PAIN12, the former PAIN11, the PAIN with the pain of smoke in the cockpit, getting down through it without any difficulty. So they decided to press on to Ardmore which had clear weather and a long runway, an excellent combination for any sort of emergency situation and/or aircraft.

Somewhere in here the PAINs presented another change of callsigns, reverting to their original callsigns, PAIN12 becoming PAIN11 and the new -11 reassuming the -12 mantle. Talk about a real pain in the callsign. The situation was confusing enough without the pilots confusing it even more.

Eventually, however, in spite of all the callsign changes, changes in destination and everything else, and after a tour of central Oklahoma and another one around the Ardmore traffic pattern, both PAINs landed safely at Ardmore, though for a while, no one was quite sure where PAIN12 went (the born again PAIN12).

What a pain.

ATC Tales III

OKC Approach didn't do me any favors a few days ago when they chucked BTA2964, a JetLink Regional Jet (RJ) off OKC, and RUFF66, a Navy E-6 off Tinker, both toward Ardmore. They called to request direct Ardmore on RUFF66 to run him ahead of BTA2964. I approved it because it would help clear the RJ . . . but they didn't ship the JetLink and he was, on this particular day, the world's slowest climbing RJ.

OKC Approach climbs their departures to 15,000 feet. About 15 minutes before the RJ departed, N48W, a twin Cessna leapt off OKC into the blue, going to McKinney, Texas, at 15,000. By the time the RJ (almost) caught up with him, they were approaching Ardmore and I wasn't talking to the RJ. I was shouting at OKC-West, "Ship the JetLink or we'll all be filling out paperwork!"

Now with the JetLink overtaking N48W at 200 plus knots, I couldn't wait any longer, dumping N48W to 14,000 and turning him 40 degrees right to get away from the JetLink; and when the JetLink came on frequency I turned him 40 degrees left and expedited his climb through 16,000. It all worked out but it was a close call.

I usually like working with OKC Approach but not today. The important thing though, is no paperwork.

A good many years ago OKC Approach did me another good turn, as it were. They gave me a C337 Skymaster at 13,000 feet with a B727 right up its tailpipe, climbing to 15,000. Then the fellow hit the landline saying, "Oh, by the way, Stillwater. I don't think that American is going to jump the Skymaster."

They were right but it was nothing a 40 degree turn to the right for the American and a 40 degree turn to the left for the Cessna couldn't take care of.

N54012, a C172, popped up on the Frisco frequency with an explanation and a request . . .

"We've heard of this program called "flight following" and we would like to enroll in it." An interesting way, I thought, of requesting VFR advisories.

ATC Tales 112

Luis Parrett was working ADM-Io this morning when he heard a strange radio transmission . . . "Can anybody hear me?"

Luis could, clearly, and answered, "Aircraft calling Center, this is Fort Worth Center, go ahead."

"This is N91BD. We are declaring an emergency. We have a cracked windshield and we are starting down out of FL350 to one-zero-thousand." The pilot was doing the right thing, getting the airplane down before the windshield popped out and the aircraft de-pressurized.

Luis shouted for help in here somewhere and Tim Ballogg plugged in to handle coordination. Luis checked the computer for the callsign but it wasn't stored. Where was he?

Where was this guy who had, maybe, moments to live?

"N91BD, squawk emergency," instructed Luis, knowing he should see the "EMRG" that would flash on the radar screen . . . and sure enough, there it was, maybe 40 miles north of Tulsa, an "EMRG" squawk at the right altitude and descending.

"N91BD, Fort Worth," said Luis, while Tim called Stillwater-low to tell them about the impending situation.

No reply. "N91BD, Fort Worth," once more the words went out into the frequency netherworld but again, no reply.

Meanwhile Stillwater-low, the sector into which the aircraft was descending, told him, "Yeah, we're talking to him." The situation was well in hand, at least as far as Luis and Tim were concerned. There was nothing more they could do other than hope the aircraft got down safely. It must have because there was no call to write a statement—and that's always a good thing.

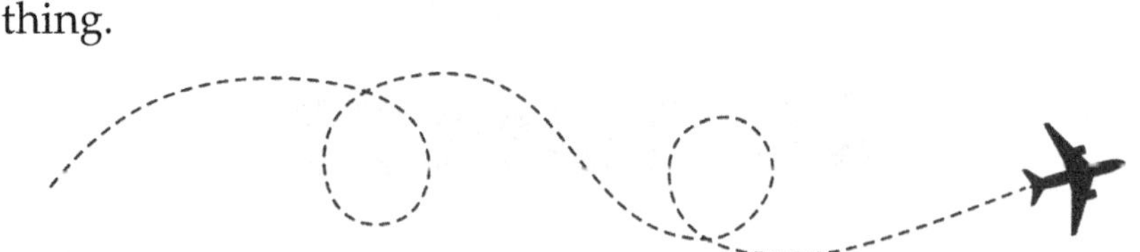

Speaking of Luis . . . this fellow is from Puerto Rico and has, as you might suspect, an accent, something a Candler commented on not so long ago, calling it "a unique accent." On his frequency a woman spoke to him, on my frequency a man asked about him. Kind of makes you wonder, doesn't it . . .

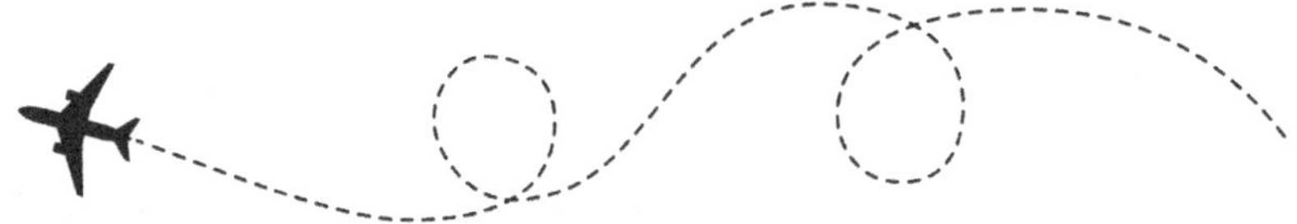

There has been more than one lost aircraft out there. One time some years ago Andy McGowan worked BUC01, a flight of four F-16s off Tinker AFB to Hill AFB near Ogden, Utah. Checking on Andy's OKC-hi frequency out of FL180, he climbed them to their requested altitude of FL430. Entering a cloud layer about FL260 as a flight of four, they came out of the clouds about FL310 as a flight of three.

"We've lost number four," said flight lead, asking Andy if he could see the other aircraft.

Andy searched for a primary target in the general area to no avail so he gave number four, still on the frequency, a discrete beacon code and started searching for that, again to no avail until Pete Moss on Ardmore-high saw the code up north of Chanute, Kansas, orbiting at FL430, well up in Tulsa-high's airspace, easily a hundred miles from where he should have been.

Quick coordination with Tulsa-high sorted out the problem with BUC01 heading northeast and BUC04 heading southwest for a join-up and then on to Hill. How did BUC04 get up to Chanute? We didn't know . . . we didn't want to know. Some things are better left not knowing because, after all, the object of the game is no paperwork.

ATC Tales 113

Brad Murray found himself on OKC-low one day when he got himself into an argument with Vance Approach. It ended when the person on the other end of the line announced, "I'm a supervisor," and Brad told him, "Well then, you had better give that up to someone who knows what they're doing."

Not to be outdone, Pete Moss tried running a LR24 off OKC direct and landing WWR, Woodward, Oklahoma, through the Vance One MOA, at FL220. Vance refused to take the Lear through the area, which had one T-38 out there that they would have to work around to get the Lear down. The argument ended when the Vance controller said, "I ain't taking him," and punched off the line. Pete shouted into the void, "Why don't you get some people up there who can work airplanes?"

That's when the Vance supervisor, probably the same one who snubbed Brad, hit the line and said, "We're pulling the tapes!" Pete got a minor counseling session, ending with a gentle reminder not to say something stupid on the line.

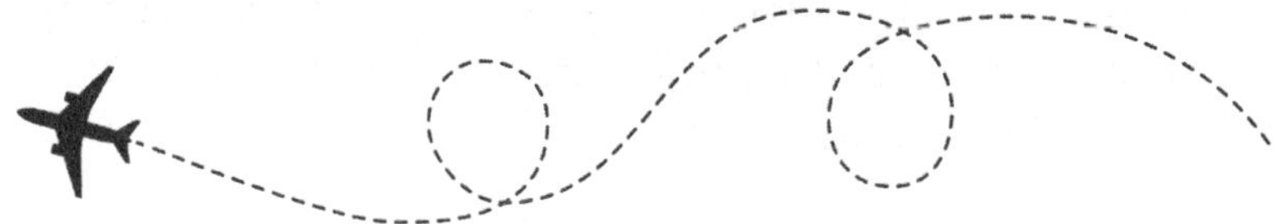

Sometimes stupid things do go out over the frequency, like the briefing in the old control room when someone recently retired forgot to de-select the frequencies and give the briefing over the air, this one including all the details about an aircraft that was on frequency and being chased by law enforcement aircraft. Soon after the briefing finished, that particular aircraft terminated VFR flight following and dropped below radar coverage.

Craig Whitwell gave a briefing on the Dallas-hi frequency one time, including a little snippet to the effect that "these two sons-o'-bitches at 3-5-0 are gonna hit but not 'til over Ardmore so I ain't gonna worry about it."

After the briefing finished, a voice chirped up . . . "I'm one of those two sons-o'-bitches at 3-5-0 that's gonna hit someone over Ardmore and I wanna know what you're gonna do about it!"

It still amazes me, even after 28 years of this ATC stuff, how big the sky is and yet how close two airplanes can be in that sky. Yesterday I had N1318W, a VFR Cherokee OKC direct Durant, OK, at 7500 feet, with N7728P, VFR BE55 at 7500 from over Bowie to Muskogee, 0K. Both of them were talking to me (at first) but then the Cherokee must have turned down his volume or not paid attention or something because when he became boresighted with the Baron I tried raising him numerous times. These guys were wired for sound, even a possible midair, but the day was saved when the Baron responded to my call and took the suggested climb to 085. A good thing, too, because while they were a thousand feet apart, they pretty much passed over the same piece of ground. Too close for comfort, that's for sure.

ATC Tales 114

There's a fellow named David Kelly out there who was working Frisco-low not too long ago when N62DM came off Grayson County in Sherman, heading to Denver's Centennial Airport, climbing first to FL230 and then FL430 on ADM-hi's frequency. The aircraft was out of maybe FL310 when he told Craig Whitwell he was beginning to have some sort of instrument fluctuation that necessitated him returning to Grayson County. It could not have happened at a worse place for coordination purposes, above three low-altitude sectors, the Sheppard AFB MOAs and requiring a pointout to Falls-hi. High took care of theirs and Craig got him down through all sorts of inbounds into DFW, finally getting him on Kelly's frequency. With a bit of help from Pete Moss on ADM-Iow, the aircraft made a safe descent through the MOA, the three low sectors and back to a safe landing at Grayson County. With everybody helping as best they could, the aircraft made a safe landing, the system worked, and most important of all, no paperwork.

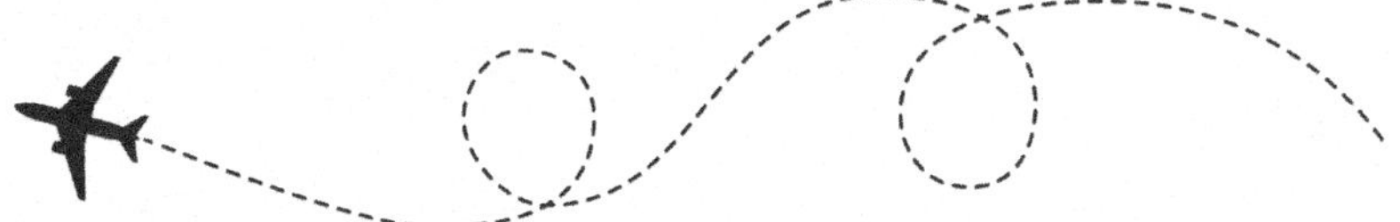

SWA48, a B73Q, one of the old 737-200s with the "quiet" engines, was out of DAL to TUL, requesting FL330. There was a KingAir at FL290 crossing his route up north that might be presenting a problem and knowing that the old 737's rate of climb isn't spectacular, Pete Moss asked,

PM: "SWA48, are you an old 737?"

SWA48: "Affirmative. Good for making noise and money."

PM: "Roger, climb and maintain FL270. That will be your final."

SWA48: "So much for the money."

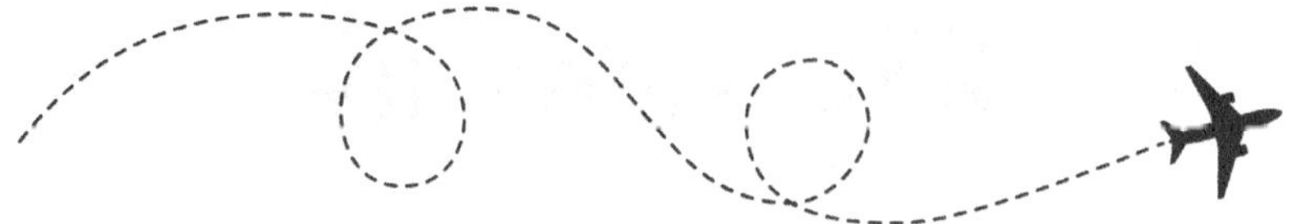

Keith Bell, the poster child for Bill King's "The Brake King" commercials, has had a go-round or two with some people out there but few more frustrating than one a week ago when he had a set-to with someone on MLC-hi. Forced by circumstances beyond his control (i.e., too many airplanes at FL330 and FL370) to apreq a wrong-for-direction FL350, Keith was told, "Unable, put him right for direction." Keith quick-looked MLC-hi, and seeing that their traffic was a DFW lander, he reached the end of his rope and for the "50" line at the same time.

"If you're making me descend this guy for a DFW lander," Keith choked out, "I'm gonna come over there and strangle you."

Seeing the error of his ways and (finally) the logic in Keith's, MLC-hi acquiesced and descended his aircraft. For once the system actually works like it should.

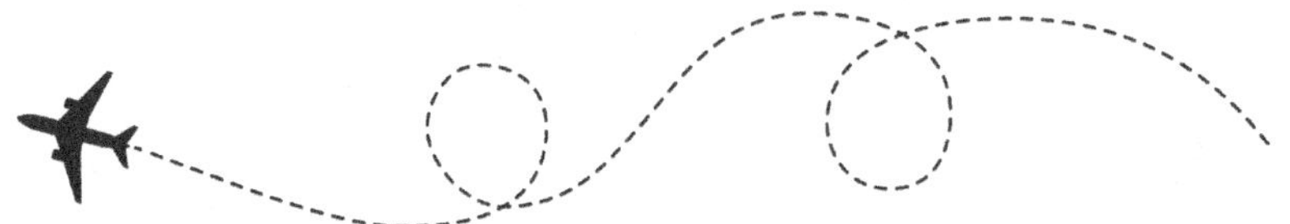

Phil Enis, who rarely works Monday nights, recently worked a body-for-body swap wherein he worked a Monday night shift for the first time in years. Seeing me in the hall he allowed as how there is "a merry band of idiots working this end of the schedule." Sometimes I agree with him.

It was Phil on Bowie-low one day that got screwed so bad by ADM-hi that he threatened to file rape charges.

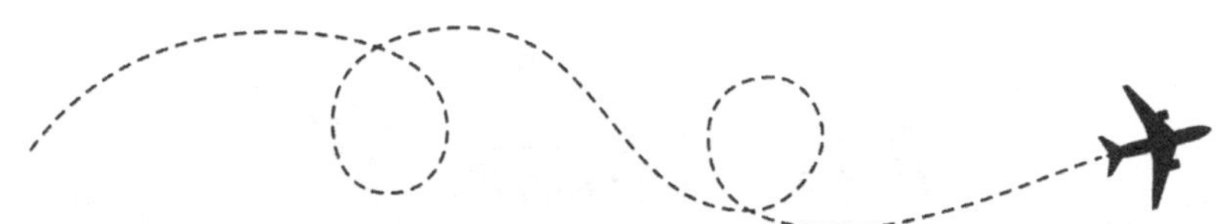

Alvy Ring had three FL330 eastbounds on MLC-hi, two Republics and one Eastern, all on parallel vectors going into Memphis Center, when he climbed an American to FL330 northeast bound. The American had just leveled when Alvy realized he was about to have a four-way deal because the American would probably get with all three eastbound 330s. He descended the American back down to FL290.

The American protested, saying "We've just leveled off. We'll take a vector or do anything to stay at 3-3-0."

Alvy keyed his mike and said, "If you knew what I knew, you'd start on down!"

ATC Tales 115

Luis Parrett (PC) cleared an aircraft "Direct the DECKK intersection, direct Will Rogers."

The pilot, unable to find DECKK in his database, asked Luis, "How do you spell that?"

PC: "It's like a deck of cards with an extra card."

Denise (DL) forced down a Delta from FL310 to FL280 for traffic when the pilot started giving her a ration of static about it.

DL: "DAL421, this NOT open to negotiation." Always a good line.

Early one morning I cleared a Houston Intercontinental arrival ". . . direct TORNN, remainder of the CUGAR1 arrival" and received a "Roger" in reply. A moment later the Learjet asked, what was the name of that intersection? I can't find it in my data base.

"TORNN," I replied, "like, the paper is torn."

"TORNN?" He exclaimed, "I was dialing in PORNN."

Now it was my turn to exclaim . . . "Porn? I hope you can't find it in your database."

Said the pilot, "This always happens when I get up at three in the morning."

You have to wonder about some pilots. The other day I worked one who didn't know what an "ident" button was. That happened to me once before, maybe ten or twelve years ago. I didn't think lightning could strike twice in the same spot.

There is a small Texas town out east of Waco named Mexia, pronounced Muh-hey-yuh. It is in an area prone to forest fires. Several routes out of DFW and into Houston go right over the town. One afternoon last year Jason Judy asked an air carrier if he could see the forest fire in Mexia (Muh-hey-yuh) to which the pilot responded, "No, but you better go put it out!"

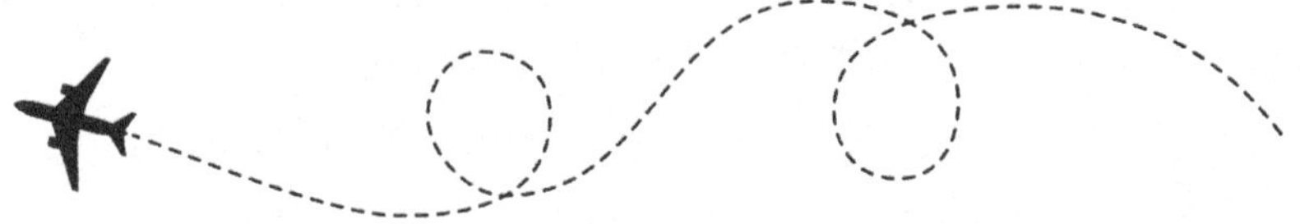

I was on Ardmore-low yesterday, stuck over in the corner of the specialty next to Frisco-low where Chuck Andrews was working. It wasn't busy and I had some time to look and listen to what was going on elsewhere. That's when I heard a low-keyed running conversation going on between him and someone on his frequency.

Chuck was working HKY301 (Hickory 301), a C-130 out of Little Rock AFB going to Davis-Montham AFB, Arizona. Chuck had been a C-130 crew chief for four years in the Air Force before hiring on with the FAA. Anytime a C-130 comes through, he perks up a little bit and so he did when HKY301 checked on his frequency.

A single question to the pilot, however, crushed the good feeling. The pilot told Chuck the aircraft was an old "E" model going out for retirement at the Air Force aircraft storage facility at Davis-Montham.

Chuck and the pilot shot the breeze for a few minutes before Chuck sent him on his way, then turned to me saying, "I feel like I'm tearing up," as we both watched a planeful of memories heading west . . . to the boneyard.

Ed Gleason was working DAL-hi when SWA1836 with a female pilot doing the talking came on climbing to FL230, looking for higher and direct College Station (CLL).

Ed: "Roger, cleared direct CLL climb and maintain . . ."

A couple minutes later Chad Etheridge, the trusty D-side, noticed the SWA drifting way to the east and pointed out the same to Ed who quizzed the SWA as to why they were drifting east, adding, "Isn't your RNAV working?"

A voice, now a man's, came out of the ether, "No, we're up here playing with it, but it isn't as tight as I'd like it to be."

ATC Tales 116

Something happened out there a few days ago (in mid-February) that made me cringe with disgust. On a solid IFR day, the pilot of N455P, a BE36 inbound to Sherman, Texas (SWI), was denied an approach into that airport because, Lu Ann Ferguson told him, there was a "flag" in our approach plate book saying that "Approach procedure NOT AUTHORIZED" to the SWI Airport.

The pilot was not happy about this, being denied an approach, because, said he, that restriction was removed months ago.

Lu Ann checked with Dave Asbell, the supervisor on duty, who in turn checked with three other sources, none of whom could verify that the restriction, the "flag," had indeed been lifted. On hearing that, Lu Ann refused to issue a clearance and the pilot was forced to execute an approach to the Grayson County Airport (F39), clear across town and out in the country somewhere out north of town.

The pilot, still unhappy (and rightfully so), asked for and was given the Frisco specialty phone number to call in after he landed. Dave, in the meantime, made several more phone calls and found out that the restriction had indeed been lifted, last October—four months prior!—but somewhere along the line someone had dropped the ball and the flag had never been removed from the approach plate book.

When the pilot called in, Dave explained to him that because we did not know for sure, that to be on the safe side, he was not cleared for the approach. The pilot said that if that was the case, then he appreciated the refusal, but he still had to explain to the passengers why they were departing F39 instead of SWI . . .

N43MC, a BE56, came through the other day. I have never seen one of those before and queried the pilot as to what kind of airplane it was . . .

"It is a 'muscle' Baron from the 60s," he said; "sort of a Baron on steroids."

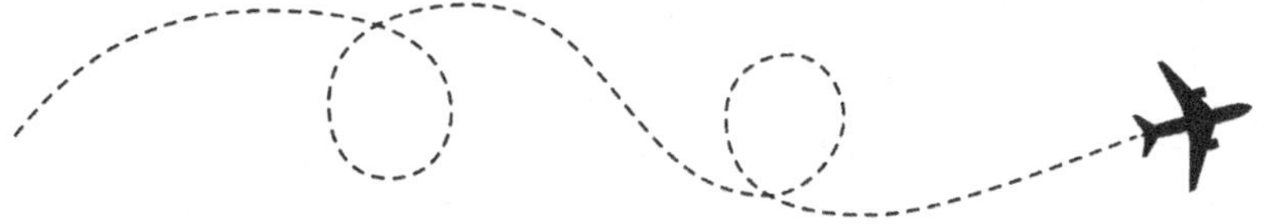

This could be titled, "Do it yourself ATC."

Pete Moss was on DAL-hi working AAL2941 inbound to Austin . . .

PM: "AAL2941, descend and maintain FL-240."

He was not surprised by the first response . . .

AAL2941: "Descend and maintain FL240."

But he was surprised by the second response . . .

AAL2941: "Descend and maintain FL240."

PM: "That's correct . . . both of you."

To which one of them replied, "This guy never tells me anything."

And talking about "Do it yourself ATC," several years ago . . .

One night on a quiet mid-shift a TXK controller heard:

"Center, AAL829, requesting direct JFK."

He was very surprised when he heard another voice say, "Roger, AAL829 direct JFK."

He was even more surprised when another voice, he thought the first voice, acknowledged, "Direct JFK, AAL829."

Turned out the two pilots were facing away from each other in the dark cockpit and had not heard each other speak on the radio, thus requesting, giving, and receiving their own clearance direct JFK.

Maybe this is what "free flight" is all about.

ATC Tales 117

Yesterday something happened out there that rarely happens but when it does, it gives you that warm fuzzy feeling that doing something good for someone leaves you with.

I had just plugged into Ardmore-low to give Carter Evans (EN) a break and was sitting there while Carter started through the sector-relief briefing. He wasn't busy by a long shot, five data blocks and only talking to three of them, one of which was a VFR.

It was that VFR that caught Carter's attention. The VFR was N9855S, a Cherokee out of Oklahoma City to Denton, Texas, at 4500 feet.

Just as Carter started through the briefing he glanced at the scope and noticed traffic for N9855S, another VFR, also at 4500 feet, very close . . . and getting closer.

EN: "November 5-5 Sierra, traffic alert. Traffic ten o'clock, one mile, northwest bound, four thousand five-hundred feet."

Half a mile later he issued it again, adding, "I suggest you climb to avoid him. 11 o'clock, one-half mile."

N9855S: "We're climbing . . . yeah, we have the traffic."

A moment later Carter asked, "Was that altitude good?"

N9855S: "You've probably saved our life actually," adding that it was a good altitude on the VFR.

Carter's voice quavered a bit as he gave the briefing and I took the sector. This had never happened to him before, two that close, and they were close. Later, after I took the sector, I asked the pilot how close the other aircraft had been. He answered that the other aircraft had passed directly under him a hundred feet and that if he hadn't climbed it would have been a bad day for all concerned.

I waved Carl Youngblood over, the supervisor on duty, and told him what had happened. I'm not one for tooting my own horn but I don't mind tooting others. This was such a close call that the happy ending bears sharing with all hands. Carl had the tapes pulled and is writing it up as a "save." That's the kind of paperwork you want to see in ATC.

Carter isn't the only one this has happened to. Over the 28 years I've been there I've seen it a time or two but there have been many others. Don Vouklizas had two Navy trainers, both NORDOs, merge at 6000 feet and then come away from each other, having been IMC at the time and never even seeing each other.

Dwan Stregles made an "in the blind" call on Frisco-low one day to "either of the two VFRs at 7,500 feet near Grayson County to come up on frequency." One did and Dwan's first words were, "I suggest you climb." The pilot did, exclaiming as he did so, "Holy s—t! He went right underneath us!"

I have made several "in the blind" calls over the years, including one in response to a request from OKC Approach. I was sitting on Ardmore-low one evening when OKC called to ask if I could see a 1200 (VFR) code northwest of ASHER intersection 10 miles. "Affirmative," I replied.

They went on to explain that he had departed 2EJ, the OKC Expressway Junction Airport and had gone right through the traffic pattern at Tinker AFB, almost hitting a LogAir aircraft. If, they said, I found out who it was, tell them because they were going to follow up on it for some sort of action against the pilot.

I tracked the aircraft for a while, then decided I might as well try to call him . . . "There is a VFR aircraft at sixteen-five northeast of Ardmore 20 miles. If you are on frequency, please come up."

He was and did. I asked if he wanted VFR advisories. He allowed as how he could take them and gave me his aircraft number. I radar-identified him, then said that, for search-and-rescue purposes, I would take all the rest of the SAR information, name, base, phone number, color of aircraft, all that stuff. He gave it all to me, every bit, and I dutifully called OKC Approach and told them not only did I have it but if they called the Quality Assurance Office, they could get it all off the tapes in the morning.

I don't know if OKC followed through but if they did, I would bet that was the last time that pilot ever requested VFR advisories.

ATC Tales 118

Today I had to read a pilot his Miranda rights, never a pleasant thing. Young John-Boy Sheddens (I call him such because he was born after I hired on with the FAA) was working DAL-hi during a push when VVPT038, a P-3, checked on to do some airwork in a block of FL240B260. Realizing he needed a buffer, John assigned the Navy a block of FL250B270 so as to give him the thousand feet where he could climb his departures from low.

The Navy had been in the new block maybe five minutes when a Cactus checked on climbing south. John climbed him to FL240, right under the Navy. It would have been all right, John having the thousand feet buffer, but the Navy dropped to FL246 before climbing back into the block. John asked him if he was in the block 250B270 and the pilot hesitated, then replied, "Affirmative" and almost immediately the data block reflected as much.

There was a loss of separation, all sorts of bells and whistles going off, the inevitable phone call from the desk and the immediate worry of, "Have I done everything right?" on John-Boy's part, as there is in every controller's mind when such an event occurs. John got pulled off the sector, the tapes got pulled downstairs, a DARTS run got pulled from somewhere and all hands got pulled upstairs to listen to and review the same.

In every event like this, blame has to be laid somewhere and the FAA (read "management") doesn't care where it goes (unless the system itself is found to be at fault, which has actually happened twice that I know of) as long as it can be laid somewhere.

Shortly after John left, I took Dallas-high and was sitting there when a supervisor came by saying I needed to read this to the pilot, handing me a little card with the standard aviation Miranda rights business on it. It sounds pretty serious and can be, I think, pretty intimidating to a pilot hearing it . . . "Navy 0-3-8, you have been involved in a possible pilot deviation. You are to call the following number . . ." and then you give them whatever phone number they need to call. The pilot calls in and they discuss it. The pilot is advised that he is being investigated for a possible pilot deviation and that it is being referred to a staff office upstairs.

The reading of the rights, as I said, can be pretty intimidating and the few times I have done it over the years, probably half a dozen times or so, the reading has been followed by a period of silence on the frequency from all hands. Today an American, when I gave him a frequency change, took the frequency saying, "I'm glad what you read wasn't for me." I told him I wished it hadn't been for anybody; I don't want anybody to get in trouble.

After everything was reviewed and John cleared, in short order fortunately, he returned to the floor and to work. Other new controllers, having been involved in an incident of some sort, have not been so lucky. Many years ago, before the strike, a new radar controller, checked out only two hours, was working a small holding stack over TXK, including a Bonanza at 6,000 feet. The Bonanza pilot never said a word about being low on gas or running out of fuel, he just crashed, killing two people. The controller never really got over it, blaming himself for something over which he had no control. I think the strike was a blessing for him.

To miss the Washita MOA, Pete Moss cleared N918SA direct LIONS intersection direct ABQ. The pilot took the clearance but did not turn, finally asking for a heading toward LIONS. Pete gave him, "Fly H310 while you're getting your machine set up." The pilot took it, then said he was going direct LI-ONS. "It works better when you spell it right. It doesn't come up," he said, "when you put LOINS in there."

ATC Tales 119

There was this student pilot from a foreign country who was asked by approach control: "Verify you have information India." (ATIS)

The student replied: "I'm not from India, I'm from Pakistan."

Jason Judy (JY) was sitting on Frisco-lo when DFW called saying they were stacking a Southwest (SWA) to OKC at 140, under an Eagle Flight climbing high. The SWA checked on at 140, looking for higher . . .

JY: "You're stopped at 140 for traffic, one o'clock, three miles, an EGF climbing high."

SWA: "We have the commuter jet in sight." There was a moment's silence, then . . .

EGF: "Yeah, like you're not!"

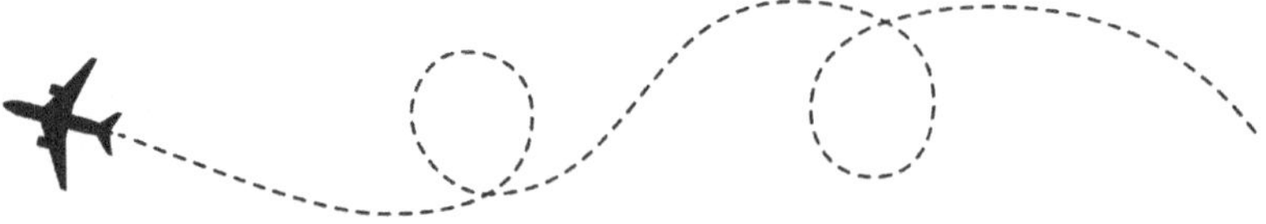

Have you ever read the book, "The Caine Mutiny"? In it a Navy officer gets a medal and a reprimand the same day. It was fiction but sometimes it happens in real life, too. Some years ago, late on a mid-shift in the Navy Pensacola tower there was a Southern Airways DC-9 lined up for an approach (the pilot thought) to the civilian field at Pensacola. He was actually about to land at the Navy field. Knowing that the aircraft shouldn't be landing there, and knowing that he, the Navy controller, could not communicate this fact to the Southern Airways pilot, he, the Navy controller, flipped off the runway lights.

One of the big no-no's at a military field is, in the hours of darkness, to turn off the runway lights. This act in and of itself, was sufficient to bring down the wrath of the CATCO, chief air traffic control officer, on this poor sailor's head; but he had done a good thing too, saving an incident (and possibly worse) from happening.

So the sailor got a pat on the back, in the form of a Letter of Commendation from the FAA Pensacola tower, and a kick in the butt, all at the same time, which makes me wonder if the CATCO was ambidextrous.

During World War II a P-51 pilot was asked if he ever prayed while flying missions over Europe. He replied, "Yes, and the prayer is always the same: Lord, if you hear me, please get me the hell out of here."

I used to think having a "senior moment" was something that happened to old controllers but today . . .

Today two US Army National Guard Shorts 360s, PAT132 and PAT344, came off OKC to SAT, both at 8,000, about 60 miles in trail.

PAT132: "Center, tell PAT344 to come up on company frequency. "

PM: "PAT344, PAT132 wants you to come up company freq. "

PAT344: "Wilco."

Several minutes elapsed, then, (and you could hear the embarrassment in his voice),

PAT344: "Uh, Center, tell 1-3-2 I don't know what company frequency is."

PAT132 didn't even wait for me to relay the message, muttering "24.24."

ATC Tales 120

I'm not real keen on sarcasm, especially from pilots. It doesn't win them any favors—or friends either, a lesson one or two pilots could stand to learn, including the Learjet I worked out of OKC today. He was a Lifeguard to Guatemala, LN16AX, but filed his flight plan as LN16.

The problem with that is that there is a real N16, a KingAir based at Fort Worth Meacham. I asked the Learjet pilot what the rest of his callsign is and he kept saying, that's it. I told him that the real N16 was a KingAir and he finally allowed as how his callsign was really N16AX, "But we never have this problem when we file as "OAE16" (Omni 16). Of course not, because that's an air taxi callsign; if he files as a lifeguard-November, he needs to file the last two numbers and whatever letters are there.

He was hacked, saying that he never has this problem in California (which, to my mind, explained a lot of the problem) and started emphasizing the "Alpha X-ray" every time he said his callsign, both on my frequency and ADM-hi, too. What a pain.

And a SWA pilot gave me a ration last Sunday, too. He asked for direct OKC. I said, "Unable," to which he replied (probably with a sneer, "Yeah, like they're really busy today."

"Your traffic, SIR, is 11 o'clock, 2-0 miles, a regional jet departing OKC, that would be head-on if you went direct Oke City," I replied, wanting to shout it into the mike but knowing the tapes can be pulled at any time, said in a normal voice.

He snorted his callsign and I gave him direct when he cleared the Jet Link but didn't particularly want to.

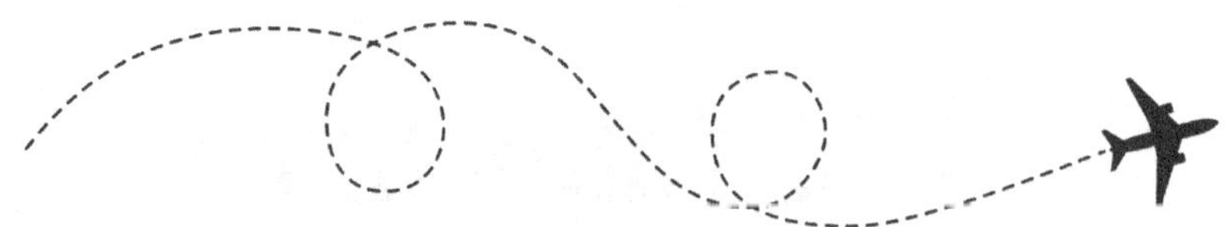

When TLX202 (Telesis 202) checked on, I asked if the "Telesis" used to be a different callsign.

TLX: "Affirmative. We used to be Projet [PJT]."

LH: "Why did you change?"

TLX: "They didn't tell us but I think the IRS was getting a bit too close."

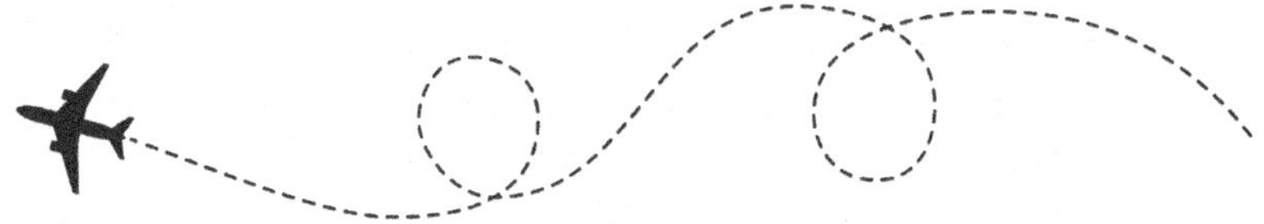

Back when I had three teenagers living at home, I worked a BJS202 and could not understand the slurred callsign when the pilot checked on.

LH: "Something 2-0-2, say again your callsign."

BJS: "It's 'Solution,' as in, if you have a problem we have a solution."

LH: "Do you have a teenager department?"

BJS: "We barely have an adult department."

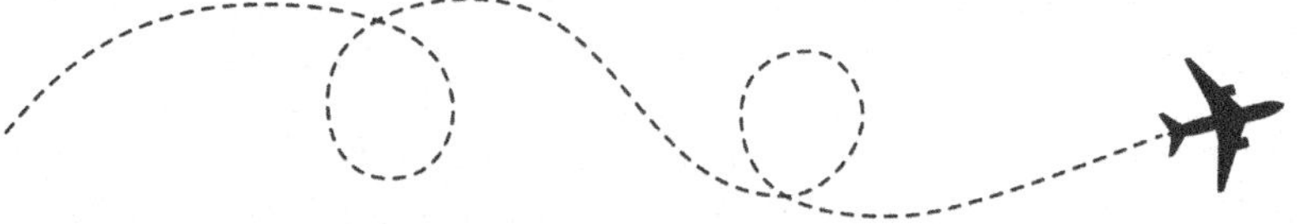

Last week we had lots of weather in the Houston terminal area and several sectors were on the verge of going down the tubes and staying there. J-180 traffic was being rerouted the west and Dallas-high was staying (maybe) one step ahead of BILEE-hi in Houston Center, the high-altitude sector feeding arrivals into the Houston area from the north.

Keith Jordan, DAL-hi R, was trying to stay one step ahead of the paperwork when Carl Youngblood, the supe, called TMU (flow control) to ask for some relief, reroute some traffic, hold some, but do something to help DAL-hi which would in turn help BILEE-hi.

Flow's response? "We're too busy to help you."

Keith called BILEE-hi to tell them the bad news, adding that they might have their TMU call our TMU because that was the only way anything was going to get done.

The weather was so bad that aircraft were holding for both the Houston and the Dallas-Fort Worth Airports. There were over a hundred aircraft holding in central Texas for those two airports when an Eagle Flight got off OKC for DFW. I offered to put him in holding or send him back to OKC. When he learned he would be holding two hours he elected to return to OKC. Wise move.

When AAL2076 got off right at the end he, too, had the same choice, though the hold turned out to be maybe an hour. When I asked Bowie-lo where AAL2076 would fit in the sequence, I was told, "Tell him he's Number Last." He was, too.

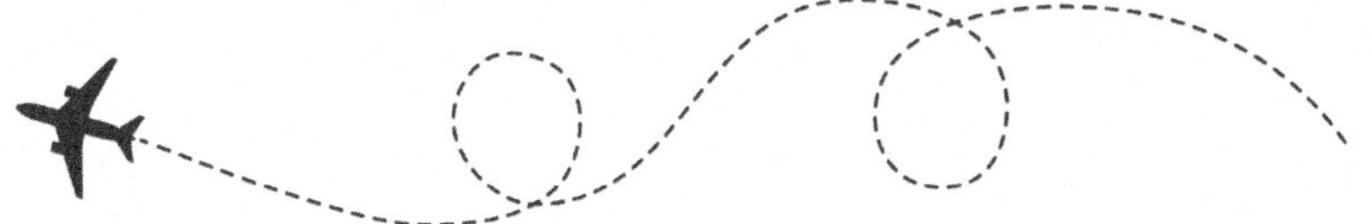

We don't go into holding very much anymore. Before the strike in 1981 we went to holding at the drop of a hat. It wasn't unusual to have two holding stacks, occasionally three, somewhere in a high-altitude arrival sector. One of the few good things the strike did was to force the FAA to improve the flow-control system, implementing ground delays, reroutes and a few other things to help the system. Unfortunately flow-control seems to have been stagnating ever since.

Speaking of holding, one horrible-weather day before the strike we went into holding and I, working ADM-hi R, set up a stack about 40 miles northeast of Blue Ridge. Myron Gates, the on-duty OKC specialty supervisor, came to me on the sector and said he wanted the holding stack moved 20 miles to the southwest, an area I thought to be dangerously close to the thunderstorm line just west of the proposed holding stack. He told me to move it and I refused. He then ordered me to move and told me that if I refused, I would be facing charges of insubordination. Telling him, again, that I thought such a move was unsafe, I told him, "Myron, if you want that stack moved, then go get your headset and move it yourself." He left then and nothing came of it.

ATC Tales 121

Sometimes I'm not sure how smart pilots really are . . . and this guy was flying a DC-10.

I have a friend who flies for American. I generally compare airline pilots to him to see how smart they are. I mean, my friend was a Navy F-4 pilot and now he flies B767s and 757s on international routes for American. I know how smart he is supposed to be; I know how smart he is; and I know how smart he thinks he is . . . think about it.

But last night I worked a DC-10 out of Fort Sill (FSI), some sort of military charter that was deadheading back to home base. It was empty and could go like a rocket so I told FSI Approach Control to climb him to FL230 and clear him direct Charleston. The flight plan showed "HVQ" (Charleston, West Virginia VORTAC) in his route of flight so when I said "clear him direct Charleston" I figured the pilot would know it meant "Charlie West," as it's called in the trade.

The pilot told FSI, "That's not in our route of flight" so I told them, "Give him direct H-V-Q" and I would sort it out.

When he came over, I asked him if he was proceeding direct Hotel Victor Quebec?

"Affirmative," he said.

"What is the identifier Hotel Victor Quebec?" I asked.

"I don't know," the pilot said, "but I'll look it up."

He checked and sure enough it was Charleston, West Virginia, the fix he had filed over. You know something? Even deep in the heart of that dark control room I could see the red face in his voice.

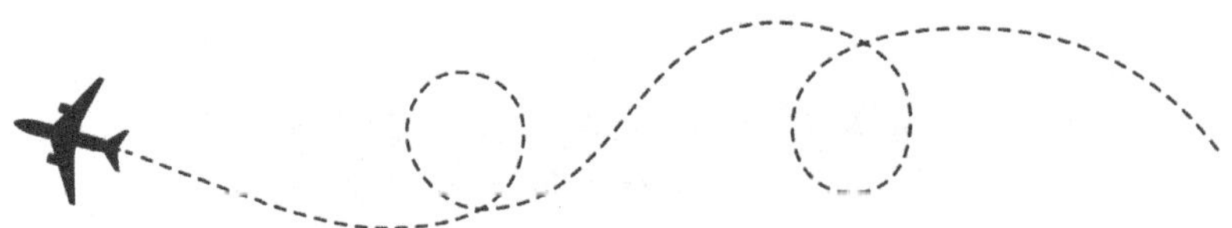

There's a female supervisor on the Bonham specialty at work named Deanne. She is married to Tony, a controller on the Quitman specialty.

Two controllers on Bonham, Randy and Mike, wanted to visit DFW Approach and asked Deanne if they could go. She said she would take a look at the staffing and if she could approve it, she would page them to call extension 7528, the desk phone.

Randy and Mike went on a break. In the meantime, the breakfast run came back and, having ordered breakfast for her husband Tony, and wanting to let him know it was back, she paged, "Tony Premin, call 7-5-2-8."

The paging system out there works half the time at best and Randy heard only, "call 7-5-2-8" and thinking it was her paging him about the DFW visit, called the desk.

Deanne, thinking it was her husband, Tony, calling, answered the phone in a sultry voice saying, "I've got what you want. It's hot; it's ready; and it's right here!"

Randy, surprised, said, "I'll be right there!"

Deanne, surprised at hearing Randy's voice, begged him not to say anything to anybody about it but of course he told everybody.

The next day, when breakfast orders were being taken, the whole specialty said, "I'll have what Tony's having!"

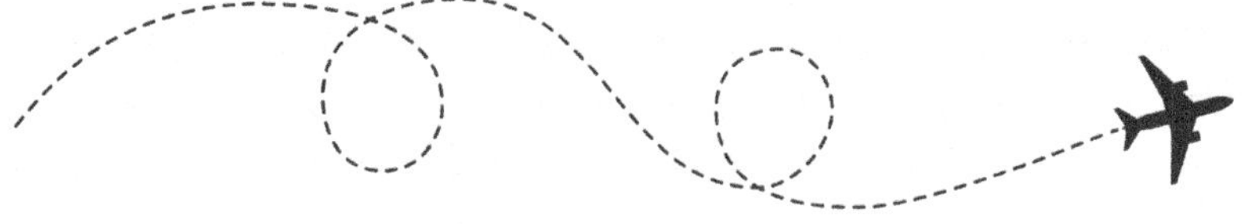

"You know what S-W-A stands for, don't you?" came the disembodied voice from SWA614 (having just requested direct Bonham for the thousandth time).

"No, what?" I replied. "Seldom Wants Airways."

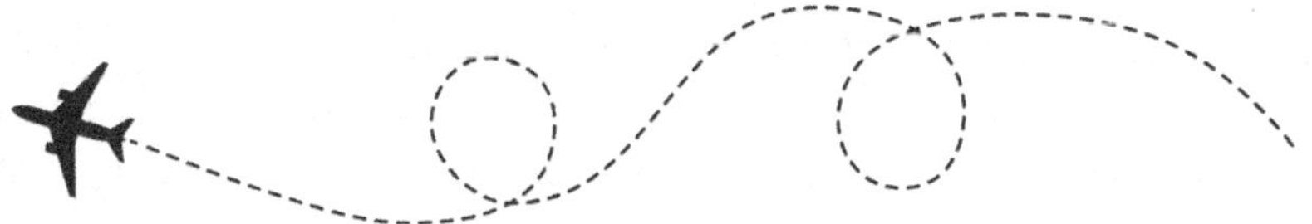

Tim Ballogg gave AAL492 the standard "landing north" crossing restriction for Oklahoma City, "Cross 3-0 south of Will Rogers at and maintain one-zero thousand and at 2-5-0 knots."

AAL492: "What's the matter, Oke City got a traffic jam?"

The best response I ever heard to an issued crossing restriction was what a Learjet said to Kim Welte. While training on her first two sectors, she had a Lear 40 south of Tulsa at FL410 and told him to cross 30 south of Tulsa at 10,000 and at 250 knots (10 miles to come down 31,000 feet and slow a hundred knots as well.)

"Lady," he said, "I couldn't make that restriction if I was a manhole cover."

ATC Tales 122

I'm still not sure what happened this last week. Days, weeks, months, even years for some, go by and you don't see an emergency. Then POW! Three or four of them raise their ugly little heads and inundate you.

I got a taste of the future while working Ardmore-high D with Dwan Stregles on the R-side. JEST16, a C-17 RTB Altus AFB checked on at FL280, right at the end of a very busy push filled with beaucoup departures mixed on with a lot of Houston arrivals that needed sequencing for Dallas-high. Dwan did a great job getting through the rush and was just starting to relax a bit when JEST16 called . . .

"Center, JEST16, we're declaring an emergency. We have a fuel leak of undetermined origin. Fuel odor and fumes in the aircraft and the tanker told us we have a fuel streak the length of the aircraft."

That was a show-stopper, sure enough, but not for long. Dwan got what information he needed while I talked with the supe and Falls-high, the next sector, and then Dwan shipped him. It was that quick, there and gone. That's the way it should be.

A few days ago there was a fleetful of FLIBs inbound to Ardmore Municipal and for a while I was running an approach control in there. Everybody was having to shoot instrument approaches because all the approaches start at 3,000 or above and the bases were down to 2,500. Great training weather, or so thought all the instructors in southern Oklahoma, so they all loaded up and zoomed off into the skies for Ardmore. The old non-radar procedures from the CSM days got hauled out and dusted-off, that's for sure.

In the middle of that airplane shuffle came COPPER1, a KC-135 with a "single side hydraulic failure," FOXY92 with an undetermined problem requiring "an immediate return to Sheppard," and BALL91, a T-37 that was so low on fuel he couldn't dip his toes in what was left.

One of the most interesting emergencies I ever heard of was one Roy Newsom told me about. It seems there was a T-38 RTB Randolph AFB that was, by the time the incident happened, low over the city of San Antonio. The student, in the front seat, leaned over to pick up something he dropped. At that same moment a bird strike occurred, slamming through the canopy and smashing into the seat back where the student's head would have been had he not leaned over.

All of a sudden there were feathers everywhere, a howling wind and an aircraft that was seemingly out of control. The instructor, in the back seat, getting no response from the student, thought the student had been killed by the bird's impact. The intercom, had been knocked out in the ensuing confusion and the instructor, fearing the worst, shouted "Eject! Eject! Eject!" and then he punched out.

In the meantime the student, leaning over when the bird hit, had a hard time getting back up from the bent-over position. After all, there was a dead bird behind him and feathers and blood (fortunately the bird's) everywhere else . . . and then came the roar of the rear ejection seat when the instructor left the aircraft.

The T-38 was still wobbling across the sky when the instructor's chute opened and he lost sight of it. He landed on a city street, in front of a 7-11 convenience store, and after gathering his chute out of traffic's way, literally walked across the street to a pay phone where he called the "SOF" (supervisor of flying) at Randolph AFB, telling him that the aircraft had crashed after experiencing a bird strike that killed the student.

The SOF was mystified because the T-38 in question was just, at that moment, landing.

It seems that the student, even through the maelstrom of charts, dust, dirt, and everything else being sucked out of the cockpit by the howling wind, had somehow managed to recover control and had made it back to Randolph (somewhat) safely.

Can't you imagine the instructor's relief (and chagrin) when he heard the news?

ATC Tales 123

Some of the strangest stuff comes out of the speaker. Yesterday there came a sentence out of the blue, in a tone rife with contempt, "You're stupid, you moron." Wow! You have to wonder what precipitated that remark.

You hear off the wall stuff maybe once a month. One day an older controller, he was 54 if I'm not mistaken, spoke (about ATC) with a young woman at OKC approach. Some wag at OKC hit the line saying, "She's too young for you, Pete."

Pete replied, "If she's under a hundred she's too young for me."

One afternoon I heard Amarillo-high tell the OKC-high D-side trainee that he was a stupid, incompetent, dumb SOB and furthermore, he was surprised the FAA actually paid him money to act like he did.

The lad in question wasn't the brightest boy in the ATC world but he didn't deserve that. He didn't make it through the training process but, all things considered, he was a nice guy.

One night on the mid-shift there came a phone call out of the speaker, clear as day, one side of it anyway. It was bleeding through on the Albuquerque Center 43-line, one of the hot lines between the two facilities.

The call was from a young woman in the Albuquerque bus station to her boyfriend (whose half of the conversation was inaudible) somewhere else. She had evidently left him at some earlier point and now she was calling to say she was coming back to him on the morning bus.

From her end of the conversation, spoken through racking sobs and a broken voice, we gathered that he was not enthused at the prospect of her impending return. She, on the other hand, was hopefully determined to come back once and for all. She cried, begged, and pleaded the better part of an hour, imploring him to meet the bus when it, and she, arrived the next day.

Her voice faded in and out over the hour, all the while the four of us listening, craning our ears when her voice went low. We sat around the OKC specialty listening to it all—or as much as we could hear. We almost felt guilty, like audio voyeurs, but there was no way to stop it or to let her, them, know the conversation was being broadcast live throughout Fort Worth Center. To be honest, I don't know that we would have, had it been possible.

It ended with (evidently) a reluctant promise on his part to pick her up. She sounded relieved, happy, and unbelieving, all at the same time. I hope they worked it out.

Occasionally some interesting stuff is heard on the radios, too, conversations and the like, usually involving a stuck mike. Bill Eaton inadvertently keyed a mike on the mid-shift as he was telling a story about a hunting dog that wouldn't hunt. Bill, who was a very colorful and very graphic individual, was also very surprised when he reached the end of the story and noticed a row of red lights over the radio transmitters which, in the old control room, meant every word he had said went out over the air.

It wasn't busy at all that night and fortunately there was but one aircraft, a TWA, on frequency. Bill unkeyed, then rekeyed to apologize.

The TWA didn't say anything except "Roger" until Bill switched him to the next frequency, then he said, "Roger, 134.55 . . . and you know something, Center? What your hunting dog needs is a good swift kick in the ass."

ATC Tales 124

N6539P, a Navajo inbound to Sulphur, Oklahoma, evidently couldn't wait to get off my frequency . . .

As soon as he had the airport he screamed, "We're canceling IFR; squawking 1200 and we're outta here!"

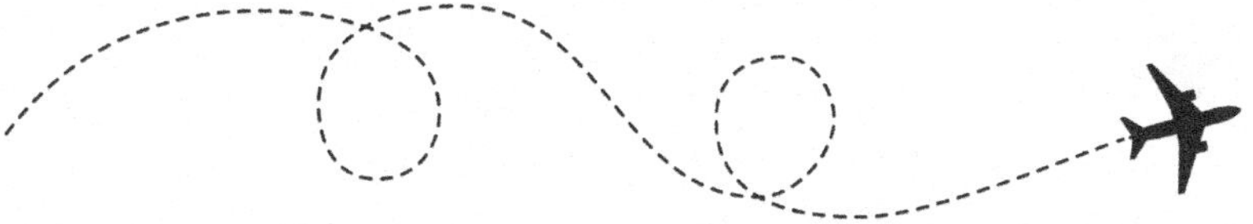

Chuck Andrews gave AA11136, who had been direct ACT-CWK, direct CWK-MARCS7-SAT. The pilot lit into Chuck saying, "We just got direct Waco Centex and now you give us direct Centex. Can't you guys all get on the same page? Why do you do this?"

Chuck, who has heard all this a thousand times, keyed his mike saying simply, "Controller amusement."

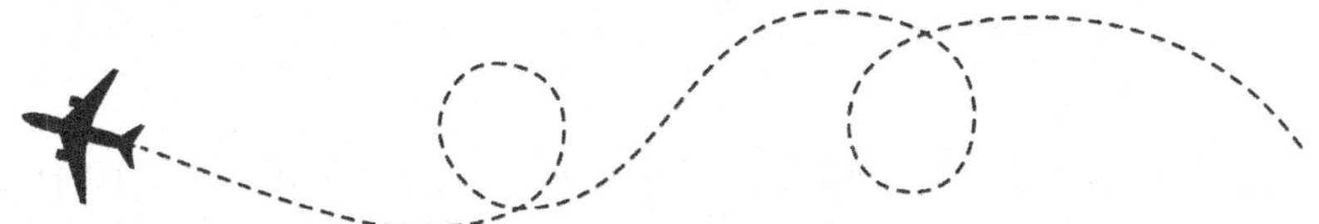

When CTLES04 checked on frequency Pete Moss called him "Cuddles-zero-four."

The pilot responded, (in a DEEP voice) "That's CUTLASS04."

Pete replied, "CUTLASS04, roger."

And in a booming voice, the pilot replied, "THANK YOU!"

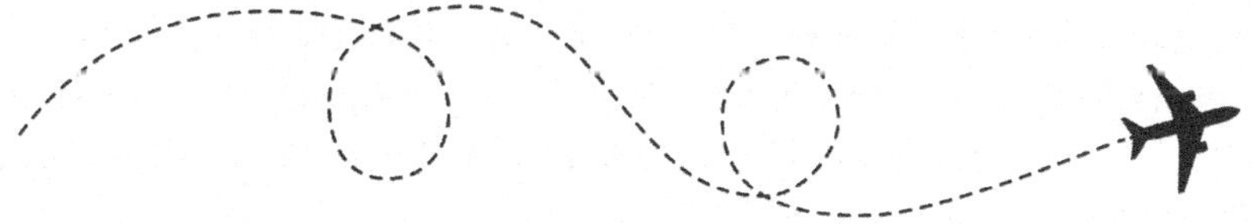

UAL492 requested "Direct echo-Oscar-sierra." (Neosho, Missouri.)

Tim Ballogg, rather busy at the time, replied, "November-Oscar."

The pilot, a quizzical note in his voice, asked, "November-Oscar? What's that?"

Said Tim, "That's NO!"

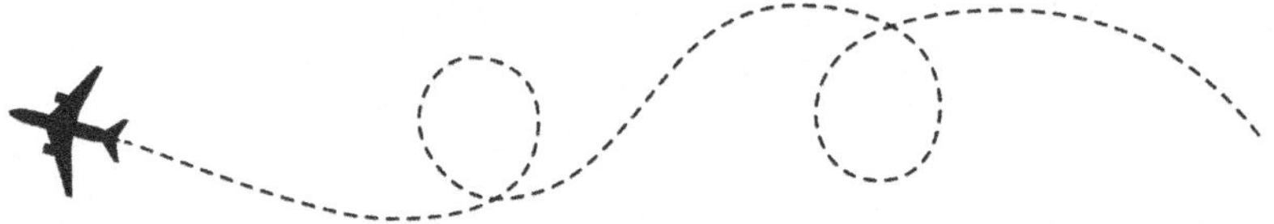

A few minutes later Tim gave N196TB, at 370 landing OKC, a PD descent to FL240.

The pilot: "Is that at our discretion?"

Tim: "Affirmative."

The pilot: "OK, our discretion. We'll start down now."

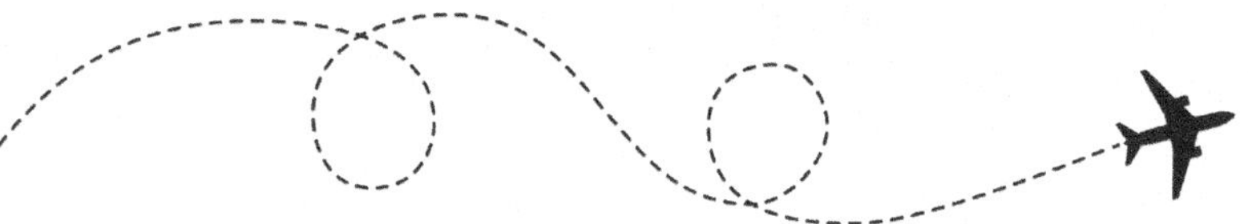

He isn't the only controller ever to deal with this type of pilot idiosyncrasy. Jimmy Gerard was working a Braniff DFW to TUL at FL250 that complained of moderate turbulence at the altitude and requesting FL210. Jim quickly did all the necessary coordination to get him down, then assigned the Braniff FL210.

Braniff: "Is that at our discretion?" (Braniff pilots were notorious for asking that.)

Jim, who had had enough of Braniff and their requests for discretionary descent, said, "YOU complained of turbulence; YOU wanted a lower. I gave YOU 2-1-0 and now YOU want pilot's discretion."

"Sorry," said the rueful voice, "it was force of habit."

I worked Air Force One (A1) today. The president was going from the ranch in Crawford to somewhere in Ohio for a speech. Since the ranch is down this way and he has to use ATC services to get to wherever he is going, we work him. I used to think it was a pretty big deal but it isn't all it's cracked up to be. You have to be pretty careful, that's for sure. There are all sorts of supervisors and managers standing around when the plane is in the airspace.

About 20 years ago (gee, was it really that long?) I was working Air Force Two (A2) (with then Vice President George Bush the first on board) into Oklahoma City when I HAD TO turn him for traffic. It was either turn A2 or turn a whole bunch of air carriers so I turned A2. The pilot almost refused the turn, saying he had to get to Oklahoma City. I wanted to tell him I was turning him so I could get him to Oke City in one piece (l wanted to say that but of course I didn't). When I wouldn't turn him back the pilot all but shouted, "Don't you know we have Vice President Mondale on board?!"

I wanted to ask him if the radios were on back in the passenger compartment because if VP Bush heard the reference to Mondale, the pilot would probably be flying KC-135s before too long.

As for Air Force One, a few years ago an F-15 at A1's altitude was turned for A1. The F-15 came back with the comment that he was tired of being turned for other airplanes and he was going to stay on the heading he was; ATC had better turn the other airplane. The controller said words to the effect, "Eagle one-five, roger . . . Air Force One, turn 30 degrees right for traffic. There's an F-15 out here that won't turn for you so you have to turn for him."

A1 came back with, "Roger, thirty right for traffic. Get the F-15 pilot's name, unit, and base. "

When a strip on Air Force One prints, shows "A1" as the aircraft identifier. Some years ago, a strip printed showing "A1" and a new assistant said (seriously), "Look, A1 Steak Sauce company has its own airplane."

ATC Tales 125

This morning I worked Ardmore-low all morning, darn near until noon. It was busy to the point where three times I needed a D-side which, for Ardmore-low, is extremely rare. Someone said it was just me but I have a feeling it was really all the military flying out of Sheppard. I guess they are making up for the last few days in this past fiscal year when they couldn't fly. They made up for it today.

There was a rather intense moment on Ardmore-high with Dwan Stregles on the R-side and Sonia Bustamonte on the D-. The sector was very busy, airplanes everywhere with a B-52 coming from the east at FL240 and its tanker coming from the west in a block of FL240B260 to meet him. Dwan got distracted elsewhere and climbed a Delta MD-80 to FL310, well in front of the B-52 but right in front of the tanker.

When conflict alert went off the Delta was out of FL233, turning northwest over Ardmore into the face of the tanker. Dwan's first transmission after the flashing started was to turn the Delta 90 degrees right "for traffic". The 90-degree turn was a clear sign to the pilot that he had better turn in a hurry and turn he did.

A 30-degree turn is about as much as you normally give an airplane, albeit for traffic or whatever reason it might be. A 90-degree turn is an indication that all is not right in the aviation world and the Delta pilot figured that out right away. It means there is an imminent situation developing and it ain't gonna be good for anybody, especially those folks in the airplane. Pilots figure that since they are sitting up front in the seats with the best view, they are going to see what's gonna happen first and a turn like that, 90 degrees, always means something bad.

It is at times like this that all sorts of things seem to happen at once, all over the control room, yet no matter what happens you start hearing both everything on your sector and also the transmissions of the affected sector, in this case Dwan's on Ardmore-high. When Dwan said, "turn 90 degrees right for traffic," the room grew deathly still, all hands waiting for the transmissions over the next two minutes. By then it would be over, one way or another, and everyone would know what had happened.

Sonia, leaning over from the D-side to see the flat-panel scope, told Dwan to ask what altitude the tanker was at, FL250 he said, and assign him that altitude, and stop the Delta at 240. Dwan, whose mind was running along these same lines, did just that, putting a hard altitude in the tanker's data block to show him level, stopped the Delta at 240 and the day was saved.

It was all over in a minute, maybe less, a welling-up of aviation horror and ATC nightmares that was gone just as quick. Separation was maintained and, in the long run, the only real inconvenience was the Delta being turned out of his route to Denver. Later I asked Dwan if he had used the word, "immediately."

"I didn't have to," he said. "The pilot could tell by the quaver in my voice what he needed to do." He was right. All in all though, it was another good day at the office; no paperwork.

I had a little shock at work today, a pilot actually volunteering to be #2 (of two) in the sequence to DFW. CHQ6459 off OKC to DFW was 12 miles ahead of an American in high, far enough in front to be number one if he leveled off at 16,000 and got his speed up. I gave him his options, speed up and number one, or slow to 250 knots, take a vector out to the east and be number two. To my surprise he opted to slow and take the vector. What a shock! He said they had gotten off OKC a bit early and were going to be early for their DFW gate time and he might as well take the delay en route (probably so he could blame ATC for the delay).

I've seen something like this once before when an Ozark DC-9 (shows you how long ago that was) DFW to STL requested a 360 en route so the cabin crew would have time to finish the meal service. What a shock that was.

ATC Tales 126

I had ADM-low a couple days ago. I took a handoff on a T-38 RTB to Sheppard AFB out of the Washita area when OKC-low took it back, calling to say that the T-38 had an emergency and had to divert to Fort Sill because it was the nearest suitable airport to the Washita area.

"Suitable" is the operative word here because there has been a time or two when it should have been considered . . . Buddy Davis was working Mcalester-low one afternoon when an F-4 out of Shaw AFB (SSC) inbound to Tinker AFB (TIK) advised Buddy that he was running out of gas. The F-4 was maybe 100 miles east of Tinker and wasn't going to make it. Was there a suitable airport around at which the F-4 could land?

Buddy hit the "emergency airport" button on the scope and there, 35 miles or so west of the F-4, was Seminole, Oklahoma. Checking the listed information on the pull-up screen, Buddy told the pilot that the airport had a hard-surfaced runway, 4,500 feet long. Would that do?

Yes it would, said the pilot and he made preparations to land. As the aircraft turned onto a long final Buddy, who had been checking for any more information he could impart, realized there was a problem and told the pilot that he had misread the information, that he had mistaken the airport identifier (H45) for runway information and that the runway was only 3,000 feet long.

Now just a couple miles out the pilot said something to the effect of, "Too late now," and proceeded to land, using every foot of available runway and then running through the chain link fence at the end, heading into a parking lot. Fortunately the aircraft had slowed to the point that the fence made an excellent "barrier" for a barrier-landing.

As matters developed, the pilot was found to be at fault, having departed SSC with insufficient fuel to make TIK. If I'm not mistaken, he was boarded out of the Air Force.

AAL2336 checked onto Frisco-to, climbing out of DFW . . .

AAL2336: "Fort Worth Center, American 2336 with you, hauling ass to 1-7-thousand."

PM: "Say again?"

AAL: "We're out of twelve and a half for 1-7-thousand."

One Christmas Eve morning some years ago I was setting up the sector to work it with a handset, putting the receivers up in the speaker, so I asked an air carrier for a short count.

He answered: "Eenie-meenie mynie-mo, how do you hear my radio?"

Knowing there had to be one, I was still at a loss for the proper response, but all was not lost. Chris Boswell, an ATA who had, at one time, been an army air traffic controller, said, "Quick, tell him . . ." and I did:

Mac: "Fee-fye fo-fum; loud and clear with a little hum."

John Davis was working Dallas-high on a chop-filled day and was getting the usual "Any ride reports?" "How's the ride?" and "Do you have any good altitudes?" Everyone wanted to know everything about the rides and since there were no good altitudes that day, John made it clear to each and every pilot.

There was, however, one pilot, who asked about the rides when he checked on and then didn't say much afterwards though he had ample opportunity to hear every other question about the rides. Then, after being on the frequency for quite a while, asked John, "When will the rides get smooth?"

That was it for John. Now he wanted to give this pilot the chop but he kept his wits about him, merely saying, in as deadpan a tone as he could muster, "Your ride will become smooth when you get out of the chop."

ATC Tales 127

A so-so day at work. There is a bit of a stir going around out there. Turns out there is a fellow who, seven or eight years ago, was sitting on a chair when the back broke and he toppled out of it backwards, hitting the floor behind him at a rather awkward angle and, after a while, going out on a 75 percent disability because of an injured back. With me so far?

Eventually he returns to work, five or six years later, giving up the disability and coming back into the FAA fold, as it were, becoming one of us again, throwing himself into the fray. You get the drift.

Then the Justice Department got involved. Turns out he was working a good deal of the time he was out on a "total" disability. Not only was he working but he was flying, first as an instructor and later as a charter pilot for some air-taxi company. The reason this is so important is because, in order to go out on an FAA disability, he had to prove to the administrative law judge, seven or eight years ago, that he could not hold a 2nd class medical certificate (as controllers are supposed to do in order to keep their ticket). The rub here is, in order to fly charter aircraft, he had to have a 1st class medical, a step up from the one he swore to the judge that he could not hold due to an injured back.

He was investigated by the feds and brought to trial. Last week he was found guilty and consequently, being a convicted felon, his security clearance was immediately pulled. In a week or two he is supposed to be sentenced. He faces ten or more years in a federal prison and a fine of somewhere in the neighborhood of a million dollars. Wow. I'll be curious to see what happens to him.

Sometimes I wonder why people do stupid stuff like this guy, trying to get away with something, trying to get something for nothing. I can't believe there are a lot of people like that. This guy was supposed to be smart; I thought he was, but evidently he wasn't smart enough. I've done some pretty stupid stuff in my time but I haul up short when it comes to anything like trying to defraud the government. I know it happens all the time, big corporations and bigger fish than this guy, but the feds always seem to catch the little guy like this one. The big ones have big name lawyers to fight for them and they have corporations they can hide in or behind. This guy was hiding behind his own stupidity and evidently it wasn't a very good cover.

[Postscript: He was "fingered" by an irate female with whom he had been living AND wouldn't marry. She wanted to; he didn't. Further, because a convicted felon cannot receive a federal pension if he has been convicted of defrauding the government, this individual, fearing a guilty verdict, retired from federal service the day before the jury returned its verdict, thus enabling him to receive his retirement.]

A couple days ago Dallas-high got pretty busy and in the middle of it all there came a KLM from Amsterdam to Houston at FL350. The KLM was wired with a Continental (COA) out of Houston to Denver, also at FL350. Since KLM was landing much earlier than the COA, the controller dumped the KLM to FL330, the minimum required separation between aircraft at 350 and 330.

When such a clearance is issued, the controller expects a fairly quick response and a descent to start pretty quick. In this case there was no response and no descent, a very disturbing fact because, in this particular case, things were already tight when the clearance was issued.

There is a point after such a clearance is issued and the no response following, that you have to do something else—and in a hurry. If one aircraft doesn't answer you go to the one that will. The problem here was that, while the KLM had a "lane" in which to descend to 330, the COA did not. There were two other aircraft already at 330 near the COA so what to do?

From time-to-time you will hear a controller say, usually as an aside, "there's nothing a 90 degree can't take care of." Well, the COA didn't get 90 degrees but did wind up turning 50 or so, enough to make him he realize that there was a serious situation afoot and he was not only part of it but he was the solution as well.

After the dust settled and the smoke cleared (and no alarm bells went off), all hands sat around telling similar stories of "NORDO" (no radio/radio failure) aircraft. At Fort Smith one time Matt McCorey cleared a Cherokee into position for takeoff on the active runway, then cleared an inbound Convair to land.

That is legal because the way it works is that you clear the aircraft on the runway for takeoff and he heads down the runway, lifting off before the inbound touches down. The problem arose when both aircraft went NORDO. Now the Convair was inbound, aiming to touch down right where the Cherokee was waiting for a clearance to take off, both facing into a setting sun.

Matt tried hitting them both with light signals from the tower but nothing worked. The Convair finally saw the Cherokee and went around on his own, irately calling the tower and chewing out Matt. Matt took it all in stride, telling that pilot and the Cherokee pilot, who came up when he saw the Convair flash by overhead, that they had both been NORDO and they should pay more attention to their radios, especially in such a critical environment.

Speaking of Matt, as a lad he attended a Catholic school. In the 7th grade he had an instructor named Sister Regina Cecilia who did not like him in any way, shape, form or fashion. They did not get along from the word go.

Every morning the class would stand for the day's opening prayer. After the opening part of the prayer, each student would say aloud something that he wanted the class to pray for. Matt, who had had it up to here with the Sister, said, when his turn came, "I pray that Sister Regina Cecilia will die and go to Heaven so I can get out of this hell."

Matt said, "I lost my paper route over that one." I'd say he lost some padding from the paddling, too.

ATC Tales 128

People keep telling me I'm going to miss that place when I retire (in 292 days) but I don't think so. The people, yes (some of them) but talking to airplanes? Nah.

The people out there are an interesting group. They came from and some still participate in various walks of life. There's one fellow out there who was an undertaker. He eventually enlisted in the Air Force where he was an air traffic controller for four years, after which he came to work for the FAA. He was a controller for a while but is now a paper-pusher and a Hawker pilot on the side. It was while stationed at Mather AFB, California, that he worked a fighter with the callsign FAGOT44.

"How did you get that callsign?" Don inquired.

"I ran over the base commander's dog," came the laconic reply.

Then there is Bob Kuhnen. He and another fellow run their own home construction business—and it must be a booming business, too, because they are backed up for quite some time.

There are teachers and car salesmen and former policemen . . . and several policemen who are still pulling reserve duty with various departments around the area. We even had one fellow who, until his retirement a couple months ago, worked one day a week as a paid officer for the Watauga City Police.

There are quite a few pilots, mostly former pilots, out there. When Braniff collapsed umpty-ump years ago some of those people worked their way into the ATC system and some of them are still there, in one way or another.

The people working out here vary greatly. Some are neat as ninepins and some are as dirty as the day is long. Some are just "there" and some make their presence felt just by walking in a room. One of the "just there" types is a fellow named

Paul Bradford. He was a controller in Indianapolis Center before transferring here in 1982. He is a quiet person who usually keeps to himself when he's at work. That's why all hands were surprised to hear of his recent encounter with, first, an American Airlines' pilot and secondly, the Homeland Security Department in Las Vegas.

Paul and his wife (who happens to be a Methodist pastor at a small church southwest of Fort Worth) were heading to Las Vegas for a weekend visit. The plane was delayed four hours and, as you might imagine, no one was any too happy about it. Paul inquired as to the cause of the delay and was told by an unhappy flight attendant that they were waiting for plates to put in the galley.

Paul, knowing that he and the other coach class ticket holders were not getting a meal, on a plate or otherwise, said as much to the flight attendant and was told that the plates weren't for the hundred or so people in the back but were for the six people in first class. This did not make Paul happy.

Once again he flagged the flight attendant down, this time saying that he was with the FAA, briefly flashing his badge as he did so, said that he wanted the captain's name. Paul'is intention, he said later, was to get the captain's name for a letter to American about the inordinate delay.

The flight attendant, now flustered because she was talking to, she thought, some bigwig Important FAA official, marched right up front and so informed the captain.

The captain, probably like every other airline captain I ever met, (about the only thing that daunts these guys is the cable repairman), sent the woman back for Paul's badge which Paul (not too happily) surrendered. It was not returned to him until after the plane landed and then by the Las Vegas Airport Police.

The pilot, while still in the air, called American dispatch about the incident. They called the Center to verify he worked there and then the FAA regional officer to report it as well. Then

American called ahead to ask the police to meet the plane, which they did.

The plane was met by the police and a group of people from the Homeland Security Department, all of whom escorted Paul and his wife off the plane, taking them down into the bowels of the Las Vegas Airport. He was given a talking-to by the police, then asked his side of the story, which he quickly spilled like a can of beans. They realized it was all overblown and gave him a warning about "interfering with a flight crew" and sent them on their way. Since then the rumors have been flying and we are all waiting to Paul give us the straight skinny when he returns.

Several good lessons here, for all hands. Paul never should have said he was with the FAA. He should not have asked for the captain's name, for two reasons, the first being that it is unnecessary. In a case like this, the captain has no say over a gate delay. Dispatch or the gate agent gives the captain a go-no go and the captain, knowing he won't be blamed for the delay, sits there—and so does everybody else. Secondly, any complaint to an airline should state the date and flight number. They can figure out who was flying that day.

I think the captain overreacted, too. He could have ascertained the facts and then had American write a letter to the FAA. Paul would get in trouble either way, probably more so that way. I think he wanted to teach Paul a lesson and he did, the biggest one being to avoid that airline in the future.

I'll be curious to see what happens.

ATC Tales 129

There is a notice on the Ardmore-low NOTAM board saying, "Runway numbers at the Sulphur, OK, airport (F30) are painted on the wrong ends." The city of Sulphur had the runway closed for a month to resurface and repaint the "17/35" runway, then painted "17" on the south end and "35" on the north end. Probably made sense to the guy doing the painting. Sure didn't make sense to the first pilot landing south, seeing the big "35" as he was landing south.

PE got a bit of shock on Ardmore-hi when an air carrier made a left turn at Ardmore into the face of a DFW inbound, instead of going straight ahead to PER, as he thought the aircraft would do. After resolving the situation, he breathed a huge sigh of relief and said, "Gee, I scared myself on that one!"

From across the room Larry Stafford deadpanned, "That's good, Dean, 'cause usually you don't even see 'em!"

Eric Parker was at Dulles Approach some years ago. There was an arrival procedure wherein inbounds came in at 7,000 but there was a "dump" altitude of 6,000 if it was necessary.

Just at shift change one day, with Eric's relief already plugged in for the briefing to let him go home, Eric had a CV-580 inbound with a faster Electra behind, catching up fast so he "dumped" the Convair to 6,000.

"Why do we have to descend?" complained the pilot.

Not realizing Eric's mike was keyed and it would go out, his relief muttered, "Because you're going to get an Electra up your ass if you don't."

"Out of seven for six," came the immediate response.

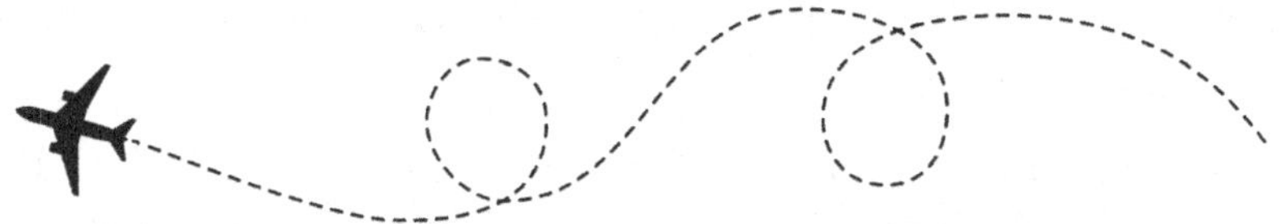

Sheppard RAPCON (SHP), an Air Force ATC training facility, called Mike Ross (RU) on the "4" line for a line check. The airman doing the line check needed a little checking himself.

SHP: "How do you hear me?"

RU: "Loud and clear. How do you hear me?"

SHP: "Loud and clear but otherwise weak and garbled."

Jim Williams (WE) worked a SWA off Midland to Love . . .

WE: "You play any golf while you were in Midland?"

SWA: "Too much snow."

WE: "Yeah, your balls would have to be orange."

SWA: "If you played in this weather, your balls WOULD have to be orange."

Jim let it go at that but on handoff to SPS-hi, told the Falls-hi controller about the conversation and told him to ask the SWA how his golf game was, which he did.

SWA: "Come on guys, please drop it. You're gonna get me in trouble."

ATC Tales 130

It has been an interesting couple of days. Bear with me a moment while I rehash this stuff and maybe we will all learn something from it . . .

I was sitting on Dallas-high, fat, dumb and happy (OK, I ain't fat anymore), when a Southwest Airlines 737, SWA1636, out of Oklahoma City to Houston, now about ten miles south of Dallas keyed his mike . . . I could tell it wasn't going to be good because there was a loud BONG BONG BONG BONG in the background before he even started talking. (That's always a clue that all is not well in the aeronautical world.)

He keyed his mike to announce, "Center, SWA1636, we need a lower IMMEDIATELY. We need to get below one-four-thousand immediately."

There are certain key words in the ATC lexicon that are not bandied about lightly and "immediately" is one of them. When THAT word is used, you (or the pilot, if he's saying it) needs to do something immediately, if not sooner, to avoid an "imminent" situation, meaning anything from a pending loss of separation to maybe loss of life.

I have used that word twice that I remember, maybe three times, all to avoid an imminent loss of separation. When a pilot uses that word, something is either about to happen or has happened, and in this case it had already happened.

"SWA1636, descend and maintain flight level 2-4-0," said I, already handing him off to Mike Ross on low altitude, calling the supervisor over and trying to explain to him while listening for the pilot's response.

"2-4-0. We need lower than that, below one-four-thousand," he said, in a very calm voice.

It was obvious what had happened, some sort of decompression and they needed to get the aircraft (and the passengers there within) down to an altitude with breathable air. 14,000 feet is breathable, at least for a while, and that would give everybody time to go on to the next step.

One mid-shift some years ago I had an American have an emergency decompression at 35,000 feet. He was just south of Tulsa heading to DFW when he announced, "Center, American 335, we're starting down." This was somewhat unusual because generally pilots get a clearance before they begin a descent and he didn't. "We'll get back to you in a minute," he said, and when he did, he told me what had happened.

Now there was another problem. There was an Air Force C-141 right below him at 20,000 feet that he was descending into.

"JEST74, turn left heading 0-9-0 . . . and make it a COMBAT turn!" He did, too.

I told the American to maintain 21,000 feet to stay above the C-141 and the pilot just laughed but added, "We can take vectors!"

"Roger, turn right heading 2-7-0, vectors for your descent." I had to issue the altitude to stay legal even though I knew the aircraft was coming down. The two missed by the required five miles but it wasn't much more, that's for sure.

One thing that has always amazed me about the emergency situations I have seen over the years, and I've seen a few in the 30 years I have worked out there, is how cool, calm, and collected all the pilots have been, even in the worst of times. I worked several crashes but one in particular stands out. The passengers screamed all the way down; the pilot? It was like he was giving scientific readings . . . We're out of ten-thousand descending . . . we've lost the engine . . . the left wing has been ripped off, etc. but he talked, fairly calmly, considering the dire circumstance, until the end.

ATC Tales 131

A few years ago a former army paratrooper was taking his first flight since World War ll.

This fellow had jumped into Normandy, Eindhoven and had a couple other combat jumps with the 82nd Airborne Division. Every time he had been on an airplane the army had given him a parachute and, he said, "I'm damn disappointed in Delta that they haven't issued me one."

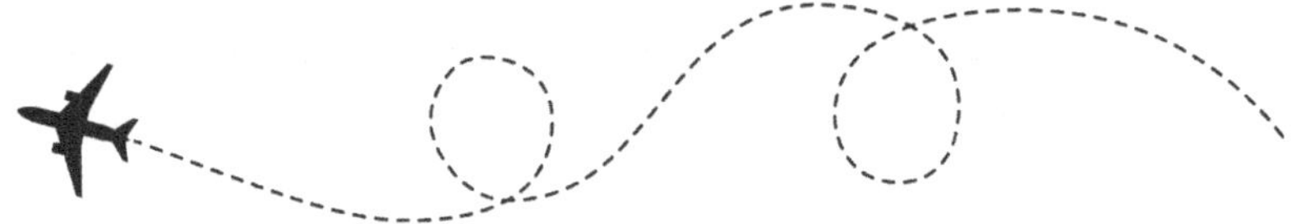

Pete Moss was working Waco-low when he got call from Addison (ADS) Tower:

ADS: "Are you working N550TL?"

PM: "Affirmative."

ADS: "Tell him he left a baby at the FBO."

PM: "Wilco."

A moment later:

PM: "N550TL, Fort Worth."

N550TL: "Go ahead."

PM: "Addison Tower just called with a message for you."

N550TL: "Go ahead."

PM: "Addison Tower called to say you left a baby at the FBO."

N550TL: "WE WHAT!?"

PM: "Tower called to say you left a baby at the counter."

There was a moment of silence and then:

N550TL: "I think we have everybody we're supposed to but let me check. "

A minute passed and then the pilot reported everyone present and accounted for, but they would call the FBO on a cellphone just to be sure. In the meantime, Tower called back to say the baby's mother had been found. She had brought the baby inside the air-conditioned building, placing it near a window and then stepped immediately outside the window, just on the other side of the glass for a smoke. All was well, fortunately.

ATC Tales 132

One fine day I found myself working Waco-lo R. It was about 1420, near enough time to power down after another fine day of air traffic control. Being the second-best controller in the building (Larry Foreman's the best, just ask him), I was ready for a short break and the walk to the parking lot.

About this time, the area manager, Jim Berm, came into all the specialty areas to say that the Saudi prince would be departing the Waco airport shortly, and he wanted NO female controllers to work him. (George W. Bush was president then and his Crawford, Texas, ranch was under our airspace. He was having the prince as a guest at his ranch.) The instructions, Jim said, came straight from the White House.

On Glen Rose, Mary Hokit was the supervisor. She started discussing this with the area manager, saying it was an illegal order, a stupid order, and she wouldn't comply with it.

In the meantime, on Frisco, a similar discussion was going on. Hearing the discussion, I got a female controller, I think Jenny Boyd, to relieve me and we got a female in on the D-side as well. In the course of the briefing, I called the Houston Center sectors south of us to tell them of the request and what we were doing. They said they would do the same.

Back on Glen Rose, Mary and Jim were pretty heated in their discussion. At one time she had been his trainee and later a friend, but after this day, she said later, she never spoke to him again.

ATC Tales 133

The Talkathon

April 18th, a great day in American aviation history. Jimmy Doolittle bombed Tokyo on this day in 1942. Many years later, on this day, I nearly bombed the west side of Fort Worth's Meacham Airport, doing minor damage to the airport, the airplane, and my pride.

I knew a couple, the wife of which was English. The husband, while American, was not exactly a credit to the species and was, in fact, hated by his mother-in-law, Marie, who just happened to be over here on a visit. I had asked her if she wanted to go out for lunch and then perhaps take a ride around the friendly skies of Fort Worth, seeing the sights from a different perspective, the bird's eye view, as it were.

Bob, the husband, is as lazy as the day is long and Marie sorely resented the fact that Ann, her daughter and Bob's wife, waited on him hand and foot. Marie took every opportunity to vent her fury and frustration reference Bob and this day was no exception. We had a nice lunch during which she talked about Bob non-stop. She seemed to have never repeated herself, telling everything she knew about him and probably making up some stuff as well. She carried on and on about him as we drove to the Parker County Airport (WEA) in Weatherford, where I rented a Cessna 150, N26J, a high-time C150 that had seen better days.

By this time in my short and somewhat checkered flying career, I had perhaps 85 hours of actual flying time. This included 40 hours of instruction, so you can tell I was still very much the novice. I really loved flying, enjoying it for the sheer pleasure of flight, if nothing else, but I was still new enough to the game where I needed to pay close attention to what I was doing, avoiding, and in this case, ignoring the non-stop talking machine in the right seat.

The pre-flight was hindered by Marie walking right behind me, talking away about Bob, telling me how he couldn't hang his clothes up, how he couldn't reach across the table for his cigarettes but instead had to have them handed to him. Sitting inside the airplane before engine start, I really had to concentrate on the pre-start procedures and did manage to tune her out, partially, but not for long.

By this time, she had gone on to other areas of his character. Even over the roar of the engine (and if you've ever flown a high-time C150, you know what I mean by the roar of the engine), I could hear her incessant drone. She was still on Bob. If ears truly burn when someone's talking about them, his must have roasted off that day.

I had hoped that the noise would have kept her quiet, but she seemed to double her effort to make herself heard. We took off north, a straight-ahead departure out of the pattern, and eventually a right-hand turn toward Fort Worth. I had to make several calls on the radio, turning up the speaker to hear. That didn't faze Marie at all. On and on she went, sitting sideways in the seat, as much as she could with her seatbelt on, gabbing away. I felt compelled to look in her direction from time-to-time as though that would placate her. I suppose it only encouraged her because her voice, now nearly a shout to be heard over the engine and the speaker, raised higher still.

Carswell AFB tower gave us clearance through their airport traffic area and soon we were over Fort Worth, seeing what was to be seen. We looked at my house, their house, and everything else. Marie talked on and on, continuing even when I started circling over Ann's house. The only time she came close to shutting up was when I banked the airplane sharply to the right, standing the airplane up on its right wing, and shouted at her to look at Ann's house 1,000 feet below. She glanced to her right, gave an involuntary sharp intake of breath as she caught sight of the ground, "Just outside the window," she said, as she quickly looked back at me. I realized then that she had never made the connection between going up in an airplane and actually being above the ground. I don't know what she thought we'd be doing but it wasn't exactly what she had in mind before we took off.

Seeing the ground, "It was so close to the plane," she said later, made her double her efforts not to think about her fear of her heights, and she concentrated all her efforts thereafter on really running down her son-in-law.

After the swing around Ann's house, I asked her if she wanted to shoot a touch-and-go at Meacham. I don't think she had a clue as to what I was shouting about so I headed over that way. Calling Meacham Tower, I requested a straight-in approach for a touch-and-go on 34L, figuring I'd shoot just the one and then go back to Weatherford.

All this time Marie had been talking away, never asking for a reply, a response or even an acknowledgement to her incessant droning. What caused her, just as the critical moment appeared, to change her style, her modus operandi, is beyond me. I lined up on the runway, pulled the carb heat, cut the throttle, dropped 10 degrees of flaps, and began settling in for a routine touch-and-go, Played with the trim wheel a moment, yes, that's it, perfect. It was all so easy, I thought, the perfect touch-and-go. This was what, excluding the yammering from the right seat, this was what flying was all about, runway banging on a beautiful afternoon. It was sunny but cool, no wind to speak of, the kind of day pilots look at the sky and say, "I wish I were up there!"

I'm not sure where things started going wrong. At some time in our descent toward Mother Earth, Mama Concrete, the runway numbers, Marie made a particularly salient point and, for emphasis, hit my right arm in a downward sweep and then began shaking it for emphasis.

We were about ten feet above the ground and I was in the process of jockeying the throttle one last time. I've always been a bit heavy-handed in that respect.

All of a sudden, we were at full power, nose down and headed for the numbers. "34L" was filling the whole windshield. I yanked back on the yoke, cut the throttle, and bounced hard, once and then again. This didn't faze Marie at all. "Well," she demanded, "what do you think?"

I thought we might make it but I didn't have time to tell her that. We were headed northeast now. Somehow, with her shaking my arm, we had changed direction, taking a right turn in the first 150 feet of the threshold, and now the fun began. I had slammed the carb heat lever sometime between the first and second bounce and had hit the flaps as well. They were coming up but that also meant the nose was coming down. Some nose-up trim in but not enough. A C150s prop makes a great lawnmower and that's what 26Juliet would have become had the grass been much higher.

We were off the runway now, off 34L, but not off the ground. And we were now headed for Runway 09-27, the east-west runway, crossing it in short order. An animal popped out of the ground ahead of us and took a look around. "Run! Get out of the way," I shouted at it, but it stood there, immobilized, transfixed, paralyzed, at the sight of 26 Juliet, the world's oldest C150, screaming down on it at full power.

I pulled back on the yoke to get the nose up and the prop out of the grass. Pushing the throttle in for full power, I hit the flaps, 10 degrees, needing lift more than speed. The little animal ahead of us had disappeared, replaced by runway lights zipping by, a foot off the left tire. Hitting one would not have been good. 26Juliet seemed intent on settling down just as I was determined to get us airborne.

As we settled down, I started cranking in in more nose-up trim. Somehow, we seemed a bit lighter and I began to feel we had a chance of doing something more at the end of our flight than crawling out of the wreckage. Back on the yoke a bit more and we were flying! The wheels were off the ground and the plane was out of the grass. We weren't assured a safe flight back just yet, but our odds were improving ever so slightly.

More concrete appeared outside the window. We had crossed a grass area and were now in flight, barely above the north end of the taxiway for runway 16R. Talk about taking the long way around! It wasn't over yet but almost. We were now five or six feet up and the power was coming up ever so gradually. 34R, off our right wing, was Meacham's main runway and it was very active, airplanes landing and taking off, and that was where we were headed now.

I dropped the left wing ever so slightly, adding just a touch of rudder, edging my way back over toward the western side of the airport. There's a small gully just north of 34L and when we passed it, now 50 feet up, I began to see I might next see my three kids in some place other than a hospital.

Marie? I don't think she ever stopped talking. She hadn't looked outside the window once since we flew over Ann's house and she hadn't now, I'm sure. I don't know what she made of my series of frantic actions to get us up, up and away. From the time she hit my arm to when we passed the gully, I hadn't heard one word, tuning her out completely. Given the choice though, of listening to her or what had happened, I think I'd have settled for her talking.

The tower asked if everything was all right and I replied in the affirmative. "Do you want to try one more?" the controller asked, the wry touch of irony in his voice his only comment on my ordeal. "Negative," I responded, as cool, calm, and collected as I could force myself to be. "I'd like a west departure and we'll head back to Weatherford."

The rest of the flight was uneventful. Carswell Tower let us fly straight through their area and back to Weatherford we went. I had learned one thing, however, and as we approached the pattern altitude at Parker County Airport, I turned to Marie, still blubbering happily away, I told her that until we got on the ground, silence would reign supreme. The loud "roar of the engine" never sounded so serene as it did those final few minutes of flight.

ATC Tales 134

A controller on DAL-hi asked a COA, "How's the ride?

COA: It feels a bit jiggly up here.

Another COA on frequency asked, "What's this 'jiggly'? I don't see jiggly in my dictionary of aeronautical terms."

The first COA said: I said it feels jiggly up here . . . I've never seen it up here but now I feel it up here.

A 7-3 shift today, wet, rainy, gray, no wind at the surface but a lot of it up there in the sky. Chad Etheridge summed it up this morning when he said, "I hate choppy days." I hate 'em, too, 'cause every pilot asks the same question: "How're the rides?" You tell 'em, "Light to moderate chop at all altitudes," sometimes stressing the "ALL." That response enters one ear and departs the other 'cause invariably their next question is, "Any smooth altitudes?" There aren't any, sometimes, but that doesn't faze them either, because they'll get to their assigned altitudes and start the same litany again.

Every once in a while you'll ask a pilot, "How's your ride?" You get some stock answers and some innovative answers. A TWA replied, "Except for the lumpy seat, it's OK." This morning a Southwest out of Oklahoma City to Houston asked, "Any smooth altitudes to Houston?" Pete Moss said, "The only way you'll get a smooth ride to Houston is to take the bus." An American pilot, in response to the "How's your ride" question, replied, "As smooth as the thighs of a high school cheerleader."

How does he know about that, I wondered.

Chop, turbulence, it's a real pain in the teeth 'cause airplanes are changing altitudes, requesting reroutes to avoid the stuff (if, by chance, they even know it's there) and there are the incessant questions.

Pirep [pilot report] that was received on ADM-lo.

262121 ZFW0 CWA 00 PIREP FROM 40NW ADM TBM7 RPTD SEV TURB AND ICING AT FL220 AT 2109Z . . . FLIPPED ACFT THEN RECOVERED, DROPPED 5000 FT IN 3 SEC . . .

What a ride!

Some years ago on ADM-lo Tony Brescia had a C177 from DAL to OKC. When the airplane checked on freq he suggested the pilot consider going over MLC first, then OKC, due to the moderate to severe turbulence near ADM.

The pilot asked if Tony was clearing him that way. Tony said he wasn't but thought it the best and safest way to go, considering the bad weather in the area. The pilot told Tony that he, not Tony, was the pilot-in-command and that he, not Tony, would determine the route of flight. Furthermore, he was going over ADM.

Just north of ADM Tony started trying to get a pilot report but the pilot wouldn't answer any of Tony's repeated calls; he just kept going north to OKC. Finally, just north of Pauls Valley he answered. When Tony asked him about his ride, he responded that he should have followed Tony's advice, that it was all he could do to maintain control and that the seats had been shaken loose from the floor of the airplane. Another convert to the wisdom of ATC.

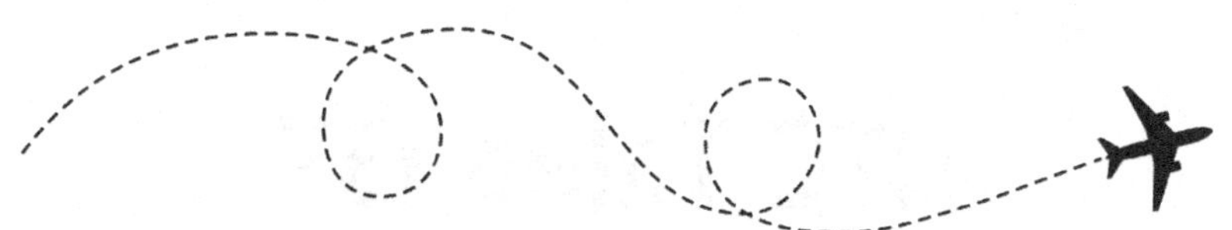

With lots of bad weather in the area, Mike Ross, Sr., asked a SWA pilot if he'd recommend the north route out of Austin to DAL to anyone else. "Not unless he has suicidal tendencies," came the reply.

ATC Tales 135

Pete Moss worked a VFR C152, N124SA, female pilot, foreign accent, 10 north of ADM to OUN (Norman), looking for advisories.

N124SA: "We are requesting VFR flight following to O'U'N."

FW: "Say type aircraft."

N124SA: "We are November 1-2-4 Sierra Alpha."

FW: "What kind of airplane are you flying?"

N124SA: "A Cessna 152."

FW: "Say position."

N124SA: "We're over Milo."

FW: "Where's Milo?"

N124SA: "Oklahoma."

Pete was laughing so hard he had to delay answering for a moment, then gave her a squawk and carried on. Not the sharpest knife in the drawer.

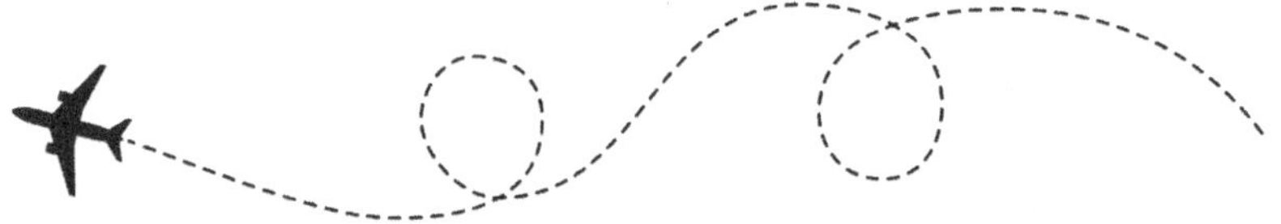

Let me tell you a little story . . .

When I hired on with the FAA in 1974, we went through a class in the training department about copying flight plans. Someday, we were told, the interphone would ring, we would answer it and the voice at the other end would say, "Copy one." When you'd say, "Go ahead," the voice would say, "Oscar, November, Echo," and then he would hang up.

A few weeks later I was manning the interphone, the phone

rings and, on me answering it, the guy says, "Copy one." I said, "Yeah, right. Oscar, November, Echo," and I slammed the phone down.

The phone rang back immediately, the man, now irate, shouted, "This is Houston Center. Our computer's flopped and I'm trying to give you a flight plan. If you do that again I'm gonna reach right through this phone and punch you in the mouth!"

Some people have no sense of humor, so I took that call.

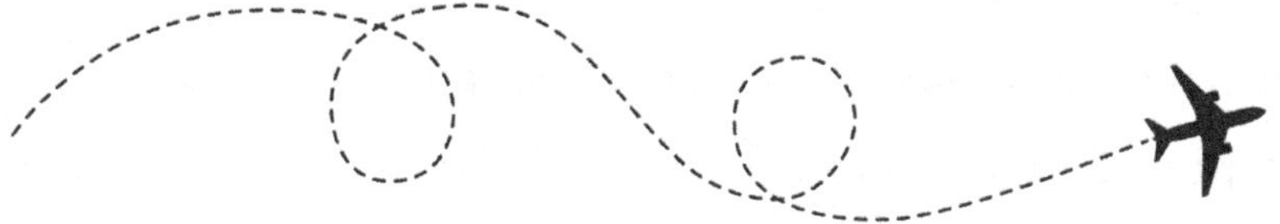

Good day at work. Pretty slow most of the time but busy enough at times. I worked out a Citation, a "Nearjet," as one Learjet pilot called it . . . "The Learjet has the Nearjet in sight." This Citation got in the way of half a dozen air carriers while he climbed on up to altitude. But he was going higher than most of them so I let him go and stepped the air carriers under him. One American Fokker, one of those slowed by the Citation, started complaining about the Nearjet's poor performance.

The Fokker is notoriously slow, a dog's dog. For air carrier jet aircraft, they don't climb well, they don't go fast, they don't do much except go from point A to point B just fast enough to warrant American keeping them in service. This guy moaned and groaned for a minute or two, then allowed as how he, being in a Fokker, really wasn't one to talk about another jet's poor performance.

The Air Force has a small primary jet trainer called the T'37. This jet does maybe 220 knots across the ground, 250 on a good day. One day I was trying to run one out in front of a Candler commuter (a prop) and it wasn't working too well. Finally I had to slow the Candler to get the T'37 out in front. Giving the Candler his traffic, he replied, "I have the sample jet in sight."

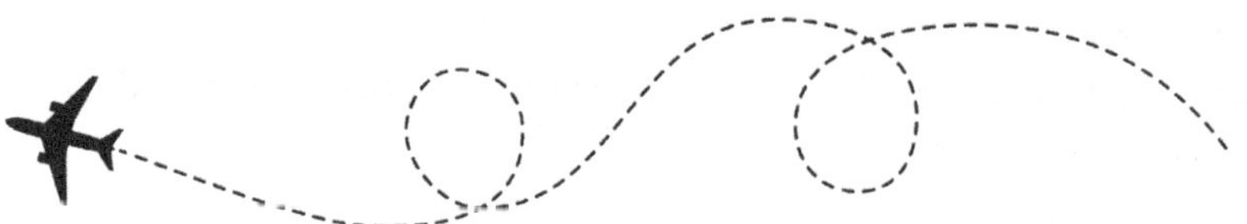

A flight attendant was on the red-eye to Manila when a water leak developed in the galley, which eventually soaked the carpet throughout the aft cabin of the 747. A very sleepy woman who had become aware of the dampness tugged at the skirt of the attendant as she passed by.

"Has it been raining?" she asked the flight attendant.

Keeping a straight face, she replied, "Yes, but we put the top up."

With a sigh of relief, the woman went back to sleep.

ATC Tales 136

Today there was an EGF821 and a CAA821 coming out at the same time, DFW to TUL, both requesting 170. Warned of the similar sounding callsigns, they started kidding each other about this, that and the other, all the way to the Red River. At one point the CAA started making his cabin announcement on the frequency only to be kidded by several other pilots.

"I used to be an Eagle pilot," said the Candler, explaining away his faux pas.

An American off Tulsa to DFW once did the same, only he didn't catch his error until almost finished. He wound up by saying, "Thanks for flying Continental!"

On the Center's computer generated strips there's a remarks section. Most remarks are innocuous but occasionally a good one shows up, like DUKE91, a flight of 2/T'38s: "1 SOB each acft."

Talk about a personality problem.

One time "No ice on board" appeared. Turned out it meant "no deicing equipment" but offhand you could say the passengers were really ticked when they started getting warm drinks.

And on a Kingair one day, the remarks showed "Violent prisoner on board." Bad news there.

Ardmore Tower called this afternoon . . . "Are you busy?" he asked. I wasn't and told him so. Tower continued . . . "Who's the airplane about ten north of here, up high?"

I thought he was talking about a Merlin over Ardmore VORTAC, 10 SW of the airport. No, he insisted, "The airplane's due north and I think it's a three-holer."

Quick-looking ADM-hi, sure enough there was a Tri-Star, DAL269, FL350, ATL to LAX, cruising westbound, and I told him so. "Sure does leave a pretty contrail," he said. adding that it was "wide and long and beautiful."

I called SPS-hi R who told the pilot. He must have been impressed 'cause he asked for a picture. Seems to me though, the ADM Tower controller had too much time on his hands.

One day on MLC-hi I was working a KC'10 tanker refueling a B-52 on AR112, FL290B310, southwest bound on the track. There was an arrival push on with several air carriers at 330 and 280, crossing over and under the refueling flight. I'd given traffic to every air carrier I could 'cause they give their passengers the information. One such passenger must have been impressed because he sent a note to the pilot saying the Air Force ought to put recruiting posters on the sides of the aircraft.

I passed the message along to the tanker whose reply was terse and to the point, "We do our best, sir."

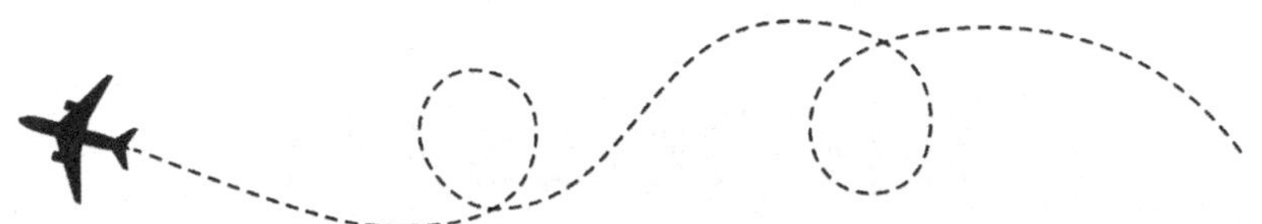

An eastbound F-15 at FL350 over Oklahoma City was approaching a westbound Tri-Star at FL330. Just before they passed, the F-15 started doing barrel rolls along the airway. The Tri-Star crew was impressed and asked that I tell the F'15 pilot as much, which I did.

"Just checking ground references, sir," came the reply.

ATC Tales 137

There was a little slip of a girl out at work last night, a mere wisp of a woman who was out there with her parents. She was a short, thin brunette who had a nice smile and teeth that looked like they been rented from a fashion magazine. She had her parents in tow, taking them out for the Center tour because she knew about the Center and they didn't. Now they do. Turned out this woman, this willow, is, get this, a captain for United Airlines. Based in Denver, she flies Boeing 727s around the highways and byways of the National Airspace System (sounds impressive, doesn't it?).

Appearances can be deceiving. She knew her stuff, that's for sure. We gave her the standard routine we give all pilots, be they United, American, Delta, whomever. She had the ability to relate, however, which made her a friend or two. Some visitors don't and consequently don't learn too much. Her parents seemed to enjoy it as much as she did.

Being a Center, we don't have as much interaction with pilots. You get a lot more contact with pilots in a tower or approach control. I've had some dealings with pilots over the years, most good, some not so good. When I was the new kid on the block, checked out on my first couple sectors (back when we were still using semaphore flags), I tried sequencing a couple airplanes to Tulsa using speed control, aircraft number two being an American DC'10 behind a Braniff BAC-111, something that even then was old and slow. Much slower than the DC-10.

The American pilot wasn't happy and let me know it. After he landed, he didn't go to the hotel, he didn't pass go, he went straight to a phone where he called the Center demanding to speak to my supervisor. He then chewed the supe out to the point where the supe finally called me up to the phone. The pilot, who was the captain of the aforementioned DC'10 then proceeded to chew me out better than a pit bull the mailman. By the time he finished I was clicking my heels and saluting faster than I ever did in three years in the army. I had been chewed so hard I felt like the dog's rubber bone but I'll tell you this, I understood the nuances and fine points of speed control and I've never forgotten the lesson, if for no other reason to avoid getting another call like that one.

I've been called in on once or twice besides that time though never for a tongue-lashing like that one. One winter's day some years ago I was working a whole string of airplanes into Stillwater, Oklahoma, four or five of them. They were icing up bad and needed to get down so I started running them into the Stillwater Airport, one after another.

After the whole lot of them were down, I got out the one departure, N4SQ, a twin Cessna that had been waiting the whole time to get out. He was not a happy camper, angrily demanding the Center phone number so he could call in. I gave him the number but at the same time asked if it was because he had been held on the ground so long. "Affirmative!" he all but shouted back.

I told him he was held on the ground because he was safe there while the four or five inbounds were all icing up and about to fall out of the sky. "I'd have done the same for you," I told him. That mollified him somewhat, enough, I suppose, to the point where he didn't call in.

Pilots are OK. One of my best friends is a pilot for American. I try to overlook that when we get together. He was a Navy pilot and on top of that he's an Aggie. Talk about "Three strikes and you're out!" Still, I overlook these deficiencies and consider his good points . . . well, let's just say he's a nice guy. He gives me a lot of insight into the pilot's mind and I actually learn from him (occasionally).

Most pilots are OK people though they vary from airline to airline, I suppose because they are required to adhere to some company policy. American pilots are pretty easy-going. They want direct from here to there and they want to go direct as soon as you can give it to them. The difference is that Southwest pilots want direct more than American.

Southwest pilots are pretty laid back, probably the most of all the major carriers we work in this area. Delta pilots seem to be a bit tense, a bit more on edge. They rarely ask for direct anywhere and if you offer it to them, they have to check the flight plan, check with the company, the president, the pope, and anybody else they can think of. It's because company policy requires them to stay on their flight plan and they do, that's for sure. But if you tell them direct is for traffic, they'll do it in a heartbeat.

ATC Tales 138

On rollout at Addison, N336LX called the tower saying, "There's a jackrabbit out here on rollout."

The tower controller, obviously a quick wit, never missed a beat. Came the reply, "Did you miss him by . . . a hare?"

Dave Asbell, a Frisco Specialty supervisor, came home recently to find his lovely wife Laura hopping mad. Turned out a Florist's delivery van pulled up to the house that afternoon and the driver exited the same carrying a great big bouquet of flowers. Happy and excited that Dave had sent her flowers (and beautiful ones, too), she opened the door even before the driver rang the bell . . . only to hear the fellow say, "These are for your neighbor. Would you mind taking them over later?"

Mike Copp, controller extraordinaire on Cedar Creek, is a dapper and dashing young (?) man who, at, let's say middle age, fancies himself to the suave and debonair type. Single, he works out at the local gym, keeping himself in pretty good shape for nights out with the ladies, etc., etc. (You get the picture.)

Recently Mike was at his gym, walking on a treadmill next to a young lovely he's had his eye on for a while. Finally he caught her eye. She asked, ever so sweetly, "Are you single?"

"Yes I am," he answered, visions of wonderful times ahead dancing in his mind.

"You'd be perfect for my mother," she told him.

What a letdown!

ATC Tales 139

Merv Newman was training Michelle Foster on MLC-lo-R. There was an Eagle Flight (EGF) on frequency who wasn't paying attention. Every once in a while he would key his mike and ask, "Was that call for me?"

Merv, tiring of the pilot's persistent query, keyed his mike as if he had done it inadvertently, and said, "You know, the other night I was at a bar with a buddy. There was some guy passed out on the floor down at the end of the bar, telling him, 'That's an Eagle Flight pilot passed out over there.'"

My friend asked, "How do you know?"

"'Cause every couple minutes he raises his head and says, 'Was that call for me.'"

A moment later the pilot said, "That couldn't've been an Eagle Flight pilot you saw. We don't make enough money to get drunk in a bar." But there were no more problems from the pilot.

ATC Tales 140

Ted Lawson had a deal today. He got so wrapped up in a very small problem that he forgot about separating airplanes—and consequently lost standard separation. He had some "help," as it were, but overall the responsibility—and lack of it—is his.

He was on Ardmore-high, having just taken the sector from Denise Hunds. Part of the relief briefing is to quickly go to DARC (a backup radar system) and back to the regular radar system (NAS). Denise went to DARC but did not switch back to NAS. Neither of them noticed that they were on DARC. Ted tried signing on in the computer, something you can do on NAS but not DARC, but couldn't do it. He called the supervisor over to find out why he couldn't do it and the supe called maintenance for the same reason.

In the meantime the two airplanes involved checked on and Ted climbed them both, not realizing that the trailing aircraft had a big overtake and a faster rate of climb than the lead aircraft.

There's an important tool controllers use to detect potential conflictions between two aircraft. It's called "conflict alert" and is a program in the ATC computer that gives a two-minute warning if it detects a potential loss of separation. Unfortunately for Ted, and all controllers, it works on NAS but does NOT work on DARC.

In this program, aircraft data blocks flash when the potential loss of separation is determined. It will continue to flash until the conflict is either resolved or manually disabled by the controller.

Maintenance showed fairly quick and immediately saw that Ted was on DARC, the backup system, and pointed it out to all hands. Maintenance types tend to like getting one over on controllers. They chuckle, they laugh, they guffaw, all of that, whenever a controller makes a stupid mistake—as Ted did this morning. But the laughing stopped quickly when Ted switched from DARC back to NAS where conflict alert WAS working. It was flashing when Ted flipped back and it kept flashing until Ted pried the two airplanes apart.

Standard separation is five miles and a thousand feet. These two got down to 4.2 miles and 800 feet, still far apart but a loss of standard separation nevertheless.

Should this have happened? No. Should Ted have been paying attention to signing on in the computer rather than separating airplanes? No. Signing on is necessary; separation is important: it's what we're paid to do.

There are varying degrees of system errors, minor, moderate, and major. Because he maintained more than 80% of the required separation, he was back at work within two hours. That's a far cry from the two to four weeks it used to be when someone had a system error.

Starting tomorrow various staff types will descend on the control room to investigate this system error, this loss of standard separation. The staff pukes will spend three to four weeks looking at various aspects of it and make their determination as to what happened and how ones like this can be avoided in the future.

What happened was that the controller screwed up. How can it be avoided? Two ways: 1) PAY ATTENTION and 2) get the conflict alert patch on DARC.

What will management say? 1) More controllers in the control room and 2) PAY ATTENTION.

I feel for Ted. I've been involved in some system errors and in no way, shape or form are they fun or enjoyable, any of that. Will he learn from this? Yes. Will he be a better controller?

Definitely. Will he feel lousy for the next few days? Yes, but as I told him this morning, this too shall pass.

ATC Tales 141

Dana Jones on Turkey-Hi was getting pretty busy when his frequencies started cutting out. With maintenance not coming up to fix them, he finally told his supervisor, "Look, I'm working a lot of airplanes. Not everybody's separated and I'm scared."

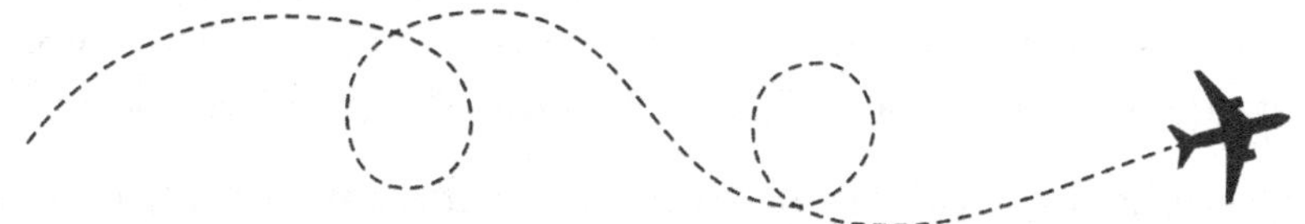

One night I had a Cohlmia over Mcalester at 10,000 feet and his transponder wasn't working. After running through my "transponder not working" bag of tricks, I gave up and the pilot as much. A few minutes later it came on so I asked him what had happened? The pilot replied that transponders always work better when the switch is in the Oscar-November (on) position.

After that, my first question to pilots with a non-operating transponder was, "Is your transponder on?"

N228: "Center, do you have another frequency we can use You have a stuck mike on this." Frequency.

PM: "N228, you're the only aircraft on this frequency."

Turns out the co-pilot had turned up the second radio, thus causing the interference.

ATC Tales 142

Real Close Air Support: In Case There Was Any Doubt: Marine Corps Close Air Support In Action . . . [from somewhere on the internet]

Recently, a Marine Corps Harrier squadron was invited to attend the annual Air Force Red Flag exercises at Nellis Air Force Base, NV. This is one of the USAF's big exercises, where they test combined arms employment of tactical air assets.

The USAF F-15 pilots showed up on the ramp with dozens of rear echelon airman types and tons of equipment such as Ground Power Units, Accessory Power Units, Hummers, Trucks, Air Conditioners, etc. The Marines appeared ready to operate in a combat environment and showed up with only their Harriers.

The Air Force commander commented to the Marine commander: "Where is all your support stuff? Geez, you guys really are just Grunts that know how to fly."

Not wanting to disappoint the Air Force commander, the Marine commander got an idea of his own. He talked to his 1st Sergeant and later that night, the 1st Sergeant had his Marines make bayonet studs fitted on with hose clamps. (There's a pitot tube sticking out of the nose of a Harrier.) In the hours of darkness, the 1st Sergeant had the clamp with the bayonet stud tightened onto the pitot tube of each Harrier.

The next morning, the Air Force pilots fell out on the ramp in front of their F-15s. The Marine pilots fell out on the other side of the ramp in front of their Harriers. Each Marine pilot had on his deuce gear with a bayonet in the scabbard. The USAF commander ordered his pilots to "Man your planes."

The USAF ground crews by the dozens scrambled to their trucks, APUs, GPUs, etc., and the pilots ran to their planes.

The Marine commander ordered his Marines to "Fix Bayonets," whereupon each pilot ran to the front of his Harrier and fixed his bayonet on the stud attached to the pitot tube.

The Marine commander then ordered "CHARGE," and the Marines jumped in their Harriers, busted airborne, and flew off. The Marine commander turned to the USAF commander and said, "This is what we Marines consider Close Air Support."

You've gotta love them!

Pete Moss: "SWA14, fly heading . . . uh, disregard."

SWA14: "It's what we do best."

A couple guys from work, Larry and Frank, went down to Cancun on Sun Country (SCX). Crafty little Sonia knew which flight they were on and asked the pilot to pass along a message to the "newlyweds," which he did, in the form of a cabin announcement.

"SCX502 welcomes aboard newlyweds Frank and Larry on their honeymoon!"

These guys are straight as arrows but they got some might strange looks from their fellow passengers.

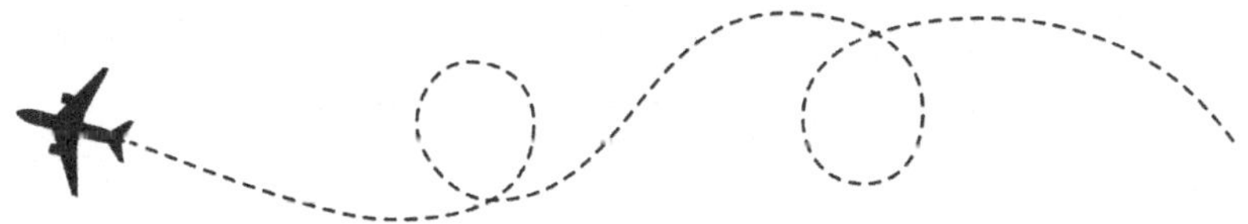

N369AC had just departed Ardmore . . . just after his initial call . . .

FW: "N369AC, say position."

N369AC: "Wee ahr ate miles nortees of Ahdmoa on de 4-4-0 radiuhl."

FW: "Are you northeast or southwest of the ADM VORTAC?"

N369AC: "Affirmative."

ATC Tales 143

I got a little busy at work this afternoon, what with DFW Approach Control shucking out airplanes like a game of "52 card pickup." In the middle of it all I took a handoff on a Southwest (SWA) out of 14,000 and climbed him to 23,000. He was passing through 16,200 when I got a handoff on an American four miles in trail at 17,000 with a 50 knot overtake.

We need five miles separation or a thousand feet at the minimum. There is a way to have three miles separation going to five miles but that entails having the slower aircraft in back. This one wasn't. The pucker factor jumps into overdrive when something like this happens. My heart went to my throat, all my attention riveted ever so briefly on this one spot as I tried calling the American, hoping first that he wasn't on frequency and second, that if he was, that I hadn't climbed him with the Southwest climbing right in front of him.

All of a sudden, the American started turning to the right, a turn so sharp I could almost see the wings banking through the radar scope. The Southwest, whose climb seemed to slow down to an immeasurable crawl to altitude when the American's data block popped onto the screen, finally got through 18,000 and I waited for the phone to ring, the front desk calling to find out what was going on. It didn't, thank goodness.

A few years ago Mike Burroughs met an Air Force pilot who flew F-4Bs over North Vietnam during the Vietnam War. On learning that the pilot had been shot down by a Mig, he asked why he hadn't fought back. The fellow explained that the F-4Bs were unarmed camera-equipped aircraft, adding, "You can't kill 'em with fil-m."

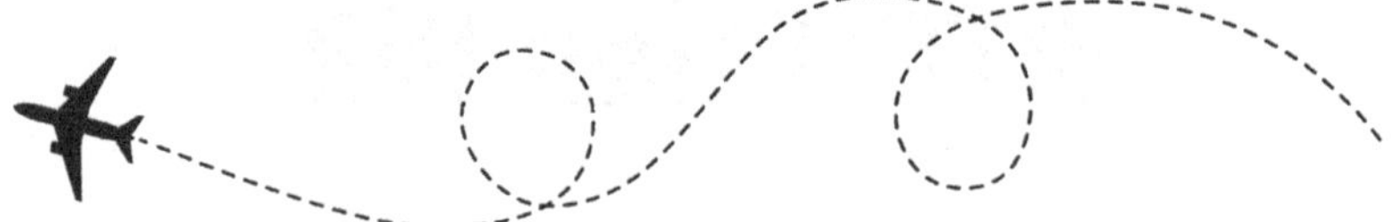

Thomas Rey worked a flight of four Idaho Air Guard fighters with the callsign SPUD61. At the frequency change, flight-lead took the frequency and then checked to make sure the flight got the freq and waited for the proper response . . .

"One potato."

"Two potato"

"Three potato."

"FOUR."

ATC Tales 144

Ardmore-high was busy last night. There was a line of weather from here to there, Albuquerque to Detroit, with aircraft deviating hither and yon, here to there and everywhere else. Brad Murray was the R-side and he was busier than a no-armed wallpaper-hanger. Tim Ballogg was "handoff" for him and I was the D-side, five bays of strips (normally there are two bays of strips at the most—even at the busiest of times). Aircraft from the east coast were coming over northwest Arkansas and southwest to Wichita Falls, Texas, before turning west. There was also a string of aircraft coming over Oklahoma City to Wichita Falls, Texas (SPS), before they turned west. These two strings of airplanes were meeting in southwest Oklahoma with little or no room to do anything with them before they turned west and the situation was getting hairier by the moment.

Brad, needing some help from the sector northeast of us, Mcalester-high (MLC-hi), called them, telling them to clear all their airplanes over Ardmore (ADM), then on to the next point. This would pry the two streams apart and allow him a better than even chance of achieving some sort of control of the situation, one that was deteriorating rapidly.

A few minutes later there came the next bunch of airplanes from them, another five or six, none of which had been cleared over ADM but were still direct SPS. Brad found this out the hard way when one from this string was a bit further west than it should have been and he almost had a system error with that airplane and one in the western string. It was at that point that Brad first pried the two airplanes apart and then proceeded to let everyone know, at the top of his voice, what he thought of MLC-hi . . . "Those incompetent, inconsiderate, ignorant m-therf-ckers on MLC-hi need to do what they're told! They're killing me!"

It was also at this point that Wayne Coley, the MLC-hi D-side, dialed in to me, hearing every single word of Brad's rantings. "Is he talking about us?" Wayne asked.

"Just ignore him; we do," I said, and repeated that their aircraft needed to go over ADM.

We took care of the business at hand and proceeded on our way, the situation calming down an hour or so later and ATC life slowly got back to normal.

Evidently Wayne had said something to the supervisor over there, David Olivas, because later Wayne stopped by ADM-hi to say Olivas was sending me a message. "Tell him," Dave said," we're not incompetent, inconsiderate, or ignorant!"

Seems like Brad has found a home on ADM-hi. This morning he was the D-side there with Chuck Andrews (BA) on the R-side when HPJ55 (Hopajet 55) checked on . . .

HPJ55: "Fort Worth, Hopajet55 with you, flight level 4-3-0, POLO."

BA: "Hopajet55, Fort Worth Center, roger."

Then Chuck and Brad looked at each other to see if they had heard the pilot correctly . . . the word POLO standing out like a sore thumb. Neither of them knew what he meant by it, what the word meant, why he would say it at all. There are some words that, when uttered by a pilot, mean something to someone somewhere but to all hands involved with this transmission, no one had a clue.

Chuck called over the supervisor, the infamous Matt McCrorey. Looking to the supervisors for answers is always a good past-time though not, as in this case, always productive. Matt had no clue (remember, he is a supervisor) so he called the watch supervisor, Roland Ballard, at the front desk. "A pilot has just declared POLO. Do you know what that means?"

Roland had never heard of it but said he would find out but 15 minutes later he was down at the Frisco desk to say they couldn't find word one about POLO anywhere. Matt said, OK, we would just ask the pilot.

So Chuck did, asking, "Hopajet55, what did you mean by 'POLO' when you checked on?"

It was the pilot's turn to be puzzled and he replied, in a querying tone, "We didn't say POLO when we checked on."

But Chuck and Brad were vindicated a moment later when the pilot came back saying, "What we said was, FL430, direct Pueblo."

An hour later the story had made its way around the center. If only the pilot knew what a commotion the slurred "Pueblo" had caused.

ATC Tales 145

Nathan King was working DFW east departures on Lake-low, all four radials running hot and heavy, shipping them to high-altitude left and right, when he got a call from the high-side controller. The American on the southernmost radial had to return to DFW immediately. Because there was a snake, a cottonmouth rattlesnake, crawling around the cabin. The pilot was unsure how the snake got on the airplane or how it got loose, but it was and back to DFW they went.

At Lubbock Tower there came a weather report in the computer: NOSOS. There was no answer when someone called the tower for an explanation. Later, when someone there called the Center, it was determined that NOSOS meant No observation; snakes on stairs.

At Love Field Vic Gathings was a baggage handler for Eastern Airlines. One day a box was off-loaded that had all sorts of stickers, labels, and dire messages about the poisonous snake therewithin. Bound for the Dallas Zoo, the snake, boxed up in two big crates, one within the other, the zoo taking only the inner crate, leaving the outer one and all its labels.

Vic and another baggage handler thought it would be great fun to play a little joke on all hands so they cut a corner off the box, resealed it and put it back on a plane. At the next stop the box was discovered sans its slithery occupant. The ground staff thought the critter had escaped and was crawling around the baggage compartment so they all abandoned ship, the plane was sealed and grounded, then some snake handlers were brought in to find and recover the missing serpent.

Alas, realizing their practical joke had gotten out of hand, they confessed—before it was tracked down to them. It didn't save their jobs, however, both of them soon on the street.

There is one other former baggage handler out there, now a journeyman controller, who was a baggage handler for a local airline. One day he was transferring a coffin from one aircraft to another when the big box fell off his forklift, popping open and spilling grandma on the tarmac. Being the future air traffic controller that he was, he looked around to see if anyone in the area had observed the unfortunate incident. No one had.

He dismounted from his steed, righted the box, scooped grandma up and replaced her in her place of repose. Then he loaded the coffin on the appropriate aircraft and away it and the box flew on to its destination, no one the wiser—until grandma arrived—in less than pristine condition.

(Seeing as how she was dead, I would have thought she was in less than pristine condition before she took a tumble.)

In any case, she arrived all the worse for wear and soon thereafter airline officials arrived at our hero's doorstep, sure that he was the guilty party. "Not me," he proclaimed, and kept up the front until the day he left for the FAA.

Spoken like a real controller!

ATC Tales 146

Steve Cooke was working SCX151. Not knowing what company "SCX" was, he inquired of those about him. One wag, Tim Ramsey, said, "It's 'Sphincter.'" Hearing it was Ramsey, Steve should have known better, but called the aircraft "Sphincter 151" from then on.

At the Dayton, Ohio, Approach Control, Red Ward was working a commuter over the Ohio River who inquired, "Is that the ferry we're flying over?" (A car ferry that makes a regular run across the river.)

"It might be. What's he wearing?" said Red.

Dick McReynolds took his cousin and some friends flying down to the Lowake (TX) Steak House, a roadside joint with a little dirt strip nearby. The flight was rough, rough, rough and Dick wasn't sure how well his cousin had taken it until he asked how the cousin's stomach was.

"I don't know yet but I might be taking the bus back to Fort Worth," came the reply.

One Easter Sunday evening . . .

DAL1709: "Happy Easter. You find any eggs this morning?"

PM: "Yeah. I found the one that said you had better report to work at 2:30 this afternoon."

DAL1709: "I know what you mean; I found the same one."

UAL991: "I must be getting older. I hid my own last night and couldn't find them this morning."

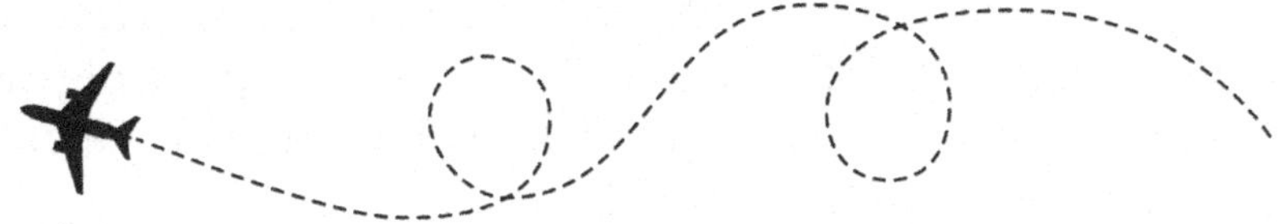

AAL2088: "We have a request."

PM: "Is this a route request?"

AAL: "I bet you want us to make it with Memphis Center."

PM: "Affirmative. You're in handoff status now."

AAL: "Yeah, we can see the line from here."

PM: "The visibility must be really good because you usually have to be a lot lower to see it."

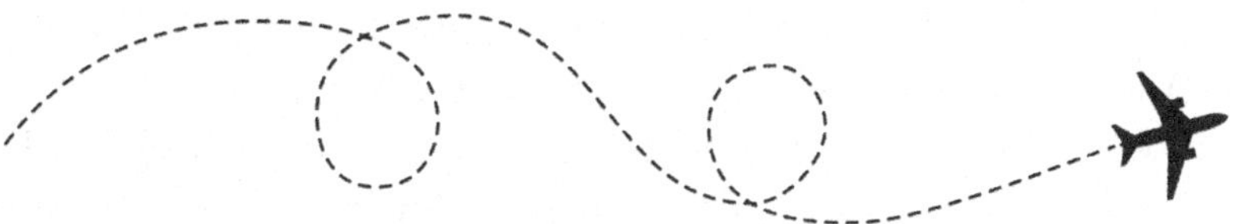

EAL414 was over OKC when . . .

PM: "EAL414, how is the visibility?"

EAL414: "It's so clear I can see the tax increases in Washington."

ATC Tales 147

I had lunch a while back with a friend who used to fly for American Airlines. He was a captain with them, an international pilot who flew for them, oh, 30 years or so. Being an airline pilot, you know how they are, his ego is bigger than his hat size. But there is another reason for the swagger. . . this guy was a fighter pilot back in the mid-70s, flying the big bad F-4 off the USS Ranger on a WesPac cruise out over the deep blue sea of the western Pacific Ocean.

The F-4 was a billy bad-ass aircraft that, before it was re-engined with the smokeless engines, would leave a smoke trail you could see for miles and miles. In fact, when I would give traffic on F-4s to other aircraft, I would always tell them, look for the smoke trail. That worked until one day a smart F-4 pilot (two words that don't often go together) told me (on hearing me issue that little bit of information), he will never see us because we have the new engines. It was his way of saying, Gotcha!

I like F-4s ever since my days of crawling around the boonies. From time-to-time we would get air support from F-4s. One time, after we were finished with an operation a flight of F-4s came rocketing over us, doing minor acrobatics, sharp turns, a roll, stuff like that; but for all of us the best show had been an hour or two before when they were dropping stuff on the bad guys.

But I digress . . . So there my friend and I were, shooting the breeze about F-4s and military aviation in general. I got to telling him a tale or two about working military aircraft and F-4s in particular and gosh, there seemed to be no end to them.

I liked working military pilots because they almost always seemed to be very cooperative. I can recall one exception, TOBIN25, a Carswell AFB T-38. I gave the pilot a 30-degree left turn and he snapped back, "What is the reason for this turn?"

I told him, for traffic (I had to turn him behind an American inbound to OKC), and let it go at that. After I shipped the American to low-altitude and the T-38 was the only aircraft on my frequency, I asked him if he had time for a question. He replied, rather curtly I thought, that he did.

Is there a student flying that aircraft? I inquired.

Negative, he snapped, and then a few minutes later he wanted to know why I had asked that question.

I told him that most pilots, when given a turn will simply take the turn.

He informed me, though I knew it already, that I was supposed to give him a reason for any vector. I told him I knew that but again, most pilots know there's a good reason for it and generally only students queried the reason. I was as polite as could be though I think I made my point.

The F-4 is a great big hulking brute of an airplane. If it had a civilian job, it would be a bouncer in a nightclub somewhere, probably in a bad part of town. But if some rifle company was in a fix somewhere, they were great ones to see. They were great ones to fly in, as well. I got an F-4 ride out of Carswell up to Fort Sill, Oklahoma, where we dropped lots of bombs and sent lots of sandbags to that great sandlot in the sky. I got sick, rip-roaring sick, but it was worth it, especially after my stomach settled down a day or two later.

When the F-4s started fading from view, the Air Force contracted with Sperry Corporation to turn them into drones. A Sperry pilot would pick one up at Davis-Montham AFB in Arizona and fly it to Tyndall AFB, Florida, with an op-stop at Sheppard AFB, Texas. One day I was working Ardmore-hi, and here came BIKE91, an F-4 out of Sheppard to Tyndall. Not having seen an F-4 in quite a while, I asked the pilot about the F-4 he was flying and he explained the above.

"Sperry Corporation," I inquired?

"Affirmative," he replied.

"And this is a ferry flight," I said.

"Affirmative," he responded.

"So that would make you a 'Sperry Ferry'?"

There was a moment of silence, a slight chuckle on the frequency, and a low-keyed droll, "Wait 'til I tell the boys that one."

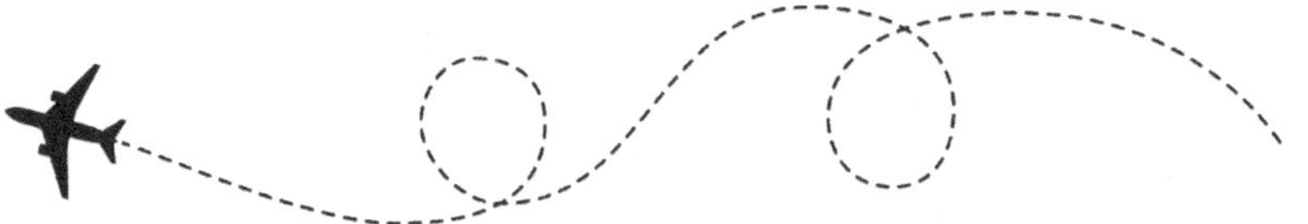

Sometimes military pilots are, well, you be the judge. Pete Costilow was working OKIE91, a flight of two F-4s inbound to Tinker AFB from the east. When they got on OKC Approach's frequency, the flight leader told Pete the wanted to split up into two flights of one. Pete asked the standard-issue question every question every air traffic controller would ask in this circumstance, "What is your wingman's name?"

You can imagine Pete's surprise when flight lead said, "Marvin B. Case" instead of what he expected, OKIE92. So all the way back to Tinker, it was OKIE91 and Marv, not OKIE91 and -92.

Jim Wacker was working an F-4 out in western Oklahoma that had become a glider—and not a very good one. The pilot said he would tell Jim when the crew was ejecting and he did, hearing Jim's usual response to a pilot leaving the frequency, "Have a good day." A letter from the pilot arrived a few weeks later saying that while he had hurt his back in the ejection, he laughed all the way down because of Jim's parting remark.

ATC Tales 148

I was so busy this morning with OKC and ADM-lows combined that we had to split it off. It was the closest I have seen it come to a mid-air in a long time. I was working AYA13 (Academy Air 13), a BE90 shooting approaches at ADM Municipal, when N116D, a Be58, wanted to get in. I cleared AYA13 to ADDMO radio beacon to hold as published, maintain 4000, and got the Baron in.

All of a sudden two USAF T-37s came up on frequency looking for clearance into ADM. The first, SHEP32, insisted on going to ADDMO to hold when I had already told him that I would not be able to give him an approach clearance for a while, that I had one aircraft on approach and one holding, waiting to get in.

When N116D landed (and canceled) I cleared AYA13 for the ILS approach when lo and behold, there appeared SHEP32 right below him. I quickly told AYA13 to maintain 4000 until he had the T-37 in sight. The T-37 reported the KingAir in sight and AYA13 finally reported the T-37 in sight after which I let him proceed with the approach.

When AYA13 got on the ground he canceled IFR instead of flying the last of the three approaches he had planned to fly. I got SHEP32 back to the VOR at 5000 and got him in. There was another T-37 on frequency, a DICEY out of Sheppard, but he went over to tower and worked with them.

I spoke with a friend of mine at ADM this evening and he said the AYA pilot was not as concerned as we were but he was concerned with his one airplane and we were concerned about all of them. CT, my D-side, said the AYA pilot should have found the T-37 pilot and "punched him in the mouth."

Once again Schroe-man is right on the mark.

On OKC-hi there was an Air Force Learjet with the callsign, JOBOB1 (Joe Bob). Before too long the young lady working the sector was calling him, BLOWJOB1.

Finally the embarrassed pilot said, "Uh, ma'am, that's JOE BOB One."

Some days you wonder if the sky really is blue and the grass really is green.

EGF949 was at FL200 . . .

EGF: "We're requesting one-zero-thousand."

PM: "Roger, descend and maintain one-zero-thousand."

EGF: "Now we're requesting one-six-thousand."

PM: "Maintain one-six-thousand."

EGF: "Now we're requesting one-zero-thousand."

PM: "Maintain one-zero-thousand; I can approve lower if you want."

EGF: "That's what we're asking for."

PM: "Roger. Maintain six-thousand."

EGF: "Is that at our discretion?"

PM: "You asked for lower; I gave you lower. Now you want discretion. Descend at any rate you want, when you want, where you want, but YOU pick an altitude and I'll assign it you. It's a one-shot deal, one time. You pick it."

EGF: "We'll go to six-thousand."

Thomas Rey had a VFR check on frequency at ELP Approach requesting VFR advisories.

N1234: “N1234 requesting flight-following.”

Thomas: “Do you have a transponder?”

N1234: “Affirmative.”

Thomas: “Roger, squawk 5234.”

N1234: “Uh, it’s in the shop.”

ATC Tales 149

A Delta B727 was being rerouted around the White Sands Missile Range. Curious as to why he was being rerouted, the pilot inquired as to "What do they shoot in the White Sands Missile Range?"

The controller replied, "727s, if you don't take the turn."

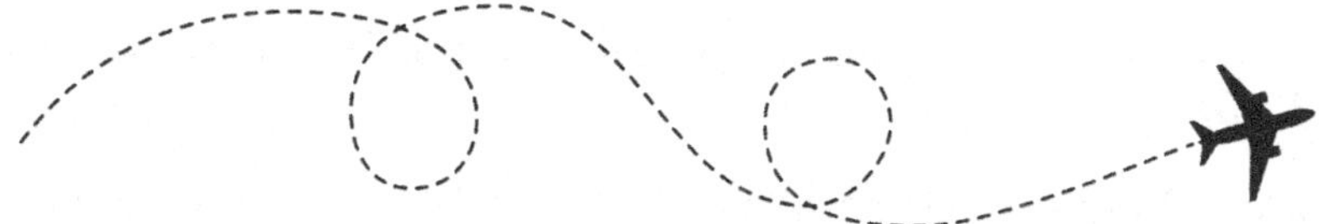

JAVET15 was a T-38 out of Tinker back to Sheppard on the JAVET route. Sometimes the students are from lands across the sea and don't sprechen sie Anglasi very well . . .

JAVET15 came off Tinker climbing to 1-5-thousand with AMW2505 just south of him, also at 150. Pete Moss assigned him ". . . FL200, expedite through 1-6-thousand for traffic. With lots of weather around Pete turned him west, away from the WX and toward the inbound radial to Sheppard . . .

PM: "Fly H260 until intercepting the Wichita Falls 0-1-8 radial, rest of route unchanged."

JAVET: "Roger, we climb and maintain FL260."

PM: "Negative! FLY Heading 2-6-0 until intercepting the Wichita Falls 0-1-8 RADIAL."

JAVET: "Roger. We fly heading 2-6-0 and climb and maintain flight level 2-6-0."

PM: "Negative! Negative! FLY heading 2-6-0; climb and maintain FL2-0-0."

There was a moment of silence, then an American voice, obviously the instructor, came on. "Tell you what, Center. We'll make this simple. How about a drop-in at Fort Sill?"

What a pain. I almost wished he had climbed to 26.

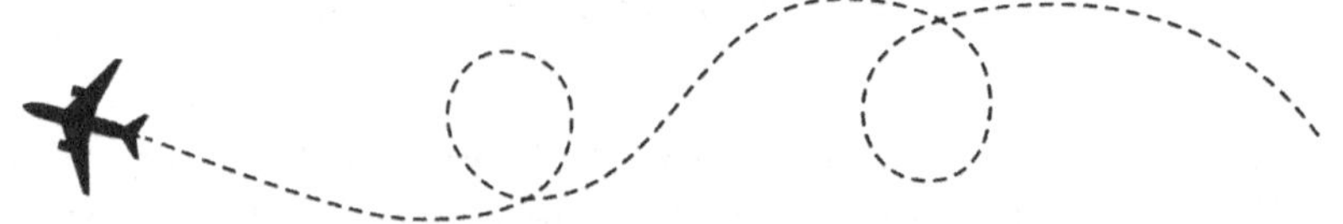

Working an outbound COA to Houston, Pete asked, "COA136, were you COA291 coming in?"

COA: "What did the guy do wrong?"

PM: "Nothing. He said he would see me in a couple hours and here I am."

COA: "Oh good. Affirmative, we were 291. I always get antsy when my wife asks me questions like that."

PM: "Yeah, I get antsy when she asks me those questions, too . . . No, just kidding."

ATC Tales 150

It's a well into the evening here in the 2nd floor studio. There's a lacrosse game going on across the street and I can hear the roar of the (small) crowd as they cheer, rant and rave at the goings-on. I'm glad that, in spite of the weather, they're having a good time. Right now I'm in a bit of a reflective mood, having heard earlier this evening that Jimmy, a young man (in his 50s – young to me) had passed away. He was a controller at Fort Worth Center his entire career and we were on the same crew for probably eight or ten of those years.

I saw something on TV earlier that triggered a memory I wanted to say a few words about. I was watching the 10pm weather when a national map came on-screen and the weatherman started talking about a line of weather that ran from down near Houston up toward Kansas City.

It was a bad line of weather with all sorts of color, red, green, yellow, and probably one or two others, and it brought back a memory or two of other weather days. I used to work that area when I was the world's second-best air traffic controller. (Larry Foreman was the best – just ask him.) To an air traffic controller, the word "weather" means "bad weather." Toward the end of my 33 years out there I was talking with the aforementioned about our forthcoming retirements and we agreed that the biggest thing we would NOT miss was working airplanes in weather.

When I first hired on back in 1974, I quickly learned that the guys who watched the weather forecasts at night would often call in sick, if the next day's weather was going to be bad. They got to thinking about it, decided they didn't want to work airplanes in that stuff and so they'd pick up the phone, call the Center, and say they were sick.

I got to the point where I stopped watching the TV weather all together, so I'd not think about what was coming the next day. Didn't bother me, not watching the weather. I could see the sky on my way to work so I was ready for it. Besides, the first twenty-one years I worked Oklahoma airspace and could always hope that it was clear up there.

The bad part about the weather is that every airplane wants to deviate for weather (understandably so), and they all want to know about the ride. That's OK with a few airplanes but sometimes even one airplane with problems can keep you pretty busy. Add another dozen airplanes, and some people are looking at going down the tubes.

Three incidents stand out. The first was on an evening shift as I was giving Roy Newsom a break on Mcalester-low. There was a lot of weather in southeast Oklahoma and seven or eight aircraft on frequency and all but one deviating around it. Roy had given me the relief briefing and was about to unplug when I noticed one particular airplane, a VFR Saratoga at 10,500 feet, had lost its transponder so I pointed it out to Roy who queried the pilot about it. That's when it started. The pilot started describing what happened when the plane got too close to the thunderstorm.

He was fairly calm, all things considered. The engine had quit, the aircraft was in a spin and a wing had been ripped off the aircraft. He was calm, probably because he was busy trying to recover from the spin. There were two passengers, a man in front and a woman in back, and we could hear the woman screaming all the way down. I had put Roy on the R-side and I stayed on the D-side, coordinating with Flight Service for the hopeful rescue. The Highway Patrol found the aircraft two days later. Nobody made it.

The second incident was one night on a mid-shift when I worked a search helicopter looking for a Bonanza in weather that had been at 8,000 feet but that had probably crashed. It had. The airplane crashed next to a road and the pilot had been thrown into the road . . . where he had been run over by a truck that couldn't stop. Fortunately for the truck driver, the autopsy showed that the pilot was dead on impact.

The third was on another mid-shift when two lines of weather were blocking most of the United States. The only way was through the weather for a thousand miles to the north and 500 miles to the south was around the south end of the western line and the northern end of the easterly line so all the FedExes, UPSs, and every other freight hauler were deviating that way. Jimmy was on the R-side and Janet Landman on the D-side and it was so busy they were actually wearing headsets on the mid, one of the two times I ever saw that in 33 years. Because of frequency congestion and overlap, Jimmy went down the tubes. He was a good controller, but he lost the picture and Janet had to take over the R-side. I took the D-side (I'd been working low) and Jimmy sat on a chair for about two minutes, regaining his composure. After that brief interlude, he came back to the R-side and, after assuring Janet he was OK, took back the R-side, doing a fantastic job. I don't remember if he got an award for that night, but he should have.

Yes, I still don't like "weather" and I don't watch it much, either. When I saw the line on TV my first thought was, I'm glad I'm not working tonight.

Rest in peace, Jimmy.

ATC Tales 151

I wanted to write a wee note and thought I'd tell a tale or two about flight attendants. Sunday night we went to a concert in the park with our across-the-street neighbors. Their daughter, who lives down in the big city, was up for a visit. After the concert, we all trekked down to "Two Scoops," the local ice cream eatery, for a scoop of the good stuff and a short visit on the front steps. Terri the daughter used to be a flight attendant for Northwest Airlines and still has a friend or two with Delta. She only did it three years, she said, but that was enough for her.

I have had a bit of contact with flight attendants and have found them to be amenable, pleasant and the other twelve points of the Boy Scout oath. As a rule, they're good people. As an air traffic controller (back in the old days – before 9/11), controllers could take familiarization flights. You had to ride in the cockpit, sitting on the jumpseat, sometimes, like on the DC-10 or Tri-Star, a very comfortable perch, and sometimes, like on a DC-9 or a smaller aircraft, on a seat in front of the door. On a Shorts 360 one time, I had to wrap my legs around the captain's seat. Very uncomfortable.

There was a book written by two American Airlines flight attendants titled "Cabin Pressure," about flight attendants and what goes on behind the scenes on airliners. Very good book. I had a copy (that I wish I still had) but I loaned it to a former flight attendant for Pan Am and she moved to Chicago, book and all. Today I discovered that I can still get it through Amazon and may do that. Good stories, good stuff.

I was on a Delta trip one time, Washington to Atlanta, sitting in the jumpseat minding my own business, when a flight attendant came in moaning about a first-class passenger who paid for a $2 drink with a $20 bill and she had no change.

Furthermore, she said, the guy was being a real jerk about it and everything else, only she didn't use the word "jerk," but other, very colorful language, and a lot of it. Let me help you out, I said, and gave her six $2 bills, six Susan B. Anthony dollar coins, and two dollars in half-dollar coins. The flight attendant thought this was great and told all the other cabin crew, who positioned themselves to see this guy's face when he got the change. He realized he was being taken for a "funny money" ride and the reason for the ride, and apologized to the cabin crew, several of whom thanked me later.

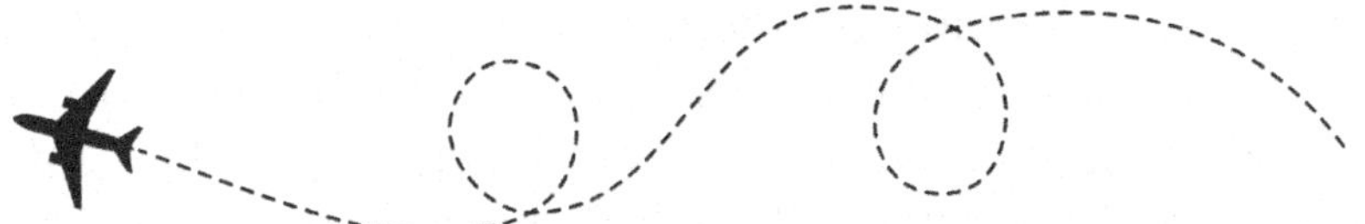

Some years later I was heading to New Orleans on Southwest to see an army buddy. I was in the fourth row and was just starting to read a book when a (male) flight attendant started passing out peanut packets from a humongous bag of the same. In the very first row a man tried paying for a $2 drink with a $100 bill, for which the attendant had no change. The passenger was being an obnoxious jerk to the point where I could easily hear every raised word he said. I caught the attendant's attention and motioned him back to my seat whereupon I told him I'd change the $100 bill for fifty $2 bills. The attendant started chuckling, dropped the entire bag of peanuts on my table and went back up the aisle, much to the chagrin of the now irate passenger who thought he was about to get a free $2 drink. The attendant, laughing, came back to my row and started to collect the peanuts, then stopped, saying, "Aw heck, keep 'em. It's worth it."

I was on a Delta flight to somewhere, sitting in a nice comfortable jumpseat, when a young, good-looking flight attendant came in from First Class. She was 20, maybe 21, and she and the captain started kidding each other. The co-pilot, flight engineer, and I weren't in on the joke and wanted to hear the story which, after prodding from the stewardess, the captain, about 45, proceeded to tell.

The previous night the crew had been on a layover in Kansas City and had agreed to meet that morning in the hotel's restaurant for breakfast before catching the van to the airport. The captain was the first one to the table and was surprised to see this girl come into the restaurant crying and inquired as to why she was so doing. She had, it seemed, just broken up with her boyfriend and she was, she said through a veil of tears, through dating younger men. She was going to start dating older men, she proclaimed, because younger men were childish, immature, and not worth the time and effort to date them.

The captain said, "I sat up straight, pulled my stomach in as far as I could, patted what was left of my hair back into place, and said, 'What do you mean by "older men"?'"

"26," the girl said, "maybe 27."

The girl, who all this time had been standing at my side in the cockpit, leaned over right in my face and said, "How old are you?" (I was a lot older than 27 at the time.)

"Too old for you," I said.

I was on another fam trip, this time on a Midwest Express DC-9 out of Chicago Midway to DFW. This DC-9 was a 10 series, old, small, and cramped. The jumpseat wasn't necessarily old but it was small and cramped and me not being the tiniest guy in the world, was packed into it when a young female flight attendant came up behind me to take drink orders from the captain, co-pilot, and myself. She was rather well-endowed, I might say, and made an effort to rub her endowments all over my back. I cannot lie and say I wasn't enjoying it because things like that rarely happened to me. (Never happened to me.) She rubbed and I smiled and then she left for the galley and our drinks.

After she was gone the co-pilot turned in his seat to face me and said, "That girl that took our drink orders? Last year 'she' was a 'he.'" When she came back with the drinks, I leaned as far forward as I could without doing a face plant on the center console. I'm still smiling though, just thinking about it.

We got to telling airplane stories on Facebook, mostly about military fam trips. At the Center you could get rides on military aircraft the facility served. Reading the paper one day I saw that a Tarrant County Commissioner got a ride in an F-105 and I thought that if he could one being a local politician, why couldn't controllers? I started bugging the airspace office upstairs in the admin wing. They said it couldn't be done but, eventually, done it was. I was scheduled for a ride with the 457th Tactical Fighter Squadron out at Carswell AFB, out on the west side of Fort Worth.

It was a great experience. I showed up, suited up and went up. Major Wilson, my pilot, was the squadron executive officer and we flew flight lead. The Wing Commander flew section leader and a major named Fred Flom flew his wing. It was a beautiful takeoff. I had a movie camera along and got some great footage, none of which I can find now. We flew up to Fort Sill, Oklahoma, and blew the heck out of some old trucks and a lot of sandbags. Wasted them.

ATC Tales 152

Brian Throop was working AAL741 who was giving Brian a ration of static and not cooperating at all so . . .

Brian: "AAL741, your attitude and disposition are incompatible with the traffic flow into DFW. Turn right 40 degrees, vector for sequencing."

AAL741: "40 degrees right vector for sequencing."

Then the light came on . . .

AAL741: "What did you say?"

Brian: "I say again, your altitude and position are incompatible with the traffic flow into DFW. Turn 40 degrees right for sequencing."

When CTLES04 (an F-14) checked on frequency, Pete Moss called him CUDDLES04.

The pilot responded, in a DEEP voice, "That's CUTLASS04."

Pete replied, "CUTLASS04, roger."

And in a booming voice the pilot replied, "THANK YOU!"

Brian Rountree on sequencing: Sequencing airplanes is like having children. If you wait until you're ready, it ain't never gonna happen.

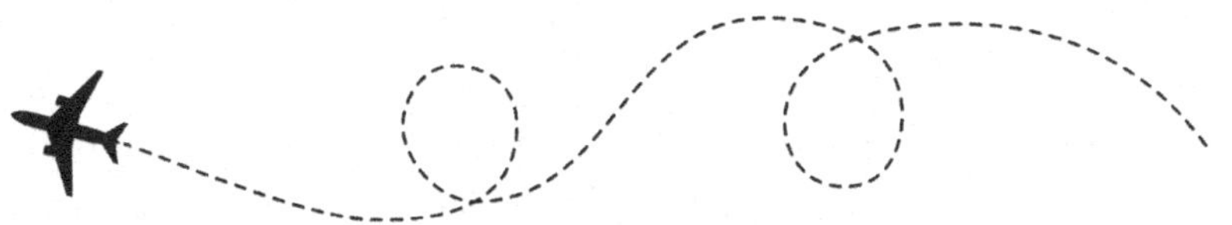

Busy at the beginning of a mid, a Learjet asked Mike Ross, Sr., for direct Harrison three times and was refused each time. Finally, the exasperated pilot said, "Is there ANY chance we can fly heading 0-3-5 for Harrison?"

Said Mike, now just as exasperated, "There's a real good chance you can fly heading 0-1-0 for traffic."

"Roger," was all the pilot said.

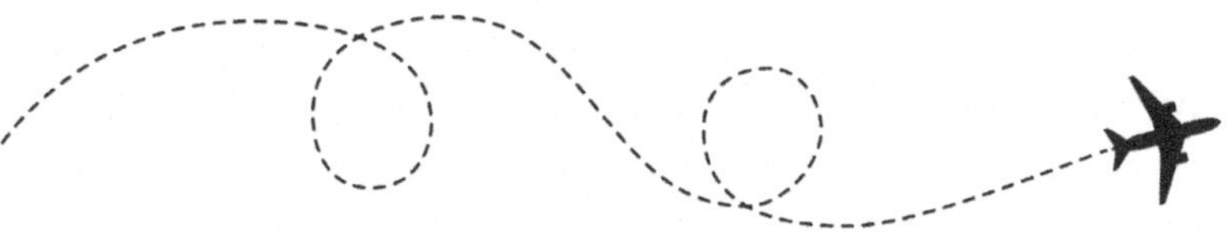

AWE614 checked on . . .

AWE: Ft Worth Center, Cactus 614 with you.

PM: AWE614, Ft Worth Center, roger. Say your altitude.

AWE: Why does everybody want to know that?

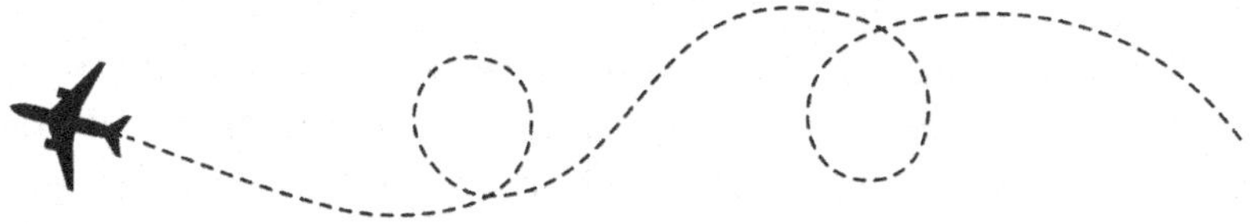

There are certain times in your ATC career that it is just an outright pleasure to be an air traffic controller.

One Sunday morning I was sitting on ADM-lo, a sector that, among other things, works the southbound departures out of Oklahoma City. There was an airshow at OKC that weekend and one of the participants, N900RW, a B-17, was leaving early to fulfill a commitment at the Galveston, Texas, airport.

When the B-17 came on frequency climbing to 7,000, I was naturally curious about it, me being a WWII aviation history buff. Evidently I wasn't the only one on frequency.

N1668R, a Cessna 182, was on frequency at 8,000, on a route that would be fairly close to the B-17's southbound flight path. When the pilot realized that, he requested (and received) radar vectors to intercept the B-17 so he could get a picture. I told the B-17 what the Cessna pilot planned to do, where he was and what he wanted. The B-17 pilot did everything he could to help out the Cessna pilot, maneuvering, turning, S-turning, all so a fellow pilot could get some good pictures. Then the B-17 had to press on south.

Long after the B-17 left frequency, the Cessna pilot was talking about it and how beautiful the B-17 was, something I already knew. Made me feel good though. Another good day at the office.

Many years ago I was an air traffic controller at Fort Worth Center, working airspace in Oklahoma. One fine day I was working Mcalester-high altitude sector, FL240 and up, handling arrivals and departures for DFW. Oklahoma City and Tulsa. It was a bear of a sector most days and some days it was a whole family of bears.

On one such day I had a whole fleet of airplanes at 37,000 and below. They were cruising, crossing, and getting in each other's way. On top of them all was an F-14 at 39,000 feet, out of somewhere to the east and inbound to Tinker AFB in Oklahoma City and he had to get down through all the mess of airplanes below him, and he had to do it so that there was no paperwork involved.

I told him, "Navy 401, I'm going to start you down in a moment and when I start you down, I need out of flight level 3-1-0 in ten seconds or less."

"Roger, Center," came the reply.

A moment later I told him, "Navy 401, expedite through flight level 3-1-0, descend and maintain flight level 2-4-0."

He replied, "Out of flight 3-9-0, out of flight level 3-1-0, leveling flight level 2-4-0." It was that quick.

Switching him to low altitude sector, I said, "Navy 401, thank you. You can fly on my frequency any day. Contact Fort Worth Center 278.3."

It was a good day at the office . . . no paperwork.

ATC Tales 153

Today in class we were shooting the breeze about various ATC topics, something you should always do in an ATC class, when the subject of "Weather" came up. The way I look at it, "weather" is a four-letter word. I don't like it, don't pretend to like it, and haven't liked it for a good many years. "Weather," to me and most air traffic controllers, means bad weather. There used to be a guy out there, Jimmy Gerard, who hated weather to the point where he called in sick on bad weather days. He taught me, albeit indirectly, never to watch the weather forecast. If I didn't know what was coming, I wouldn't think about it. Every day would be a new day and that was fine with me.

Weather is a problem and the worse the weather, the more problems there are. You learn early on what to do with airplanes when there is weather around. One of the most important things is tell pilots everything, as soon as you can, so that they have the knowledge they need to deal with the weather. This brought to mind something that happened to me a few years ago . . .

I was working Dallas-high one evening with a lot of weather north of Waco. AWE880 (Cactus 880) checked on about 80 miles east of Waco, heading right for the bad stuff, so I gave him the standard warnings of "Moderate to severe turbulence 80 miles ahead on your route of flight."

The Cactus pilot acknowledged the transmission and the next one I gave him when he was about 30 miles out. He didn't deviate before he reached the area, and when I told him he was in the area of reported turbulence and he rogered it. I shipped him to HICOE-hi and that was it.

That was it until he landed in Las Vegas. Then he notified the company that in the aforementioned turbulence a flight attendant had broken an ankle. The pilot told his company that he had received no warning of the turbulence from ATC, i.e., me. The company requested a copy of the tapes which were pulled and reviewed, then sent to the company.

I would have liked to have had a conversation with that pilot. I would also like to find out what happened to him after the company had a conversation with him.

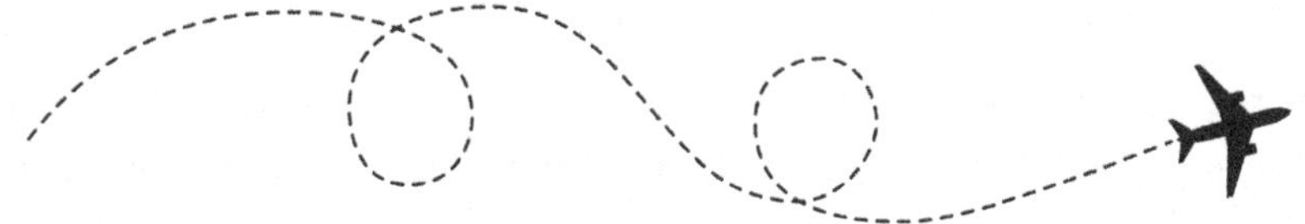

Shades of the Caine Mutiny wherein the main character got a Silver Star and a Letter of Reprimand for the same action in that World War II novel.

Mickey Davenport was working the mid-shift at Ellison NAS, a satellite field off NAS Pensacola. It is a training field for Navy helicopter pilots, so it has short runways, the longest about 3,000 feet long. It doesn't have much traffic after dark though the field is open and the runway lights are always on.

So it was that Mickey was reading a book this mid-shift. He had the Pensacola Approach Control frequencies on in the background and could hear a Southern Airways DC-9 talking to them as it was making a visual approach to the civilian airport. Looking up from the book and down the Ellison runway, he realized that the DC-9 was about to touch down at Ellison, not the civilian airport, landing on a runway that was too short to handle such an aircraft.

Thinking quickly, he leaned over and flipped the switch to turn off the runway lights, causing the runway to darken and the subsequent radio call proved he had done the right thing. "Pensacola, why did you turn off the runway lights/"

Mickey could see the aircraft starting a go-around at the end of the runway, lifting up into the sky while hearing, "We didn't turn off the runway lights . . ."

When the aircraft was high enough it reported seeing the Pensacola Airport's lights dead ahead at which time Mickey flipped the lights back on. Meanwhile, the DC-9 continued to the civilian airport where it made a routine landing. No big deal.

But to the Navy it was. There is a regulation that says runway lights at Naval Air Stations shall not be turned off during hours of darkness for any reason.

Southern Airways wrote a Letter of Appreciation thanking him for saving an aircraft and the lives of the passengers, some of whom undoubtedly would have been injured or worse had it landed on the too-short runway. The FAA wrote a letter stating the same.

The Navy didn't quite see it that way. They wrote a letter but it was a Letter of Reprimand chiding him for disobeying the aforementioned regulation.

Some days it just pays to do the right thing, unofficially anyway.

ATC Tales 154

There's a fellow out there named Scott Moore. He likes all sorts of outdoor stuff: skydiving, scuba diving, all that stuff. A few days ago, he was telling a story about encountering a shark on an ocean dive in the Gulf of Mexico. Someone asked him, "Aren't you afraid of sharks?"

"No," he said, "because I can swim through water faster than sharks can swim through shit!"

It took me a minute to figure it out, but I got it.

There's a female supervisor at work who is, among other things, very attractive. Back when the cafeteria was closed, all the specialties ordered breakfast from the local eateries and one particular morning she did, too, ordering breakfast for her and her husband Tony, also a controller.

Shortly after the breakfast run left, two employees, Ron and Mike, (who happened to be going on a break) decided they wanted leave. She told them she could not approve it right then but would look at it. If she could approve it, she would page them (to call the specialty desk at x7528) to let them know.

The chow run came back and this young lady paged her husband to call x7528 to tell him that his breakfast was back.

Unfortunately, the paging system was all but broken and the only thing that actually went out over the intercom was a lot of static and the words. ". . . call 7528."

Ron, hearing the ". . . call 7528" and thinking the page was about the leave request, found a phone and called the desk.

Dee, thinking it was her husband calling about breakfast, answered the phone, saying, in a very sexy, sultry voice, "I've got what you want. It's ready to be eaten and I've got it waiting for you right here!"

Ron, hearing an invitation he probably had not heard in years, said, "I'll be right there!"

Dee, expecting Tony's voice, was shocked to hear Ron. She asked him not to say anything to anyone but there was little chance of that so the story, as well you might expect, got around quickly.

The next morning, when breakfast orders were being taken, everybody said, "I'll have what Tony's having!"

When SWA checked on . . .

Center: "One of us is old; one of is tired, and both of us would like a shortcut."

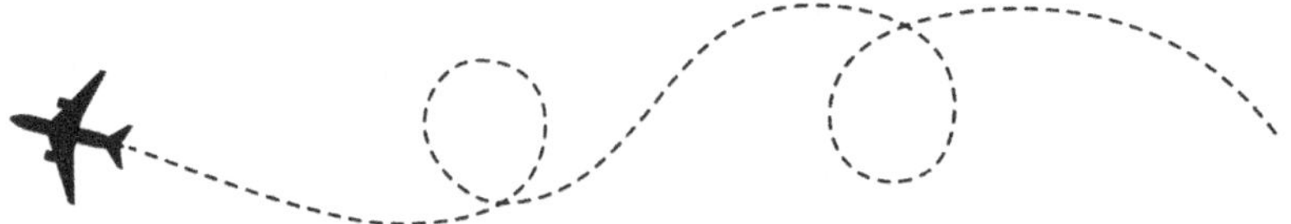

ZFW: "How's the ride at 1-5-thousand?"

AAL: "As smooth as my wife's behind."

ZFW: "Maintain 3-5-0 knots or greater."

SWA: "I'd like to but we'd like to keep the wings on the airplane."

Unidentified: "No guts, no glory."

SWA: "We've got the guts but we want to keep them all in one piece."

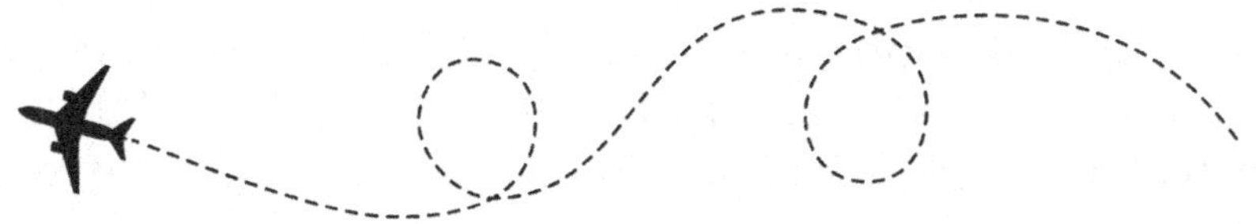

ABQ DEP: ". . . Liner123 climb and maintain FL330, cleared direct Atlanta."

123: (after readback) "Wish you worked Atlanta; we always get a stairstep out of there."

ABQ DEP: "That's why they call us 'controllers.'"

123: "I already have a wife."

ATC Tales 155

There are times that try men's souls, difficult times, and all of us, almost all of us, encounter such times in the course of our lives. I've had a time or two myself trying to parallel park, but I'm not here this morning to talk about that. No, this morning I want to visit about THUD01, THUD02 and TANKR01, and the bad day they all had near Shreveport, Louisiana, lo those many years ago.

THUD01 was a flight of two F-105s that had been working the Rivers Military Operating Area (MOA) in southeastern Oklahoma, and then heading back home to Barksdale AFB, at 21,000 feet. It was during this leg of their flight that THUD02 discovered he had a serious fuel problem. That is to say, he had all but NO fuel, a serious problem indeed. He got on the horn to flight lead and THUD01 got on the horn to Fort Worth Center, asking if there was a KC-135, a military fuel tanker, in the area that would be willing to give the wingman some gas.

There was indeed such a tanker available, but he was some distance away, and another problem soon reared its ugly head, the separation issue.

Controllers, as a rule, are bound by a whole manual of rules, regulations, laws, and bylaws. There are paragraphs and sub-paragraphs that cover darn near everything a controller says, does, or even thinks about doing. One of those paragraphs says, thou shalt not have less than the minimum required separation between two aircraft or flights of aircraft. Further, it says that only the military, not the FAA (the controller), can declare MARSA (Military Assumes Responsibility for Separation of Aircraft). In other words, even if the KC-135 and the F-105s got in the same area, the controller could not put them together because he would be intentionally causing a loss of separation.

One of the good things about most military pilots is that they are forward thinkers. They think outside the box. Sure, they are bound by rules and regulations, just as are controllers, but, in times of duress, the rules become a guideline, a framework from which to begin, not the be-all-to-end-all. Besides, it is much easier to get forgiveness than permission.

Trying to help, the controller aimed the fighters east, in the general direction of the tanker, and the tanker, now at 20,000 feet, west, in their direction, with the tanker offset slightly to the north.

Aerial refueling (AR) is, in a sense, a ballet in the sky. It is a series of maneuvers with big, bulky airplanes loaded with gas, ammo, bombs, cargo and whatever else they carry. It is inherently dangerous because of just that, all that potential for a deadly explosion that does bad things to aircraft, equipment, and especially the crews and personnel thereupon. It is a well-rehearsed maneuver that becomes a skill honed to perfection. It is, at best, a work of art, and, at worst, a one-way trip to the end of the road. Most of the time it is accomplished without incident. You link up, hook up, drop off and go on your way. It is a pre-arranged affair that requires a great deal of coordination, meeting at the aerial-refueling contact point (ARCP) of a charted AR track, flying the track during the AR and then going your separate ways.

This day, however, there was no coordination, no track, nothing more than three airplanes hurtling toward each other at a combined speed of 900 miles an hour.

The controller, knowing he was bound by all the rules in the world and that he could not put the two flights together, mainly because there was a rule-following supervisor hovering over his shoulder watching his every move, explained the situation to the three aircraft. The tanker, making sure that THUD01 was at 21,000, said it was no big deal, that he would (and did) declare MARSA.

Then there came another FAA dilemma. Legally, MARSA has

to be worked out before a flight takes place. It was obvious that these two flights had not done so. It didn't bother the controller but, to the supervisor, it was a different story. He started to hem and haw while the controller argued with him that perhaps they did work it out pre-flight. The supervisor finally acquiesced, just as the flights approached each other.

In AR the trick is for the tanker to time his turn to the receiver's (in this case, THUD01) direction (east) so that he rolls out right in front of the receiver. This day the turn was so tight and so perfect that, had they been at the same altitude, the first fighter could have slipped his fuel receptacle right into the tanker's boom, but the fighters were a thousand feet above the tanker.

The fighters were running on fumes now, 02 with no fumes to speak of and 01, flight lead, with barely a bit more. They quickly descended to the tanker's altitude. The tanker boomer (the man responsible for working the tanker's fuel boom) it extended and waiting. THUD02 slipped in for the perfect hookup and started taking on fuel as flight lead hung off his wing, waiting his turn.

Moments later 01's engine quit, out of fuel, and he started down. 02 had enough fuel to fly for a moment so he dropped off and the tanker started down after 01, telling 01 to keep clear of him (the tanker) until he could hook up from behind. The controller, seeing the aircraft all start to descend, began clearing aircraft out from below the maneuvering planes, giving a free and clear patch of airspace into which to maneuver.

The tanker pulled in front of 01 and he hooked up, taking on fuel, sucking it in as if his life depended on it, and, in a way, it did. By now 02 was hanging off 01's wing, and he ran out of fuel. 01 had enough to fly for a moment so he dropped off and 02 slid into position. Soon 02 had enough gas to fly for a few minutes so 01 got back on and took on more fuel, and so it went. The steep descent became a gentle descent, then level flight as the two fighters were soon gassed up to the point where they had enough fuel to get back to Barksdale.

A harrowing flight for all hands. A quick-thinking tanker pilot that dove his KC-135 down in front of THUD01 to give him the gas he needed to fly, and a mission that all concerned would, no doubt, talk about for years. I hope THUD01 wrote the tanker pilot up for an award, but I don't know if that ever happened. It should have.

ATC Tales 156

The tenth anniversary of 9-11 and the horrific events of that day is nigh upon us. A friend in Texas sent me a link to a YouTube video about the air traffic events of that day, the two people speaking having worked in New York Approach and Boston Center that day. They spoke of it from management's point of view so I thought I would spend a minute or two talking about it from the controller's point of view.

I was an on-the-boards air traffic controller for over 30 years. I started in 1974 and got the boards at the end of 2004. I work all sorts of stuff: crashes, fatal and otherwise, emergencies, military, civilian, students and pilots who had been flying for years. There are several events that stand out and right near the top of that list is what happened on 9-11.

I was working Dallas High R, the radar, and radios for that sector of airspace over Dallas, Texas, and south to Temple. It was maybe 80 miles wide and 150 miles long. It had mostly DFW departures to the south, Houston arrivals from the north and Houston departures to the northwest. It was a fun sector, the three threads of airplanes having to be woven through, around and by each other, all with the east-west over flight traffic mixed in. As I said, it was a fun sector.

It was about 0830 and I had been for two hours, working Dallas-High R the whole time. Tim Gravens came by asking if I wanted a break. Sure, I said, I could get some breakfast, read a bit, and then come back to have even more fun. I gave him a briefing and unplugged.

As I turned around to move out of the area, Bob Washin was coming into the control room. Bob had a reputation as the world's biggest pathological liar. Someone once remarked about him that Bob would rather crawl up in a tree and tell a lie than stand on the ground and tell the truth. He was in the

US Coast Guard Reserve for some years, having first done 11 months active-duty training in Pensacola, Florida. During those 11 months, to hear him tell it, he saw more combat than anyone I ever met while in World War II, Korea, Vietnam, Iraq, and Afghanistan (combined). We used to tell outrageous stories to just to see how he would top them, and he would try.

So when Bob announced that half an hour before one airplane had run into a World Trade Center tower and then added a postscript, that just before he came back a second airplane had run into the second tower, Jerry Stephens actually said to him, "You're lying, Bob, just like you lie about everything else."

For once, Bob was actually telling the truth.

A few minutes later word came down from FAA Headquarters in Washington, put all airplanes on the ground at the nearest airport. They were not to continue to destination (with one exception), they were to get on the ground at the nearest airport that could handle that type of aircraft. Soon there were airplanes turning this way and that as they were being sequenced into various airports, particularly Dallas-Fort Worth, Dallas Love and Fort Worth Meacham. Small aircraft, business types and pleasure aircraft, were all directed to the nearest small airport that could handle them.

The one exception was a single Continental Airlines flight out of Seattle for Houston was about to turned out to the east for sequencing into DFW, a long trail eastbound before a turn back inbound over the corner post. I argued with the supervisor that the aircraft would be on the ground quicker if he went on to Houston because he was, in a sense, already in-trail for sequencing and landing at Houston's Intercontinental Airport. The supervisor reluctantly agreed; Houston Center agreed to take him and the lucky passengers on that one flight actually made it to their destination, probably never knowing how close they to hitchhiking from DFW to Houston.

The control room, normally a continuous hubbub of noise, slowly became quiet as there were fewer and fewer airplanes in the sky. Finally it was continuous quiet. No one, it seemed, wanted to talk. No one could believe what had happened and no one, for the moment anyway, wanted to talk about that or anything else.

Slowly the control emptied as most controllers went downstairs to watch the TV and news thereupon. We were all on-call but there was no activity and no promise of any. It was the same all day, and all the next day except for the military. The military began flying on that day, particularly fighters. They started with Combat Air Patrols over major cities across the nation and several other areas as well.

Military transport types came up on the second day as well, as troops and equipment were moved from place to place. On the third day, a Thursday, when we came in, we were told that civilian medevac flights and a limited number of other special civilian aircraft would be allowed to depart, effective 10 o'clock local.

I was working Waco-low that morning, the airspace underlying Dallas High, and I had on my frequency a flight of two Marine Corps F-18s orbiting one of the special areas. About 0940 I asked the flight leader if he was aware that at 10 o'clock, just 20 minutes away, some civilian aircraft were going to be released. He exclaimed, "What?!" When I repeated it, he said he was going off frequency to command post and that number two would monitor the frequency. Away he went.

A few minutes later, probably around 0955, a supervisor came running around, literally, to every control area shouting for us not to let any civilian aircraft off the ground, that the military didn't know anything about the releases and that it all had to be coordinated with them before aircraft could be released.

Maybe it was a good thing I asked the question.

ATC Tales 157

Let's talk about close calls. A while back I wrote about having two airplanes a quarter of a mile and no altitude feet apart. That's a close call. I know of two airplanes, NORDOs (No Radios) that passed directly over/under each other with maybe 200 feet to spare, at 35,000 feet. That's a close call. I heard a guy tell another, there are two airplanes there together at 8,000 feet. The R-side (the fellow doing the talking) asked one of the two, Are you in the clouds? When the pilot replied that he was, the controller said, Be careful because there's another aircraft at 8,000 in there with you. That's a close call.

The president's wife was on a Boeing 737 that was three miles from a C-17, military cargo jet. Three miles! Even though it's less than the required five miles, it's still a lot of space. The two aircraft must have been working Washington Center because they were both en route to Andrews AFB and approach controls only need three miles. The 737 must have been overtaking the C-17 big time because supposedly the 737 had been vectored all over the sky to get the required in-trail spacing and the controller still didn't have it when he handed them off to Dulles Approach with just the three miles.

Eric Parker, right at the start of a relief briefing, handed a Convair 580 off to Dulles Approach at 7,000 feet when he realized that an Electra was screaming up the Convair's 6 o'clock. He told the Convair to descend to 6,000 and the pilot started arguing about it, demanding to know why he had to descend. Just as Eric keyed his mike his relief muttered, "'Cause you're gonna get an Electra up your tail if you don't."

"Roger, out of seven for six," said the pilot.

For one reason or another, air traffic controllers have been catching a lot of flak lately. Mostly that has been for sleeping on duty, specifically the mid-shift. I know they shouldn't but stuff happens and these particular individuals, all five of them (in the five separate sleeping incidents) should be disciplined appropriately. The FAA, however, tends to react first and then think about appropriate punishment.

Personally, I think that were I working a mid-shift in a tower and especially if I were there by myself, I would stand up all night, never even think about sitting down. It's tough, I know, and I once asked some people who worked the Oklahoma City tower how they dealt with that issue.

The fellow said he turned up all the lights to full brightness, turned up all the landline and radio speakers to full volume and then, if he did fall asleep, the noise would scare him awake and the lights would keep him that way.

I worked in a big radar room with six areas of controllers. We always had three on duty in each area so one might take a break, leaving the other two in the area. Sometimes, in the middle of the night, the traffic would be so slow that we would combine it all on one sector and work all of Oklahoma off Ardmore-low. Didn't work with bad weather, of course, but weather presents problems of its own so more people would be in the area anyway.

One night all three of us were plugged in, headsets and all, which was unusual for a mid because you normally used handsets for a mid. There were two overlapping lines of weather about 50 miles apart that aircraft from all over the country were daisy-chaining through. Jimmy, on the R-side, got caught up in frequency congestion, three frequencies with airplanes on each calling ALL THE TIME. It got so bad that he finally lost the picture, a rarity for most controllers and Jimmy in particular. Janet slid over to the R-side and I took her place, Jimmy coming over to low where it was a lot slower. He worked low until he regained his composure, about ten minutes, and then he took back the R-side, getting back into the saddle. By that time, I had alerted everybody around us to use the one frequency, Ardmore-high, and frequency congestion was not a factor.

Close calls though, they are another matter. One time, in the days before digitized radar and radar screen presentations, a twin Cessna came out from behind a cloud and almost ran into an aerial-refueling flight on AR313, also at 21,000 feet. The Cessna pilot later said, "They were so close, all I could see was 'U.S. AIR FORCE,' one letter at a time." That's a close call.

Or the commuter plane near Wichita Falls at 6,000 feet who reported being nearly being hit by falling engines and aircraft parts. That was a close call. Turns out two airplanes at 8,000 feet almost directly above him had had an even closer call, impacting and then almost taking the 6,000 with them.

I was working a Cessna 208, a Cohlmia at 6,000, near Cushing, Oklahoma, one day. I had just advised him of the possibility of parachute jumpers in his area when he started cursing, shouting that a jumper had passed directly in front of his aircraft, "Right in front of my prop not more than 50 feet!" Now that's a close call.

One day I was on an American Airlines familiarization trip, riding in the cockpit as we used to be able to do, listening to the pilots go on about the evils of ATC. (Why shouldn't they? That's what controllers do when we get together with pilots.) They mentioned a time when they were flying along at 33,000 feet and a United Airlines DC-8, also at 33,000 feet, came out of a cloud on their right not a quarter of a mile ahead of them and disappeared into a cloud on their left. They were both surprised, stunned, and shocked, but before they could say a word to ATC, a new voice came on the radio apologizing, asking if they wanted to file a report. The paperwork was already in the mill on the ground, said the voice. That was a close call.

Please don't be alarmed over anything I have said in this little missive. There are now a lot more safety features built into the ATC system now than there used to be. Even I feel safe flying and you should, too, especially since I'm not working the radar anymore.

ATC Tales 158

I've been writing some stuff called "Flying Stories." I like aviation and I like telling stories so what better mix than the two?

Today I want to visit about something that happened a while back when I was a lowly controller for the FAA. I had finished a BA at TCU in Fort Worth and, wanting to make the most of the GI Bill, I was working on a Master's program through TCU before my benefits ran out. Of the ten courses I took through the program, six or seven of them were out at the Carswell AFB education center. TCU had an extension campus out there where military personnel (and anybody else who knew about it) could take classes. I liked taking them out there because the length of the class, while 20 or 30 minutes longer each night, was four to six weeks shorter than classes on campus. That pleased me to no end.

Most of the Air Force types were young officers who were looking to fill a square in their personnel file. A Master's degree looked good in their file so they took a class or two every semester and, in two years or so, they got the degree.

Carswell AFB was a SAC base, Strategic Air Command, where they flew B-52s, a great big behemoth of a bomber that made a lot of racket whether it was taking off, in flight or landing. Their bomb loads, I know from experience, made a lot of racket, too, having been near several B-52 strikes in Vietnam. A great airplane that started its service life back in the early 1950s and is still flying today.

As an aside, I used to ask B-52s if there was anybody on the airplane that was younger than the aircraft they were flying. As time progressed, it turned out to be that everybody on the airplane was younger than the airplane. At the end of my career, it became a rarity to find anybody on the plane older than the aircraft.

I got to know quite a few of the people with whom I was taking classes and quickly learned that most all of them had a great sense of humor, especially one young captain named Paul Erbacher. He was a navigator in the 4417th CCTS (Combat Crew Training Squadron) and was a good guy with a good smile, a great laugh and a mustache that ran nearly from ear to ear. On top of all that he had a penchant for the practical joke that wouldn't quit (just like me).

It turns out that the aircraft commander on Erbacher's crew was a captain named Robert Davis. Captain Davis had a girlfriend named Sandy. Sandy had a unique talent that drove Davis crazy and was causing him to seriously rethink their entire relationship. She could track him down everywhere. He lived near the air base in far west Fort Worth and she did, too. One day he decided he would journey to the Macy's Department Store in the far reaches of Dallas, way east at the other end of the Dallas-Fort Worth Turnpike.

He didn't tell anyone he was going, said he, so he was very surprised when he heard, over the store's PA system, "Captain Bob Davis, Captain Bob Davis, please contact the store operator." He did, and was given a message to call Sandy as soon as possible.

He was tracked down several other places as well, to the point where it was getting old in a hurry, and everybody on his crew knew it. Erbacher decided to do something about it.

Our class was on Monday night. I worked 7-3s on Mondays and Tuesdays so I would be at work the next day when Davis, Erbacher and crew would be coming through my airspace on aerial refueling track AR313, cruising down the way at 22,000 feet in ENEMY20. And I would be there waiting. We worked out the details, all of us laughing heartily, and then went on our merry ways.

The next day about one here came ENEMY20, fat, dumb, and happy, and I was ready and waiting. Shorty Bush had been Mcalester-low but he let me take it for the little while EN-

EMY20 was on frequency. I waited a few minutes after the aircraft checked on frequency, then began.

"ENEMY 2-0, Fort Worth Center."

"Fort Worth Center, ENEMY 2-0, go ahead."

The time was right; I was ready, and so I began. . .

"ENEMY 2-0, is there a Captain Davis on board your aircraft?"

There ensued a long silence, something I wasn't expecting. Everybody except Davis was supposed to be in on the joke and a reply would have, should have, come quicker than this.

"Fort Worth, why do you want to know?" asked ENEMY20.

Not knowing what was happening or going on, I pressed on. "ENEMY 2-0, if he's on board, I have a message for him when you're ready to copy; over."

A short pause, then a curt, "Go ahead with the message."

I relayed, "Tell Captain Davis that he needs to call Sandy as soon as possible after landing, over."

A short, "I copy," and it was done.

Monday night finally rolled around, and I was eager to learn what had transpired on board the aircraft upon receipt of the message. A lot, as it turned out. Erbacher was brimming with excitement as he told the tale.

It tuned out that the co-pilot, the one normally doing the talking and who was in on the joke, had been bumped at the last moment by the squadron commanding officer (CO). The good thing was that the CO was going to get several things out of the way at once, a surprise check ride for the crew, some in-flight safety work, and earn his flight pay by getting the required flying time. The bad thing was that the CO would be sitting in the right seat, doing all the talking while Davis flew the airplane. The worst thing was that the CO wasn't in on the joke and when I started talking, the muck would hit the fan, for Davis because of the message and, once the joke came to light, for whomever set it, specifically Erbacher.

The rest of the flight was a long, cold silence broken only by the required transmissions. The CO had already told Davis that he wanted to talk to him after they landed so he was expecting the worst. Erbacher knew he couldn't let Davis get in trouble, so he wasn't going to let that happen but how to break it to the CO?

After landing, the CO went down the ladder first and Erbacher made it a point to hustle down right behind him. On the ground he stopped the CO before he got in the waiting car, explaining the situation, and asking that he not jump on Davis. The CO, fortunately, had a sense of humor but knowing he had to say something, waited until Davis descended, said something to the effect that he ought to square Sandy away and not to let it happen again, then, chewing out over, left. Davis was relieved, Erbacher and the crew were delighted and all hands, including the CO (and Davis himself, when he found out he had been taken), had a good laugh at Davis's expense.

ATC Tales 159

Greetings from the northland. This is Groundhog Day. I wrote that as a date on a check that I sent to my grandfather. His sense of humor wasn't as well developed as mine evidently, because he didn't cash it until I blew into town and explained the humor. I'm not sure he ever got it, but he cashed the check.

A friend sent me an email a day or so ago that was titled: SF-160 Memories. SF-160s were familiarization trips (we called them, fam trips) that controllers could take eight times a year, on different airlines, and it included one international trip. I started taking them early in my career, when I had been there about a year, and took them until we could take them no more. The New York City WTC 9-11 attacks stopped the program in its tracks. It was sorely missed.

The theory was that controllers would take the trips to learn about airline operations and how airline crews and air traffic controllers might better interact with each other. There were some rules like, you had to have on a coat and tie, no jeans. Women had to be neatly attired and so on. We had to ride in the cockpit with the crew. You weren't supposed to go in the back except to use the restroom, and you weren't supposed to do anything to make you or the FAA, especially the FAA, look bad, stupid, or otherwise out of their minds.

The first trip I ever took was a night flight to Washington Dulles. I was going up for a look around Washington DC, and was coming back that evening. It was an American DC-10, I remember that, and the crew had been yanked, banked, and cranked by somebody in Boston Approach and the captain was an unhappy camper about it. He wanted me to explain it to him and he wasn't satisfied with the answer. First, I knew nothing about approach control – including Boston's, which was halfway across the country. Next, he didn't care that I knew next to nothing about air traffic control in general. I had been at the Center a year and was on this flight to learn from the captain, not him from me. Didn't faze him.

I took several fam trips to London Gatwick and back; a dozen in all, actually. I had friends and relatives over there who were kind enough to put me up—and put up with me, long enough to warrant taking the trip. Eastbound to London was an overnight flight, flying into the sun. The route was always on the north Atlantic tracks that went far north over Greenland and near Iceland and many times I saw the Northern Lights. A beautiful sight they were, one trip lasting from Greenland to Iceland, a roaring gas fire that seemed to be just off our left wing all the way across. Truly one of the most beautiful things I have ever seen.

On one trip Sian, my oldest daughter, was in the back. She was 10 y.o. and was going over to visit her grandparents for a month. That was a great trip. I was only there a week and had to leave her in Scotland, but the week was fun. Leaving her there was one of the hardest things I have ever had to do and she didn't want me to go, crying for several hours the night before I left. It broke my heart to have to go back but I had to.

Later her gran told me that after she woke up, she came into the kitchen and looked around for me, then said, He's gone eh? What's for breakfast?

So much for being missed.

When I started taking the international trips, I saved my American Airlines trip for London so I could go visit. On the return trip, it was always a nice feeling to be walking to the gate and see the AA logo on the aircraft's tail. Then I knew I was a step or two away from getting back to the Land of the Round Doorknob.

For a while after I went to work out there, you could take fam trips from almost the day you hired on. After a while the rules were tightened a bit to where only journeymen could take them, but at first any air traffic controller type could. One day a young man named Tom Carmenetti was heading out for his first fam trip. On his way out to the car he had to pass the supervisor's office where his supervisor, Ed Bickers, happened to be working. Ed, knowing it was Tom's first fam trip, shouted at Tom who then went into the office for a little pre-trip lecture. "Keep your eyes and ears open and your mouth SHUT," Ed told him, "and don't do anything to embarrass the FAA," Ed added.

Tom took the message to heart because halfway through the trip he had hardly said a word to the DC-9 crew, nor they to him. When smoke started coming out of a panel above his head, Tom kept wondering if he should say something but he remembered Ed's stern warning to keep his mouth shut, and he sat there, quietly, silently, until he could take it no more. He tapped the captain on the shoulder and with his finger pointing up and to the right, he asked, "Should that be coming out of there?"

The captain, who moments before had pulled a manual out of his flight bag and was studying it intently, seemed a bit irritated at the neophyte's interruption but when he saw the smoke, now beginning to fill the cockpit, he moved in a hurry. Tom said later he didn't know how the captain moved so fast, seemingly without standing up, without unfastening his seatbelt, without doing anything, but before Tom could say anything else the captain was standing on the center console and Tom, trying to figure out the problem.

He started telling Tom to get up and get out of the jumpseat, to go back into First Class and get somewhere out of the way. Tom was happy to oblige but there is not much room in those old DC-9 cockpits and Tom, a big boy himself, had a hard time getting unfastened, turned around, getting the seat folded up, all with the captain breathing down his neck saying, "Move, move, move," and then out of the cockpit into the passenger cabin.

The captain was at Tom's back out the door and into the First-Class galley where, he learned in short order, the microwave was on fire. He put it out himself and calm and order was restored throughout the land, but it had been a near thing, one that would not have been near as bad had Ed not hammered the mouth shut instruction into Tom's brain.

Dwan Stregles was on a fam trip returning to DFW when he got an eyeful of airplane, and he was thankful that was all it was.

DFW Approach Control was extremely busy this particular day and Dwan, in AAL415, a Boeing 727, could tell they were in the process of "turning the airport around." In this case they were going from a north to south configuration and airplanes require a lot of extra vectoring. Dwan heard the DFW controller tell another American to "turn 90 degrees right and make your turn as tight as you can!"

Dwan thought that a strange control instruction until he heard the same controller tell his aircraft, "American 415, turn 90 degrees left and make your turn as tight as you can!" Both Dwan and the first officer started looking out the right windows for any traffic out there when, all of a sudden, a Boeing 727 came out a cloud headed straight for AAL415. Both the first officer and Dwan started shouting, "Tighter, Captain, tighter!" The other 727 was turning as tight as he could to the right and the Captain, even more aware of the need for a tight turn now than he had been a moment before, pulled and turned as hard as he could, but the two airplanes kept sliding toward each other.

It was an old 727, Dwan said later. He could see individual rivets and the oil streaks from each one. It was a dirty airplane, the bottom of it, and it was so close he felt he could reach out with a rag and wipe each oil streak away, and that would have taken a lot of wiping.

Then, barely, hardly, minutely, the two aircraft, stopped their forward progress as the turns took hold, and they flew belly to belly for a moment before beginning to inch away from each other. It had been a close thing for all hands. Dwan didn't know if the passengers knew how close they came, or if many of them even saw the other aircraft, but Dwan knew and the crews knew, and the guys at DFW Approach knew. That was enough.

ATC Tales 160

A friend posted a note on Facebook earlier today about a young woman at Fort Worth Center who had worked a crash wherein a passenger died. It was weighing heavy on the woman's mind and he was asking for prayers for her and all others involved. I sent along my prayers for her and all concerned, then got to thinking about a crash or two I worked or was involved in.

No crash is fun. There's something inherently horrible about listening to someone on their way down, someone who's about to die, and they know it.

Roy was going on break and I was getting a briefing prior to relieving him, when the beacon on a VFR PA32 at 10,500 feet disappeared. I asked Roy, where's his beacon, and Roy asked the aircraft the same question. The pilot started talking, saying first, "We're going down." There were two passengers, I found out later, a man in front and a woman in back. We never heard the male passenger, just her. She screamed all the way down.

The storm killed the engine first, then threw the aircraft into a downward spin, finally ripping a wing off while the aircraft was still fairly high. The pilot was calm, considering what was about to happen. We could hardly hear him over her screams, but he was calm and sort of collected as he trying to save the aircraft, his passengers, and himself.

I had called Flight Service and they called the Oklahoma Highway Patrol, which was already out looking for the aircraft and now the crash site. Search and rescue kicked into high gear, but it still took two days to find it, and them, at the MLC117022. (It's amazing how you still remember things like that.)

Roy and I got pulled off the boards and went upstairs to write a statement. We had to sit there for an hour and inevitably the bad thoughts creep in . . . did I do or say anything wrong that might have contributed to the accident? The controller rarely does but the thoughts remain until they are laid to rest.

After writing my initial statement, I went back in the control room and was sent directly to Mcalester-low, the sector I had been working the crash. I was not ready to go back to work, having just listened to what had transpired. The storm was still there, having moved a bit east, but not far. Perhaps an hour had passed, that was all. Shortly after I plugged in another VFR said he was going to go direct Tulsa, putting his flight path right through the same thunderstorm that killed the PA32.

It was probably the only time I ever lost my temper with a pilot. I got on his case and, my voice rising with my blood pressure, I counseled him about weather, thunderstorms, and what had just happened to the Saratoga. "That storm just killed three people in a Cherokee Six," I all but shouted at him, and he got the message, electing to steer well clear of the storm on his way to Tulsa.

Two years later Roy and I were still writing statements. There were several lawsuits and our statements, old and new, were called into question. The bad part of writing the statements was that we had to listen to the tape every time. It never became old hat, as it were, but was hauntingly fresh – and horrible, every time. The fact remained, fortunately for us, that we had nothing to do with the aircraft's flight path. Roy had made no suggestions to the pilot on a route, the pilot had chosen his own route.

It came out later that Roy knew the two passengers. The male had been a controller at Houston Center when Roy worked there, and the woman was his wife. I'm glad Roy didn't know that at the time.

I think perhaps this and the several other crashes with which I was involved were easier on me than most. I have had a bit of experience with death in the military and at one point met the fellow myself. It was a short visit but long enough to make me appreciate being alive.

ATC Tales 161

Greetings from the 2nd floor studio high above the Anoka High football field. It's dark out with just the one streetlight across 4th Avenue providing any light outside. If the moon's out, I can't see it.

I was writing a letter a day or two ago, a handwritten letter to a friend with whom I've corresponded with for 35 years. Mike was an Air Force career type, and I was the world's second-best air traffic controller. (Larry Foreman was the best, back then . . . just ask him.) Mike would write to me about Air Force leadership (and the lack thereof) and I would write to him about supervisors and all the other things wrong with FAA management. (There were a couple of exceptions to the "all supervisors are incompetent" rule: Gene Hutchins, Dave Olivas and one or two others.)

The letter I was writing was being penned on stationery cut from an old sector overhead chart I picked up along the way. When I left the land of Fun, Action, Adventure, I fished a couple of those old charts out of the trash and cut them up for stationery and printer paper. They're different, unique, and interesting. Good conversation pieces. The particular page on which I was writing had, on its reverse, part of Ardmore-high depicted. I used to work Ardmore-high, quite a bit in fact, and had one of my most interesting ATC experiences thereupon.

One fine day I was working the D-side on another sector when Frank Dixon, the Oklahoma City system supervisor, tapped me on the shoulder and said, "Get over to Ardmore-high and take it, quick! Bob's lost the picture!" [Bob isn't the real name.]

At the time, facility supervisors were required to work at least eight hours of live traffic a month and Bob was doing his time on Ardmore-high, a sector that can be very busy – and had done so four of five minutes before I got there. Bob had two strings of DFW arrivals from the north, over OKC and Tulsa, needing to be sequenced over Bridgeport. He had assigned all of them 24,000 feet without regard to their position, altitude, or position in the sequence.

To complicate matters, there was an Air Force flight of two, a KC-135 and a B-52, doing random aerial refueling from over Texarkana to the west as they headed for the ARIP on AR-13. The flight was in a block of 24,000 to 26,000 feet and was about to pass through the airspace into which ALL the inbound aircraft would be descending.

I plugged in and told Bob I was there to take the sector. Did he have a briefing for me to let me know what was going on? His briefing was short and not so sweet: "I gave all these guys 24," and that he unplugged and left the area.

Seeing what might be about to happen (bad things and a lot of paperwork), I issued the strangest clearance I ever gave. It was the only time in 30+ years of air traffic control experience that I ever said anything at all like this: "ATTENTION ALL AIRCRAFT, maintain your present altitude and look out for other aircraft!" I issued it twice and quickly aircraft began to level at whatever altitude they were at. That bought me a little time which is what I needed, and I soon got a handle on it, turning several aircraft behind the refuelers and others to get them lined up for Bridgeport-low.

Nothing was ever said about it and nothing ever happened to Bob, which was the right thing, but he never worked Ardmore-high again.

ATC Tales 162

I was writing a letter yesterday, a handwritten letter (what a novelty!) on some stationery that had once been part of an overhead chart where I used to work. I like the paper, the charts, and would take them out of the trash once they'd been discarded, cut them up and use them for letters. This particular piece was part of a chart covering southeastern Oklahoma, an area I used to work back when I was your basic ATC Stud. On this piece of chart was a military operating area (MOA) named the Rivers MOA, an area I worked for 21 years.

As the name implies, it is an area used strictly by the military so they can maneuver high-performance aircraft, mostly fighters, and maneuver they did. The area was used primarily by the US Air Force Reserve units at Carswell and Tinker AFBs, as well as Air National Guard units out of Tulsa and Fort Smith.

When I hired on in 1974 F-100s were using the area and when I left, there were F-16s out there on a regular basis. When a flight came into the area, the procedure was to put the flight on a discrete frequency and then put the receivers in the speaker so you wouldn't have them in your ear. You could hear them in the speaker and if something happened, as it occasionally did, the raised, excited voices of the pilots would catch your attention. Sometimes, if you weren't busy, you would listen to them just for the heck of it, as I did one Saturday morning.

Four A7s out of Tulsa were in the area and they must have had a break in the action because they started talking about how much fun it all was. One pilot said he loved it and another answered him, saying how much he loved it, how his wife thought he hated it and was only doing it for the extra money. "She thinks I'd rather be home mowing the lawn!"

Another flight was out there one day, this lot flying F-4s out of Tinker. By the time F-4s got to the reserve units they had been pretty well wrung out in Vietnam and had lots of maintenance problems, as evidenced by one fellow's observation that "this thing flies like a piece of s—t!" He was not a happy camper.

F-105s flew out there for a while, but they had been really been put through the wringer in Vietnam as well, before they came home. One day "Black Cloud" was working the floor, on loan from the Training Department. He was so named because bad things had a way of happening when he was working a sector. This particular day one of the four F-105s literally fell apart in the air and crashed, and another aircraft in the same flight declared an emergency and returned to Tinker, crashing on the runway. That pilot lived, the other did not.

I suppose the funniest thing that ever happened out there was when SLOP71, an Air Force tanker came through the area. I asked the pilot if he ever refueled the F-4s out of Fort Smith? Why, he asked. I said, "Because their callsign is HAWG!" He was not amused.

Speaking of callsigns, I worked a SCUM41, a C-130, one day. I asked him about the callsign and he was quick to reply that he sure would like to talk to the guy who assigned them because the day before they had been SCOW41. But the best callsign of all was DUD01, a B-52. I asked him how it was he got that one. "We came in last at the Bomb Competition," said he, a rueful note in his voice.

ATC Tales 163

I read a lot and I always have. When I hired on at the FAA in 1974, I was reading a series of fiction books by C. S. Forester, about Horatio Hornblower in Britain's Royal Navy. Set in the Napoleonic Wars, the closest it came to aviation was the occasional mention of a bird overhead.

As a junior air traffic controller wannabe, I worked the A-sides for a year, ripping and stuffing strips in strip holders and putting them on the sectors, removing the same when the sector was finished with it, and then stuffing the discarded strip in a bin in front of the printer. The bin was high enough to hide a book under it, and I did so until one day someone saw me with a book hidden there.

Don McAfee was a crusty old soul. He was grumpy, crotchety, didn't take guff, and didn't put up with youngsters like me. He stayed away from new hires and we stayed away from him, unless you were working on a sector next to him, as was I this day on Blue Ridge Low A.

"Whatcha reading, boy?" He asked, and I pulled out the book from its hiding place and showing him and explaining what it was about.

"The navy?!" He exclaimed, and went on to say, "You ain't never gonna make it, boy. You're gonna wash right out of here!" After that, I avoided him like the plague, but I never forgot what he said.

Five years later I got signed off on my last position, Mcalester-high R-side. Now I was a journeyman and I went looking for him, finding him on Flow Control. Marching up to him, I thrust the paper in his face and said, "I just got signed off on my last position, Mcalester-high R-side and now I'm a journeyman just like you, you son-of-a-bitch!"

He looked at the paper and then at me, saying, "What the hell are you talking about?" He had forgotten all about his remark, probably as soon as I left that A-side, but I hadn't. Over the ensuing years he had given me a little extra push toward making journeyman, a push for which I was grateful and a push he had forgotten years before.

Rivershore Books

www.rivershorebooks.com
info@rivershorebooks.com
www.facebook.com/rivershore.books
www.twitter.com/rivershorebooks
blog.rivershorebooks.com
forum.rivershorebooks.com

Made in the USA
Middletown, DE
23 June 2021